Partners

ONE-on-ONE *Discipleship*

Dr. Mike Fabarez

Partners: *ONE-on-ONE Discipleship*

© Mike Fabarez 1991, 1994, 1997, 2000, 2010, 2013
All rights reserved.
No part of this publication may be reproduced in any form without the prior permission of the author.

Except where otherwise indicated, all Scripture quotations in this manual are taken from the English Standard Version (ESV), Wheaton, IL: Crossway Bibles, a publishing ministry of Good News Publishers, 2007.

Printed by Dr. Mike Fabarez
P.O. Box 2850
Laguna Hills, California 92654

For publication or distribution information contact:
Dr. Mike Fabarez
Focal Point Radio Ministries
P.O. Box 2850
Laguna Hills, California 92654
Toll Free: (888) 320-5885
Voice: (949) 389-0476
Fax: (949) 389-0475
Email: info@fpr.info
Web: www.focalpointradio.org

Partners
Table of Contents

Introduction to Partners..iv

A Few Pointers v

1. Being Sure About Your Relationship with God........................ 1

2. Deepening Your Knowledge of God..................................... 25

3. Learning to Study the Bible on Your Own 51

4. Developing an Effective Prayer Life 73

5. Living a Life Led by the Holy Spirit.................................... 95

6. The Importance of a Good Church 119

7. Being Intentional About Biblical Fellowship 143

8. Getting Actively Involved in Serving Your Church 165

9. Sharing the Gospel with People Who Need It 193

10. Living a Holy Life in an Unholy World..............................213

Introduction to
Partners

"walk in a manner worthy of the Lord, fully pleasing to him, bearing fruit in every good work and increasing in the knowledge of God"
Colossians 1:10

In a phrase, that is what Partners is all about. Partners is a program designed to help people enhance their walk with Jesus—learning how to live an effective and pleasing Christian life. The emphasis is on application, but there is plenty of learning that takes place at the same time.

The Partners program includes ten chapters and takes anywhere from ten to thirteen weeks. There's no doubt that the program is intensive. It will take some time and some hard work, but it is definitely worth it!

The workbook chapters are to be studied and completed throughout each week, and each chapter culminates in your weekly meeting with your "partner." At your meeting, you and your partner will discuss and develop the concepts studied that week.

The Partners program is designed to prepare you to take another person through the same chapters when you have completed the program. I trust that each chapter will be so exciting and relevant that you will be eager to share your progress in each area with another Christian.

A Few Pointers

Studying the Manual

1. Do Your Homework

Be sure to thoughtfully study the chapter that you will be discussing during your Partners appointment. If you confront a difficult question, answer it the best you can—this is not an exam booklet! If you are totally stumped, leave it blank and be sure to discuss it with your partner during your next meeting.

2. Use a "Good" Bible

If you don't have a readable and reliable translation of the Bible, get one! An understandable translation will help you to answer the questions in the manual that call for you to look up passages of Scripture. The *English Standard Version* is a reliable and yet readable translation that I suggest. Do not rely exclusively on paraphrases or translations that seek to be extraordinarily current or modern in their translation such as the *Living Bible* or *The Phillips Translation,* or *The Message.* The *King James Version* may be beautiful sixteenth-century English, but among other disadvantages it proves hard to understand when attempting to discover the meaning of a verse.

Other helpful suggestions would include the *The New American Standard Version, The New Revised Standard Version, New International Version,* or even *The Amplified Bible.* Using more than one of the suggested translations may be helpful when looking at what seems to be a confusing verse.

3. Pray!

Don't forget to pray as you begin working on each chapter. Ask God to give you insight into the topic being presented and the Scripture passages that you will be asked to read. Pray for clear thinking and undistracted study time.

Meeting With Your Partner

1. Pray

In anticipation of your appointment, pray that God would allow you and your partner to have a meaningful time of communication and learning. Pray that unnecessary walls would come down and that open and honest communication would take place.

2. Be Practical

During your discussion with your partner, remember that the goal is not simply to educate, but also to change our lives. We must be honest about where we are spiritually and the struggles we face. The Christian life is not easy, and this partnership is not the place to make it look that way. Make sure your discussion touches the real you.

3. Take Notes

The words of your partner are not inspired, but they have been prepared with much thought and prayer. The direction of your discussion and the additional comments and topics brought up are probably worth jotting down. Make it a habit to take notes. Remember, you will be teaching this material soon!

PARTNERS MEETING #1

Being Sure About Your Relationship with God

At Partners Meeting #1…

You will be discussing the importance of knowing for sure that you are a Christian. There are plenty of misconceptions out there about what God requires to be right with him, so whether you have been a Christian for a long time or a short time you can look forward to digging into what God's word has to say about biblical Christianity.

To Prepare for Partners Meeting #1…

- Read chapter 1 carefully.

- Fill in the questions for chapter 1.

- Be ready to discuss your testimony.

- If any of the "Deeper Study" topics are of interest to you, prepare to discuss those as well.

- Memorize 2 Corinthians 5:17.

> Therefore, if anyone is in Christ, he is a new creation. The old has passed away; behold, the new has come.
> – 2 Corinthians 5:17

PARTNERS:

ONE-ON-ONE DISCIPLESHIP

The concern over being "right with God" is as old as the third chapter of the Bible. Ever since Adam and Eve's first rebellious act in the Garden of Eden men and women have been faced with the problem of a severed relationship with their Creator. People with sin on their record can't create nor maintain a relationship with a holy and sinless God. For centuries people have tried, and they still do, but by themselves imperfect people just don't have a chance.

The good news is that Jesus came to solve the problem (that's even what the word "gospel" actually means)! What he did made all the difference in the world for people wanting to be right with their Maker. Unfortunately, too many people don't understand what the good news is all about. They struggle through life hoping that their good deeds will outweigh their bad deeds—as though God will simply overlook their sin and embrace a 65% righteous person.

Being "right with God" is certainly not defined by doing more good than bad. Jesus made that clear in his promise to a dying thief.[1] Doing good things may be an important part of living the Christian life, but if one wants to be "right with God" it all comes down to a question of one's relationship to Jesus Christ. Heaven and hell will ultimately be about who really "knows" Jesus and who does not.

Most People

Though there are always some who admit to being on God's bad list, most people believe that they are "right with God." They may be counting on a divine sliding scale, or some religious ritual, but whatever their reason, most people think that come judgment day they'll probably come out on top. Unfortunately, that is not what the Bible says. Read *Matthew 7:13-14*. What does this passage have to say about how many really do inherit God's blessing after their death?

FYI...
The blank spaces after certain paragraphs in the Partners manual are provided to give you room to write out your responses to the questions or statements.

With Your Partner...
Discuss the deception that is depicted in Matthew 7. Do you think that you are, or ever have been, deceived about the reality of your "right standing" before God?

Read a few verses further in *Matthew 7:22-23* where those standing before Jesus present their case. Though they seem certain about their right standing before God, Jesus tells them to depart from him because in reality "he never knew them" and they still had sin on their record. What is your reaction to Jesus' prediction of there being so many deceived people on judgment day?

---

[1] See Luke 23:39-43 if you are unfamiliar with this story.

CHAPTER 1

BEING SURE ABOUT YOUR RELATIONSHIP WITH GOD

With so much deception and so much on the line, it is critically important that we look to the Bible to discover just exactly *what a Christian is*, *how a person becomes a Christian*, and *how we will know when we are a Christian*.

What is a Christian?

The word "Christian" is not often used in the Bible (actually only three times[2]) and yet it was the label that caught on to refer to someone who is closely aligned with Jesus Christ. It may mean different things to different people today, but when the term was coined a person who was closely aligned with Jesus was someone who truly "knew" him and was "known by him" (remember the words of Jesus in Matthew 7:23).

This is obviously more than just knowing *about* Jesus. Really knowing Jesus implies a relationship with him—a good relationship. Notice how Jesus described it.

> ### John 10:14-15a
>
> "I am the good shepherd; I know my own and my own know me, just as the Father knows me and I know the Father"

Remember...
Whenever a concept or a Bible verse is confusing to you be sure to bring it up for discussion with your partner.

Jesus compares his relationship with his people to his relationship with God the Father. It is clear then that to "know Jesus" is to have a real and vital relationship with Jesus. But it doesn't stop there.

> ### John 8:19b
>
> Jesus answered, "You know neither me nor my Father. If you knew me, you would know my Father also."

If we have a vital relationship with Jesus Christ, we also have a real and vital relationship with God the Father. The sin problem that severed our relationship with our Creator has been solved for those who "know Christ."

A Christian is Someone Who is Acceptable to God

Christians then, are those people who through Christ have had their sins forgiven and have been made acceptable before a perfect and sinless God. Christians are imperfect people made perfect in God's sight through their alignment with Jesus Christ!

> ### Acts 13:38
>
> "Let it be known to you therefore, brothers, that through this man forgiveness of sins is proclaimed to you,"

---

[2] Acts 11:26; 26:28; 1 Peter 4:16.

PARTNERS:

ONE-ON-ONE DISCIPLESHIP

> **Romans 8:1**
>
> There is therefore now no condemnation for those who are in Christ Jesus.

How does it make you feel to know that as a Christian you can be completely, 100% acceptable before God?

A Christian is Someone Who Follows Christ

One of the most popular words in the New Testament for one aligned with Jesus Christ is the word "disciple." The word "disciple" is a descriptive term for one who follows the teachings of his master and seeks to emulate the lifestyle of his master. In the Bible those who had been made right with God through their faith in Christ sought to follow Christ. Though a Christian's following of Christ and his teachings is never consistently perfect, the New Testament speaks volumes about this being a clear indication of those who know Christ and those who don't.

FYI...

Implications of this facet of what a Christian is will be covered in more detail on pages 12 and following.

Read *1 John 3:1-10* and summarize what is being said in that passage.

A Christian is Someone Who Has Been Adopted by God

First John 3:1 reminds us of another popular biblical phrase used to described Christians, namely the "children of God." This title emphasizes the strong legal bond that exists between God and his people. With their sins forgiven and their lives made acceptable to him through the work of Christ, Christians are brought into a close and permanent relationship with God as his adopted children. The indwelling of the Holy Spirit is described in Ephesians 1:5, 13-14 as the pledge of God's adoption.

Ponder the power of this concept for a moment. God, our infinitely wise Creator, has chosen to embrace Christians not just as subjects in his kingdom but as sons and daughters in his family!

> **Romans 8:15b**
>
> ...but you have received the Spirit of adoption as sons, by whom we cry, "Abba![3] Father!"

---

[3] "Abba" is an Aramaic term of endearment for one's father.

4

CHAPTER 1
BEING SURE ABOUT YOUR RELATIONSHIP WITH GOD

A Christian is Someone Who is Closely Identified with Other Christians

The most frequently used term in the New Testament for those aligned with Christ is "brothers." This may come as a surprise considering that it speaks of our relationship with each other instead of our relationship with God. Jesus obviously wanted us to realize that Christianity was not to be as "personal" as our generation has wanted to make it.

Christians are called to find an identity together. Assembled groups of Christians are called the body of Christ, a temple of God, a household of faith, and a flock of followers, just to name a few. The love, unity, togetherness, and mutual respect of Christians for one another should be one of our distinguishing marks.

> **John 13:35**
>
> "By this all people will know that you are my disciples, if you have love for one another."

This brief overview of what a Christian is should quickly reveal that one cannot be "sort of a Christian." There must be a point in one's life when one becomes a Christian. Though one can consider Christianity and learn tons about it from the inside of a church (possibly for years), a person is either a Christian or not a Christian. There is no middle ground.

With Your Partner...
Discuss some popular misconceptions about what a Christian is.

How Do I Become a Christian?

To be sure about our relationship with God we must be certain that we are clear about what the Bible says a person must do to become a Christian.

To Become a Christian You Must Understand the Gospel

The New Testament boldly proclaims a message (called "the gospel") that if rightly understood and rightly responded to makes one a Christian. This is what most of the preaching recorded in the book of Acts is all about. In some of the gospel presentations in the New Testament we will find much time allotted to laying a foundation and giving background, in other instances we will simply find a record of the speaker calling the people to rightly respond to an abbreviated gospel message. In any case, a pattern emerges that gives us a basic outline of the gospel content.

Deeper Study...
To get a firm grasp on the message of the gospel you might consider taking a firsthand look at all the presentations of the gospel message beginning in the book of Acts. Look for passages that are recording the presentation of the message in attempts to see more people saved.

5

PARTNERS:
ONE-ON-ONE DISCIPLESHIP

With Your Partner...
Look together at Acts 17:22-34 as one example of the gospel message being presented to non-Christians. Attempt to locate as many of the elements in this summary outline as possible. →

Summary of the Gospel Message
1. The Background
• *God is our Creator*
• *God is Holy*
• *God is Just*
• *God is Loving*
2. The Bad News
• *We are Sinful and Separated from God*
• *We Deserve God's Punishment*
3. The Good News
• *Jesus is God*
• *He Lived and Died as Our Substitute*
• *He Conquered Death for Us*

Remember that this is just the gospel message. It does not spell out the necessary and biblical response (to be discussed later beginning on page 9). Nevertheless, one cannot become a Christian without understanding and embracing the basic message of the gospel. So it is important to look at each element a little closer.

God is our Creator. The background to the gospel message is rooted in the fact that we are created by God. This is so important that we find it in the very first verse of the Bible. Why do you think that this is so essential if one is to properly understand the rest of the gospel message? What are the implications for people if God really is their Creator?

Deeper Study...
If the creation/evolution debate has you a bit confused, be sure and consult the resource page at the end of this chapter. You may also want to ask your pastor, your church, or a local Christian bookstore for the latest books and articles that show that the evidence that we find in our world best fits the biblical account of creation.

God is holy. This means that God is absolutely perfect. Read *1 Peter 1:15-16* and notice that God's own perfection is to be the standard for all those he has created. This concept of perfection being the only acceptable standard is central in the gospel message!

CHAPTER 1
BEING SURE ABOUT YOUR RELATIONSHIP WITH GOD

God is just. God has not left the people he made to do whatever they want without accountability and consequences for their choices. Foundational to the gospel message is the fact that God will one day judge each person, and according to the Bible he will do it with perfect justice. Job 34:12 says, *"God will not do wickedly and the Almighty will not pervert justice."* That may sound like a comforting verse if someone has seriously wronged us, but assuming that we by nature have all seriously wronged God (failing to measure up to his standards of perfection) the justice of God leaves us in a precarious position. What does *2 Thessalonians 1:8-9* say about the end result of God's justice for most people?

God is love. Understanding that we all answer to our Creator, that he requires perfect holiness, and that because he is just he can't bend the rules, should make it overwhelmingly clear that if there is going to be any "good news" it will have to stem from his love! Thankfully, God *is* loving (1 John 4:8). His love prompted him to provide a solution for our problem of sin and the coming judgment.

With Your Partner...
Discuss the potential problems if one were to try and understand the gospel without recognizing that God was first their Creator, holy, and just. Why does the gospel begin here and not first with the fact that God is love?

A person cannot become a Christian unless he first understands something about that problem. We've called this "the bad news." The gospel is good news because it provides answers for people's terrible dilemma.

We are sinful and separated. Many people are slow to admit that they have this problem because they have come to believe that sin is doing something they consider "really bad" or culturally unacceptable. Remember that God, by virtue of his position as our Creator, is the judge of whether something is bad or good. Some things our culture may consider moral may in fact be immoral to God (Luke 16:15). In the Bible sin is defined in two ways. First, it describes doing something God considers wrong (1 John 3:4 – i.e. breaking his standard). Secondly, it describes the state of being separated from God (Ephesians 2:1 – i.e. living without a relationship with God). Realize that people who do not have a relationship with God are considered to be in a state of sin even though they may do many things that are morally acceptable.

How does *Isaiah 59:2* summarize what happened in the garden of Eden when Adam and Eve sinned?

By reading Isaiah 59:2 and noting that sin causes separation, we might be led to believe that we become separated from God (enter the state of sin) when we commit our first sinful act. But in reality the Bible teaches that every person since Adam has been born into a state of sin. Comment on the relationship between the state of sin and the acts of sin in *Ephesians 4:18-19.*

Deeper Study...
Investigate the idea of "original sin" in Romans 5:12-19. Be able to articulate the important relationship between inherited sin in Adam and inherited righteousness in Christ. What is the problem with our gospel when this point is missed?

7

PARTNERS:

ONE-ON-ONE DISCIPLESHIP

We deserve God's punishment. Many people believe that "guilt" is simply a bad feeling we have when we do bad things. In reality, the Bible defines guilt as being responsible for sin. We do not necessarily have to feel guilty to be guilty. According to the Bible all people who live in a state of sin and choose to do sinful things are guilty before a just and holy God. That means that all people are deserving of God's punishment.

> **Ephesians 2:3**
>
> among whom we all once lived in the passions of our flesh, carrying out the desires of the body and the mind, and were by nature children of wrath, like the rest of mankind.

When someone becomes convinced of the bad news regarding their situation before God they are ready to hear the greatest news of the gospel message. The great news is all about Jesus Christ!

Deeper Study...

Disputing that Jesus was really God has been a common point of departure for many groups over the centuries. Outline and give examples of the various ways that Jesus is presented as God in the Bible. Begin with his claims of deity, the exercise of divine attributes, the acceptance of divine titles, etc.

Jesus is God. This is an essential part of the gospel message in the New Testament (notice that it becomes a test of one's Christian profession in 1 John 4:2-3). Jesus was the expected Messiah that had been foretold in the Old Testament which, if carefully examined, clearly pointed to someone who was more than a mere human (see for instance Micah 5:2; Isaiah 9:6; Daniel 7:13-14). Jesus had to be God for his work on our behalf to be qualitatively and quantitatively adequate to save us. It was "qualitatively divine" in that he lived a perfectly holy life (1 John 3:5; 1 Peter 2:22), and "quantitatively divine" in that his death was applicable for many (Heb.7:27; 9:14). Read *Philippians 2:6-8* and comment on what Jesus went through in becoming a man to accomplish our salvation.

With Your Partner...

Discuss the importance of Jesus being God and any experiences you might have had with those who try to convince people that Jesus is not God.

With Your Partner...

Look at Matthew 3:13-15 and discuss Jesus' reason for being baptized and its relationship to his life being a substitute for ours.

Jesus lived and died as our substitute. This is the core of the gospel message. When we thought through God's holiness it became clear that a 65% righteous life would not cut it with a perfect God. He, by the nature of his holiness, requires 100% righteousness and 0% sin. Knowing that all humans are sinful and separated from him, God the Father sent Jesus to become a man and live a 100% perfect life. This perfect righteousness can then be credited to people who are not perfectly righteous.

Not only did Jesus live so that he could give us his righteousness, he died so that he could take on our sins. When Jesus died on the cross, God the Father was exercising his justice against the sinful acts of sinful people by punishing Jesus instead of them. In this way God could credit Christ's account with our sin and leave us with none! Notice carefully how this is stated in the Bible:

CHAPTER 1

BEING SURE ABOUT YOUR RELATIONSHIP WITH GOD

> **2 Corinthians 5:21**
>
> For our sake he made him to be sin who knew no sin, so that in him we might become the righteousness of God.

Our Creator demonstrates his incredible love for us by counting Jesus' life and death as a substitution for ours, making us in Christ 100% righteous and 0% sinful, while at the same time maintaining his holiness and justice. This is the heart of the gospel message!

Jesus conquered death for us. The result of all of this is that God is now able to free us from the penalty of our sin, which includes both spiritual death (i.e., relational separation from God) and physical death (i.e., our spirit's separation from our bodies). In taking care of the sin problem Jesus has eliminated for Christians the relational separation that existed between him and us. The intimate relationship with God that Christians enjoy every day is proof that Christ's life and death did the job and bridged the gap!

Jesus also demonstrated that he had fully paid the price for our sins in that he reversed the biological consequence of sin—physical death. This is what his resurrection was all about! While one might claim that the "proof" of a real and intimate relationship with an invisible God is hardly proof, it is difficult to argue with Christ's resurrection! This is God's objective, historical stamp of approval on the substitutionary life and death of Jesus Christ. Read *1 Corinthians 15:12-28* and comment on how important Jesus' resurrection is in the Bible.

Deeper Study...
If you ever have doubts about the truthfulness of the gospel message (or if you know someone who does) a thorough investigation of the resurrection of Jesus should be a top priority. Researching this objective proof of the gospel has won over many skeptics!

To Become a Christian You Must Rightly Respond to the Gospel

Knowing and accepting the facts of the gospel message are critically important, but it is not enough. God requires that if a person is to become a Christian he or she must respond to the gospel message as directed in the Bible. God calls people to *make a decision* based on the gospel facts. This decision involves two parts. Note the two components of this decision as stated in Acts 20:21.

> **Acts 20:21**
>
> "testifying both to Jews and to Greeks of repentance toward God and of faith in our Lord Jesus Christ."

Let's look at each part one at a time.

9

PARTNERS:
ONE-ON-ONE DISCIPLESHIP

Turn to God in repentance. Repentance is presented over and over again in the New Testament as a necessary response to the gospel. Carefully read this partial list of examples below.

Deeper Study...
There are some that would say that repentance is an <u>unnecessary</u> response to the gospel, or if it is necessary it is synonymous with "faith." Do a word study on the word "repentance" noting its usage in the NT and then attempt to respond to those two assertions.

NT Examples of the Gospel's Call to Repentance

Matthew 4:17 From that time Jesus began to preach, saying, "Repent, for the kingdom of heaven is at hand."

Mark 1: 14b-15 Jesus came into Galilee, proclaiming the gospel of God, and saying, "The time is fulfilled, and the kingdom of God is at hand; repent and believe in the gospel."

Luke 13:3b but unless you repent, you will all likewise perish.

Luke 16:28-30 for I have five brothers. —so that he may warn them, lest they also come into this place of torment.' But Abraham said, 'They have Moses and the Prophets; let them hear them.' And he said, 'No, father Abraham, but if someone goes to them from the dead, they will repent.'

Luke 24:46-47 and said to them, "Thus it is written, that the Christ should suffer and on the third day rise from the dead, and that repentance and forgiveness of sins should be proclaimed in his name to all nations, beginning from Jerusalem.

Acts 3:19 Repent, therefore, and turn again, that your sins may be blotted out,

Acts 11:18b And they glorified God, saying, "Then to the Gentiles also God has granted repentance that leads to life."

Acts 17:30-31 "The times of ignorance God overlooked, but now he commands all people everywhere to repent, because he has fixed a day on which he will judge the world in righteousness by a man whom he has appointed; and of this he has given assurance to all by raising him from the dead."

2 Corinthians 7:10a For godly grief produces a repentance that leads to salvation without regret, whereas worldly grief produces death.

Hebrews 6:1 Therefore let us leave the elementary doctrine of Christ and go on to maturity, not laying again a foundation of repentance from dead works, and of faith toward God,

2 Peter 3:9 The Lord is not slow to fulfill his promise, as some count slowness, but is patient toward you, not wishing that any should perish, but that all should reach repentance.

It is easy to see from this list that repentance is of primary importance! To properly respond to the gospel and become a Christian one must repent! In its most literal sense the word "repent" is a command that tells people that they should "completely change their thinking" which inevitably changes their behavior. Or as one lexicographer puts it, to repent *is "to change one's way of life as the result of a complete change of thought and attitude with regard to sin and righteousness."*[4]

_____

[4] Johannes P. Louw and Eugene A. Nida, *Greek-English Lexicon of the New Testament based on Semantic Domains*, (New York: United Bible Societies) 1988, 1989.

CHAPTER 1
BEING SURE ABOUT YOUR RELATIONSHIP WITH GOD

This Greek word that we translate "repent" in the Bible is the same word that the ancient Hellenistic army commanders used to get their marching soldiers to turn around 180°. When they wanted their men to do an "about-face" they shouted, "Repent!"

To repent is to make a mental decision to turn around. It is critically important that we know what the gospel is telling us to *turn from*, and what the gospel is telling us to *turn to*. Use the following passages to answer those two questions: *1 Thessalonians 1:8-9; Acts 20:21; and Acts 14:15.*

With Your Partner...
Discuss what it is like to make a decision to become a Christian that involves this kind of mental 180°.

Have faith in our Lord Jesus. The second component of God's required response to the gospel is to place one's faith in the Lord Jesus Christ. If one has truly understood the gospel message it is not hard to see the absolute necessity of discarding any trust in one's personal righteousness (which is totally deficient before a perfect God) and having all one's trust in Jesus' righteousness (which is 100% complete). Notice this fundamental definition of saving faith as the Apostle Paul describes his new attitude toward all his "accomplishments" in trying to be righteous and acceptable to God without Christ.

> **Philippians 3:8b-9**
>
> For his sake I have suffered the loss of all things and count them as rubbish, in order that I may gain Christ and be found in him, not having a righteousness of my own that comes from the law, but that which comes through faith in Christ, the righteousness from God that depends on faith.

To put my faith in Christ means that I cease trusting in my own résumé and from that point on I keep my confidence in Jesus Christ alone as the sole provision for my sinful condition!

Notice that the words used to describe faith are words like "trust" and "confidence." This is important. Unfortunately, misunderstandings about "faith" abound because over time our English word "faith" has lost its impact and is often understood as merely "believing" the truthfulness of some facts (unfortunately, sometimes even the original Greek word is translated this way in our Bibles). Though our English dictionaries still offer a secondary definition of "belief" as having "firm faith, confidence, or trust: *I believe in your ability to solve the problem*"[5] most understand "belief" as simply agreeing, or giving mental assent to some proposed facts.

This has led to the false impression that to be a Christian one has to simply agree with the facts presented in the gospel message. This is a terribly

With Your Partner...
Discuss the problem and prevalence of the assumption that to be saved one only has to agree with the facts of the gospel message.

---

[5] *American Heritage Dictionary: Third Edition,* Softkey International Inc., 1994.

11

PARTNERS:

ONE-ON-ONE DISCIPLESHIP

costly misconception. The Bible points this out by reminding us that even the demons have a proper set of beliefs in the facts (James 2:19). "Faith" is not just believing the facts, instead real faith means transferring our trust and confidence to Jesus Christ. If a person is to become a Christian he or she must be trusting in Jesus' perfect life and his substitutionary death that he suffered in order to pay the just penalty for sin.

As you read the numerous examples of the gospel's call to "faith" you will discover that the necessary response to trust in Christ is not just for the future day of judgment, but its emphasis is very much on the here-and-now! The gospel is calling us to trust in Jesus not only to save us in the future, but also to lead us in the present. Jesus demonstrated this aspect of faith while he was here on earth by continually calling people to "follow him." After Jesus' departure the Apostles often spoke of trusting "the Lord" Jesus. The emphasis here is on his position as leader or boss of one's life. Though he is not on earth presently to physically follow and emulate, he laid down a clear pattern of living that is to be followed with the help and guidance of God's Spirit.

Deeper Study...
In recent decades in the Western church some people have begun to dispute the fact that our trust in Jesus is to include both trust in him as our Savior (future) and trust in him as our Lord (present). Study and present passages in the Bible that put this dispute to rest.

> **1 John 2:6**
>
> Whoever says he abides in him ought to walk in the same way in which he walked.

When we place our trust in Christ it is a confidence for a future deliverance from judgment *as well as* a confidence in the present lordship of Christ for our daily lives.

How Do I Know That I Really Am a Christian?

Of course the most obvious way that we can know that we are Christians is to be certain that we have properly understood the gospel and have rightly responded to it. Assuming that a person is convinced of this we will briefly examine the objective indicators that give assurance of one's salvation.

Real Christians Bear Real Fruit

Wanting to avoid the tragic self-deception of would-be Christians, who discover on judgment day that they were never really Christians after all (Matthew 7:22-23). Let us seek to compare our lives with the primary test of true Christianity— namely, a transformed life!

When we become Christians our lives are changed forever in a variety of profound ways. Some patterns in our lives cease and others begin.

> **2 Corinthians 5:17**
>
> Therefore, if anyone is in Christ, he is a new creation. The old has passed away: behold, the new has come.

CHAPTER 1
BEING SURE ABOUT YOUR RELATIONSHIP WITH GOD

The Bible often calls these obvious changes caused by our new relationship with Christ "fruit." Fruit is an appropriate analogy for these changes in our lives because, like fruit that is borne on a tree, these new patterns of behavior are produced as the result of God's Spirit working in and through us.

John 15:8

"By this my Father is glorified, that you bear much fruit and so prove to be my disciples."

These changes are so profound that Jesus once equated the beginning of this new relationship with him to being "born again" (John 3:3). These changes include the transformation of one's core motivation, the curbing of one's sinful habits, and the initiation of new righteous habits – all of which are promised to last for a lifetime! Let's examine each of these.

Real Christianity transforms your core motivations. The Bible is clear that everyone is born sinful. We all come into this world separated from God and wired to please ourselves. We may choose to do this in culturally acceptable ways, but we are still motivated by a desire to live for "self." When we become Christians this motivation is turned upside-down!

2 Corinthians 5:15

he died for all, that those who live might no longer live for themselves but for him who for their sake died and was raised.

In what ways do you see that your core motivations are different than before?

Real Christianity curbs your sinful habits. Christians still sin (1 John 1:10 – 2:1), but not at all like they used to! Sinful habits and continuous indulgence in sinful behaviors are broken when God gets involved in a person's life. Where you once found addictions and vices in a non-Christian's life, you now find freedom and deliverance in the Christian's life (see 1 Corinthians 6:9-11). If there is a continuing pattern of habitual disobedience in a person's life, even though they may claim to be a Christian, they are deceived about the genuineness of their relationship with Christ.

1 John 2:3-4

And by this we know that we have come to know him, if we keep his commandments. Whoever says, "I know him," but does not keep his commandments is a liar, and the truth is not in him.

With Your Partner...
Discuss the overall changes that you and others witnessed in your life when you became a Christian.

Deeper Study...
How do you respond to someone who claims to have rightly responded to the gospel and yet does not have a transformed life? How do you approach this situation tactfully yet with a proper concern for that person's salvation?

PARTNERS:

ONE-ON-ONE DISCIPLESHIP

The curbing of sinful behavior is inevitable because Jesus came not only to remove sin from our record, but he also came to remove sin from our lives!

---

1 John 3:5-10

You know that he appeared to take away sins, and in him there is no sin. No one who abides in him keeps on sinning; no one who keeps on sinning has either seen him or known him. Little children, let no one deceive you. Whoever practices righteousness is righteous, as he is righteous. Whoever makes a practice of sinning is of the devil, for the devil has been sinning from the beginning. The reason the Son of God appeared was to destroy the works of the devil. No one born of God makes a practice of sinning, for God's seed abides in him, and he cannot keep on sinning because he has been born of God. By this it is evident who are the children of God, and who are the children of the devil: whoever does not practice righteousness is not of God, nor is the one who does not love his brother.

In what ways have your sinful habits been curbed?

Real Christianity initiates new righteous habits. If we have truly repented of our sins and placed our trust in Christ, righteous habits naturally follow. Notice what the Bible says about the "proof" of real repentance and real faith.

Acts 26:20b

"...they should repent and turn to God, performing deeds in keeping with their repentance."

James 2:14, 17-18

What good is it, my brothers, if someone says he has faith but does not have works? Can that faith save him? ... So also faith by itself, if it does not have works, is dead. But someone will say, "You have faith; and I have works." Show me your faith apart from your works, and I will show you my faith by my works.

Deeper Study...
Seek to assemble a biblical list of specific things that the Bible considers "good deeds" or righteous acts that reflect a new life in Christ (e.g. "loving your brother," etc.)

CHAPTER 1
BEING SURE ABOUT YOUR RELATIONSHIP WITH GOD

A sure indicator that we have truly turned to God is the presence of good and righteous deeds. These new patterns of doing what God desires for us to do are not drudgery! Because of the transformation of our core motivation doing what is right is a joy for the genuine Christian.

> **1 John 5:2-3**
>
> By this we know that we love the children of God, when we love God and obey his commandments. For this is the love of God, that we keep his commandments. And his commandments are not burdensome.

What righteous habits has God initiated in your life?

Real Christianity creates changes that last a lifetime. When God genuinely transforms people, the effects of that transformation last for the rest of their lives. Of course there will be times of struggle and occasional defeat but their new life in Christ is never temporary. Notice the Bible's perspective when people's association with Christ *is* temporary.

> **1 John 2:19**
>
> They went out from us, but they were not of us; for if they had been of us, they would have continued with us. But they went out, that it might become plain that they all are not of us.

For those adopted into God's family (or flock in this case) there is nothing that can sever that new relationship. It is an act of God that cannot be reversed.

> **John 10:27-29**
>
> "My sheep hear my voice, and I know them, and they follow me. I give them eternal life, and they will never perish, and no one will snatch them out of my hand. My Father, who has given them to me, is greater than all, and no one is able to snatch them out of the Father's hand."

If the Christian's relationship with Jesus is secure, then it follows that the implications and effects of this relationship with Christ are equally secure.

With Your Partner...
Discuss the practical difficulties of admitting that "fruitless" Christians aren't Christians at all. Have you had to admit this about someone you know who claims to know God but really doesn't? Look together at Titus 1:16.

PARTNERS:
ONE-ON-ONE DISCIPLESHIP

How does this principle of guaranteed longevity in Christ help to convert verses like the one below from passages producing fear and concern into passages that produce security and confidence?

> **Hebrews 3:14**
>
> For we have come to share in Christ, if indeed we hold our original confidence firm to the end.

Big Errors Regarding Christianity & Good Deeds!

So far we have studied 1) the right gospel, 2) the proper response to the gospel, and 3) the good deeds that follow. It is critical that we understand the relationship between these elements and never confuse them. Confusing the role of any of the elements we have discussed can have disastrous results. There are two primary ways that people tend to misunderstand them.

The first error is a fatal one. Almost every cult group in the world falls into this trap. Notice that though they may include the proper elements they certainly don't understand them as presented in the Bible because they place them wrongly into the biblical equation. The first popular error looks like this:

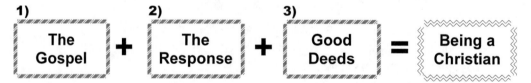

Those who believe this equation say that if you want to become a Christian you must:

1) understand the gospel;
2) respond to the gospel with repentance and faith;
3) do a lot of good deeds;

...and then you will become a Christian!

With Your Partner...
Discuss the various groups with which you are familiar who say that our good works are the basis for our salvation (wholly or in part).

When we took a closer look at faith earlier in this chapter it became clear that the call to faith was a call to put our trust in Christ, and Christ alone. We saw that we must abandon any confidence in our own righteousness and trust fully in the righteousness that comes from Jesus Christ. The equation above bases our salvation (at least in part) on the accomplishment of our own good deeds. This is thoroughly unbiblical! Notice in the following verses that our good deeds play no role in bringing about our salvation. We are saved through the work of Christ and what he has done for us, not what we have accomplished ourselves!

CHAPTER 1
BEING SURE ABOUT YOUR RELATIONSHIP WITH GOD

> **Titus 3:4-5a**
>
> But when the goodness and loving kindness of God our Savior appeared, he saved us, not because of works done by us in righteousness, but according to his own mercy,

> **Ephesians 2:8-9**
>
> For by grace you have been saved through faith. And this is not your own doing; it is the gift of God, not a result of works, so that no one may boast.

These verses make it clear that our salvation is not based on the good deeds that we do. Unfortunately, some have understood these verses to mean that good works are not important in the equation at all. That is the second big error people can make when thinking through the elements involved in salvation.

When people take good deeds and fruit out of the equation altogether it looks something like this:

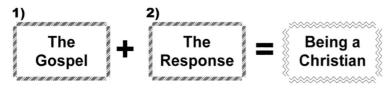

They would say, if you want to be sure you are a Christian ➩ just make sure that:

1) you have understood the gospel;
2) you have responded to the gospel;

…then you can be sure you are a Christian regardless of whether you see any fruit of that decision or not.

We have already seen that this is an unacceptable equation according to the Bible. Real Christians produce real fruit! Jesus said:

> **Matthew 7:16-20**
>
> "You will recognize them by their fruits. Are grapes gathered from thornbushes, or figs from thistles? So, every healthy tree bears good fruit, but the diseased tree bears bad fruit. A healthy tree cannot bear bad fruit, nor can a diseased tree bear good fruit. Every tree that does not bear good fruit is cut down and thrown into the fire. Thus you will recognize them by their fruits."

Deeper Study…
Evaluate the movement sometimes referred to as "easy-believism." Seek to discover its recent origins and explore its implications and dangers in modern evangelism.

PARTNERS:
ONE-ON-ONE DISCIPLESHIP

Summary!

The gospel message properly understood, coupled with a biblical response to the gospel (repentance & faith) makes one a Christian who then bears fruit (good deeds). An accurate summary of the gospel elements should look like this:

1) **The Right Gospel** + **2)** **The Right Response** = **Being a Christian** + **3)** **Good Deeds**

If you want to be sure that you are a Christian ☞ you should evaluate your life and make sure that:

1) you have understood the gospel as presented in the Bible;

2) you have rightly responded to the gospel with repentance and faith;

3) you are producing fruit or good deeds as evidence of your Christianity.

If after working through this chapter you are convinced that you are *not* a Christian, either because you have never understood the gospel, or because you have never rightly responded to the gospel, or because you realize that there has never been any genuine fruit in your life, then make the decision to become a Christian right now!

With Your Partner...

If you have responded to the gospel with genuine repentance and faith today be sure and tell your partner!

If you sense that God is right now working in you a biblical response of genuine repentance and faith, be sure to review the components of the gospel message on pages 5 through 9; then express to God that you are now wholeheartedly repenting of your sins and placing your faith in Christ. If this is God's work in your heart and mind, then you will undoubtedly begin to see the fruit of repentance and faith from this day forward!

Your Story

Writing out your testimony (the story of how you became a Christian) can be helpful in harmonizing your experience with the teachings of the Bible. Often the temptation is to reinterpret the Bible to maintain your story. Remember that your testimony is a subjective recollection of what you think happened in the establishment of your relationship with God. The Bible is clear, objective, and timeless. God would much prefer that you reinterpret your testimony to be in sync with the clear statements of Scripture. That may mean that you need to admit that you did not really become a Christian when you thought you did. It may mean that something that you considered a "rededication" was really the point when you became a Christian and began to see fruit in your life. It may mean that what you believed to be genuine fruit at some point in your life was actually artificial and short-lived.

Whatever the case, don't be afraid to reevaluate your story especially the timing of 1) when you properly understood the biblical gospel, 2) when you rightly responded to the gospel with repentance and faith, 3) when your life began to reflect the transformation that happens when a person becomes a Christian.

18

CHAPTER 1
BEING SURE ABOUT YOUR RELATIONSHIP WITH GOD

Describe the point in your life when you really understood the biblical gospel.

Describe the events that surrounded your response of repentance and faith.

Describe the fruit in your life that gives evidence of your new life in Christ.

PARTNERS:
ONE-ON-ONE DISCIPLESHIP

Notes

CHAPTER 1
BEING SURE ABOUT YOUR RELATIONSHIP WITH GOD

Notes

PARTNERS:
ONE-ON-ONE DISCIPLESHIP

Notes

RESOURCES & FURTHER STUDY

Being Sure About Your Relationship with God

Rating Key
★ Helpful (four being most)
◉ Difficulty (four being hardest)

Resources on the Content of the Gospel Message

★★
◉◉◉ Basinger, David, and Randall Basinger, eds. *Predestination & Free Will: Four Views of Divine Sovereignty & Human Freedom.* Downers Grove, IL: InterVarsity Press, 1986. (This book presents four major evangelical views on the conundrum of God's sovereign election and man's freewill.)

★★
◉◉◉◉ Calvin, John. *The Bondage and Liberation of the Will: A Defense of the Orthodox Doctrine of Human Choice Against Pighius.* Grand Rapids, MI: Baker Books, 1996. (This classic work helps to clarify the problem of sin.)

★
◉ Gromacki, Robert. *Salvation is Forever.* Schaumburg, IL: Regular Baptist Press, 1989. (This book explains the reasons that Christians endure.)

★★★★
◉◉ MacArthur, John F. Jr. *The Gospel According to Jesus: What Does Jesus Mean When He Says, "Follow Me"?* Grand Rapids, MI: Academie Books, Zondervan Publishing House, 1989. (This book helps to explain the necessary and biblical response to the gospel.)

★★★
◉◉ _____. *Faith Works: The Gospel According to the Apostles.* Dallas, TX: Word Publishing, 1993. (This book shows that works naturally follow real repentance and faith.)

★★★
◉◉ Metzger, Will. *Tell The Truth.* Downers Grove, IL: InterVarsity Press, 1984. (This book highlights the "God-centered gospel" of Scripture versus a popularized "man-centered gospel".)

★★★
◉◉ Miller, C. John. *Repentance & 20ᵗʰ Century Man.* Fort Washington, PA: Christian Literature Crusade, 1975. (This short book presents insights on repentance as it relates to salvation and the Christian life in general.)

★★
◉ Needham, David C. *Alive for the First Time: A Fresh Look at the New-Birth Miracle.* Sisters, OR: Multnomah Books, 1995. (This book gives some helpful insight into the reason Christians bear fruit.)

★★
◉◉ Packer, J. I. *Evangelism and the Sovereignty of God.* Downers Grove, IL: InterVarsity Press, 1961. (This book addresses the conundrum of God's sovereign election and man's freewill.)

★★★
◉◉◉ Sproul, R. C. *Faith Alone: The Evangelical Doctrine of Justification.* Grand Rapids, MI: Baker Books, 1996. (This book is helpful in showing that works are not the basis of salvation.)

★★★
◉◉◉ _____. *Getting the Gospel Right: The Tie That Binds Evangelical Together.* Grand Rapids, MI: Baker Books, 1999. (This book counters the recent organized movements that attempt to unify churches at the cost of compromising the gospel.)

★★★★
◉◉ Watson, Thomas. *The Doctrine of Repentance.* Carlisle, PA: The Banner of Truth Trust, (1668) 1994. (This is a devotional and provocative look at what it means to really repent of our sin.)

Resources on the Creation/Evolution Debate

★★
◉◉◉
Behe, Michael J. *Darwin's Black Box: The Biochemical Challenge to Evolution.* New York, NY: The Free Press, 1996. (This book is not written by a creationist and yet it clearly shows the biochemical impossibilities of the evolutionary theory.)

★★
◉◉◉
Denton, Michael. *Evolution: A Theory in Crisis.* Bethesda MD: Adler & Adler, Publishers, Inc., 1985. (This book is also not written by a creationist and yet it presents the major flaws of evolutionary thinking in microbiology.)

★★★★
◉
Institute for Creation Research. 10946 Woodside Ave. North, Santee, CA 92071; (619) 448-0900; www.icr.org. (This us an organization that has many popular resources supporting biblical creationism, including works for children, and a bookstore on the Internet.)

★★★
◉◉
Lubenow, Marvin. *Bones of Contention: A Creationist Assessment of the Human Fossil Record.* Grand Rapids, MI: Baker Book House, 1992. (This book shows the fallacies that surround the modern beliefs and presentation of the fossil record.)

★★★
◉◉◉
Moreland, J. P., ed. *The Creation Hypothesis: Scientific Evidence for an Intelligent Designer.* Downers Grove, IL: InterVarsity Press, 1994. (This book logically presents the reasonableness of a personal Creator from a Christian perspective.)

★★★
◉◉◉
_____. *Scaling the Secular City: A Defense of Christianity.* Grand Rapids, MI: Baker Book House, 1987. (This book presents a variety of evidences that argue for the existence of a personal Creator.)

★★
◉◉◉◉
Schaeffer, Francis A. *The God Who is There: Speaking Historic Christianity into the Twentieth Century* Downers Grove, IL: InterVarsity Press, 1968. (This book lays a foundation for the book that follows.)

★★
◉◉◉◉
_____. *He is There and He is Not Silent.* Wheaton, IL: Tyndale House Publishers, 1972. (This book presents an argument for the necessity of a personal Creator from a philosophical and epistemological perspective.)

Chapter 2

PARTNERS MEETING #2

Deepening Your Knowledge of God

At Partners Meeting #2...

You will become aware of our great need to deepen our knowledge of God. You will work together with your partner to deepen your understanding of our Creator, focusing especially on the practical implications that come from a better comprehension of him. This subject is vast and limitless so prepare to stretch the boundaries of your current view of God.

To Prepare for Partners Meeting #2...

• Read chapter 2 carefully.

• Be very practical and specific in your answers about the implications of the knowledge of God for your particular life situation.

• Be prepared to discuss your answers.

• If any of the "Deeper Study" topics are of interest to you, prepare to discuss those as well.

• Memorize 2 Peter 1:3.

His divine power has granted to us all things that pertain to life and godliness, through the knowledge of him who called us to his own glory and excellence,
– 2 Peter 1:3

PARTNERS:
ONE-ON-ONE DISCIPLESHIP

Your understanding of God is arguably the most important thing about you. Your view of God affects everything in your life—how you think, what you value, and how you act. It is almost impossible to overstate the importance of how you understand God.

As Christians we derive our view of God from the Bible. Believing for good reason that the Bible is a record of what God has revealed about himself (see chapter 3), it is critically important that we always attempt to align our understanding of God with what he has recorded about himself in the Bible. Deferring to our personal preferences or intuitions is always a bad idea if our goal is to come to an accurate and truthful understanding of what God is really all about. And seeing that so much depends on a proper view of God, the Bible must be our guide in deepening our understanding of him.

A Regal God

One of the first things we discover about God when we look to his word is that he is a lofty and majestic God. All over the Bible God is presented as overwhelming and amazing! The magnificence of God is the foundation for our awe and worship. The more we learn about God, the more impressed we become. Compare the following awe filled comments from 1 Chronicles to the average Christian's view today.

With Your Partner...
Describe how your view of God has changed (either improved, deteriorated, or fluctuated) since you became a Christian.

1 Chronicles 29:10-14, 20

Therefore David blessed the LORD in the presence of all the assembly. And David said: "Blessed are you, O LORD, the God of Israel our father, forever and ever. Yours, O LORD, is the greatness and the power and the glory and the victory and the majesty, for all that is in the heavens and in the earth is yours. Yours is the kingdom, O LORD, and you are exalted as head above all. Both riches and honor come from you, and you rule over all. In your hand are power and might, and in your hand it is to make great and to give strength to all. And now we thank you, our God, and praise your glorious name. "But who am I, and what is my people, that we should be able thus to offer willingly? For all things come from you, and of your own have we given you..." Then David said to all the assembly, "Bless the LORD your God." And all the assembly blessed the LORD, the God of their fathers, and bowed their heads and paid homage to the LORD and to the king.

With Your Partner...
Discuss how well you worship (i.e., express your respect, love, and adoration to our majestic God) both in worship services and throughout the week.

Words like that stand in contrast to today's popular, but inadequate, concepts of God. If we really begin to grasp the biblical portrait of God in the Bible we will certainly never be able to refer to God as "the man upstairs" or our spiritual "buddy." A thoughtful study of this chapter of *Partners* ought to enrich and deepen our appreciation of God and our expressions of worship.

26

CHAPTER 2
DEEPENING YOUR KNOWLEDGE OF GOD

From Theology to Thursday

Remember that when we maintain a deflated view of God it always has its adverse effects on our lives! We cannot afford to forget the inevitable connection that exists between how we view God and how we live our daily lives.

Consider for a moment the relationship between sinful activities and a wrong view of God. See if you can identify the way particular sins correspond to particular errors in one's view of God. For example, when a Christian is consumed with worry and anxiety, then he or she certainly isn't living in light of the truth that God is good, sovereign, all-powerful, and always present.

When we are forgetful or uninformed about what kind of God we have, we make ourselves vulnerable to all kinds of problems in the Christian life.

> **A. W. Tozer**
> *Knowledge of the Holy – p.6*
>
> "The low view of God entertained almost universally among Christians is the cause of a hundred lesser evils everywhere among us."

Jot down a few other connections that exist between familiar sins and the corresponding errors in our thoughts about God.

Deeper Study...
Study acceptable and unacceptable worship as described in the Bible. Identify situations in which we can be sincerely attempting to worship God, but in reality we are actually in danger of offending him.

With Your Partner...
Discuss some of your answers to this question.

Not only is an accurate view of God a deterrent for sin in the Christian life, it is also an unmatched motivation to love and serve him! The more we accurately understand and fully comprehend God's perfect character, the more we will live in awe of him and the more we will be challenged to respond with enthusiasm to what he says.

The Triune God

No one should think that the God of the Bible is simplistic. He certainly is not! Some things about God are quite difficult, and sometimes impossible, to fully comprehend. The nature of God is one of these profound challenges. The facts as presented in the pages of the Bible are simple enough, but the intellectual resolution of those facts is beyond our ability. This reminds us that God is definitely more complex than we can fathom—which in and of itself is something we might expect of God.

PARTNERS:
ONE-ON-ONE DISCIPLESHIP

Fact 1: There is one God
The Bible is clear that there is only one God.

> **Deuteronomy 6:4**
>
> "Hear, O Israel: The LORD our God, the LORD is one."

> **Romans 3:30a**
>
> ... God is one...

> **Isaiah 44:8b**
>
> "Is there a God besides me? There is no Rock; I know not any."

> **1 Corinthians 8:4b**
>
> ...we know that "an idol has no real existence," and that "there is no God but one."

Fact 2: The Father is God, Jesus is God, and the Holy Spirit is God
While the Bible plainly teaches that there is only one God, it also unabashedly designates three persons as God: The Father, Jesus, and the Holy Spirit.

Note these examples.

> **Ephesians 5:20a**
>
> ...giving thanks always and for everything to God the Father ...

> **Hebrews 1:8a**
>
> But of the Son he says, "Your throne, O God, is for ever and ever,..."

> **Acts 5:3-4**
>
> But Peter said, "Ananias, why has Satan filled your heart to lie to the Holy Spirit...? Why is it that you have contrived this deed in your heart? You have not lied to men but to God."

Further Study...
Research other passages in the Bible that show us that Jesus is God. Give special attention to the "divine titles" that both the Father and the Son share.

CHAPTER 2

DEEPENING YOUR KNOWLEDGE OF GOD

Not only are all three persons presented in the Bible as "God," but many times all three persons are grouped together and presented as a divine authority.

Matthew 28:19

"Go therefore and make disciples of all nations, baptizing them in the name of the Father and of the Son and of the Holy Spirit..."

2 Corinthians 13:14

The grace of the Lord Jesus Christ and the love of God and the fellowship of the Holy Spirit be with you all.

1 Peter 1:1b-2a

...to those who are elect... according to the foreknowledge of God the Father, in the sanctification of the Spirit, for obedience to Jesus Christ...

Fact 3: The Father is not Jesus, Jesus is not the Holy Spirit, and the Holy Spirit is not the Father

One important fact that cannot be overlooked when considering this mysterious truth is that all three persons of the Godhead are distinct personalities. In other words, the one God is not simply manifesting himself in three different ways. This is made clear in several passages where the personalities of the Godhead are interacting with one another. As one theologian put it, there are three "personal self-distinctions within the Divine essence."[1]

How are these distinctions seen in these Old Testament passages that are predicting the Messiah's coming?

Isaiah 48:16

Isaiah 61:1 (Luke 4:17-21)

---

[1] Louis Berkhof, *Systematic Theology,* (Grand Rapids, MI: Eerdmans Publishing, 1938), p.87.

PARTNERS:
ONE-ON-ONE DISCIPLESHIP

How are these personality distinctions seen in these New Testament passages?

Luke 3:21-22

John 14:16-17a

Conclusion: God is "Three in One"

Amazingly, God is Triune! One God in regard to essence, but three in respect to persons. In his triunity God has, from all eternity, been expressing his perfect attributes in the perfect relationship that forever exists in the Godhead. "In his essential life God is a fellowship."[2] Without a doubt, it is a mystery, but arguably a reasonable one! This truth can be visually summed up in this diagram.

With Your Partner...
Discuss how an understanding of the triunity of God makes a difference in your worship.

With Your Partner...
Explain the meaning of this diagram.

Deeper Study...
There have been three long-standing errors in understanding the Godhead, traditionally called: 1) Tri-theism, 2) Modalism, and 3) Arianism. Research these errors and describe how these have been repackaged in the modern era in the various groups that hold to these positions.

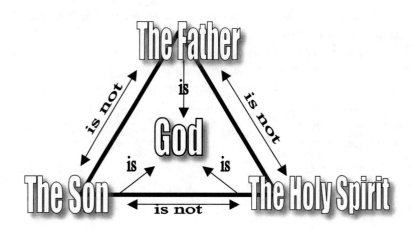

By studying the Triune God we see that God is not a force or a thing. He is a God who exists in three persons. Each person of the Godhead is presented in the Bible as having the characteristics of "personality"—namely, intellect, emotion, and will. All persons of the Godhead think. All persons of the Godhead feel. All persons of the Godhead act.

---

[2] *The New Bible Dictionary*, (Wheaton, IL: Tyndale House Publishers, Inc., 1962), p.428.

CHAPTER 2
DEEPENING YOUR KNOWLEDGE OF GOD

Match each passage in the left-hand column with the appropriate description in the right-hand column. Connect the dot next to each passage with the dot next to its description.

John 11:35 •   • An example of the Father's intellect

Ephesians 4:30 •   • An example of the Father's emotion

John 1:43 •   • An example of the Father's will

Genesis 6:6 •   • An example of the Son's intellect

Isaiah 11:2 •   • An example of the Son's emotion

Isaiah 1:18 •   • An example of the Son's will

Matthew 22:45-46 •   • An example of the Holy Spirit's intellect

Mark 1:12 •   • An example of the Holy Spirit's emotion

Genesis 1:1 •   • An example of the Holy Spirit's will

How does this knowledge of the "personhood" of the Godhead affect the way you pray?

The Attributes of God

A thoughtful study of some of the specific attributes of this triune God is critical if we are to really know who God is and what he is like.

Deeper Study...
List as many attributes of God as you can (and a corresponding Bible reference) that are not mentioned on the following pages in this chapter of Partners.

An attribute of God is *a statement that accurately and succinctly describes some aspect of God's character.* Millard Erickson clarifies what attributes are not: *"We are not referring here to the acts which he performs, such as creating, guiding, and preserving, nor to the corresponding roles he plays – Creator, Guide, Preserver."* [3] When we speak of an attribute of God we are talking about a characteristic that constitutes who God is.

Here are a few reminders when considering the attributes of God:

1. The Bible is the only reliable source of information about God's attributes! To know for sure what God is like we must rely on the information that he has provided. The Bible is the only unalterable and indisputable source of revelation from God that we have. Since God has revealed himself to us in the Bible, that is the place we must go to learn what is true about him.

With Your Partner...
Discuss the ways that people are led to believe things about God that are derived from some other source than the Bible.

---

[3] Millard J. Erickson, *Christian Theology,* (Grand Rapids, MI: Baker Book House, 1985), p. 265.

31

PARTNERS:

ONE-ON-ONE DISCIPLESHIP

2. The information found in the Bible about God is profound and immense! Though the Bible does not tell us everything there is to know about God (see Deuteronomy 29:29), the information we do have is extensive. It can easily take a lifetime to delve into the implications of just one of God's attributes.

> **Ephesians 3:17b-19a**
>
> that you, being rooted and grounded in love, may have strength to comprehend with all the saints what is the breadth and length and height and depth, and to know the love of Christ that surpasses knowledge...

What does this passage say is needed for us to grasp the meaning and implications of God's attributes?

Hint...
This passage can serve as a guide for how you study each of the specific attributes listed on the following pages.

Though this chapter admittedly only covers a few of God's important attributes, and your time spent on each will only scratch the surface of their implications, it is hoped that the chapter will motivate you to make "attribute studies" a regular part of your Christian life.

3. Some of God's attributes are revealed to be a model for our lives! It is obvious that many of God's attributes cannot and should not be the goal of our Christian lives (e.g.: everywhere-present, all-powerful, etc.). On the other hand, God has told us to reflect many of his attributes in our everyday lives.

With Your Partner...
Discuss which other attributes of God we cannot share as well as those we could emulate but shouldn't.

Deeper Study...
Find passages of Scripture like 1 Peter 1:15-16 that give us the command to emulate, or the prohibition not to emulate, a divine attribute.

> **1 Peter 1:15-16**
>
> but as he who called you is holy, you also be holy in all your conduct, since it is written: "You shall be holy, for I am holy."

The distinction between the attributes we are to imitate and the attributes which are God's alone should be carefully noted in your study. Some scholars have made this distinction with terms such as "moral" and "non-moral attributes," "communicable" and "non-communicable attributes," "transitive" and "non-transitive attributes." In this study we will categorize the difference with the terms "shared" and "non-shared attributes."

When it comes to his "shared attributes," Romans 3:23 makes it clear that we cannot always reflect his attributes with perfect consistency, but that does not mean that we cannot and should not make the reflection of his character our goal in every situation we face.

32

CHAPTER 2
DEEPENING YOUR KNOWLEDGE OF GOD

God's Non-shared Attributes

God is Sovereign

A Definition
God retains all rights and exercises supreme and ultimate authority over everyone and everything.

Comment on each of the following verses, summarizing what they teach us about God's sovereignty.

Psalm 103:19

Isaiah 14:24

1 Timothy 6:15

Mark 4:39-41

How will a continual and deepening understanding of God's sovereignty change the way you think and live?

Hint...
Use an English dictionary to look up the word that represents the attribute being discussed (in this case "sovereignty"). Looking up the word in a dictionary will help you understand its origin, as well as give you insight as to why that particular word was chosen to represent the attribute.

Deeper Study...
Study and discuss the implications of God's sovereignty as it relates to human decisions regarding the gospel and salvation. Study passages such as Ephesians 1:11. For related books which may help, see chapter one's Resources & Further Study Page.

With Your Partner...
Discuss this question's answer with your partner.

33

PARTNERS:

ONE-ON-ONE DISCIPLESHIP

God is Omniscient

A Definition
God possesses all knowledge, knowing all there is to know whether actual or possible.

Comment on each of the following verses, summarizing what they teach us about God's omniscience.

Psalm 139:1-6

Deeper Study...
Study how God's omniscience is foundational to the distinctiveness of the Bible (see passages such as Isaiah 44:6-8). Notice how all other "holy books" are void of this signature of the one true God.

Romans 11:33-36

Psalm 147:5

John 16:30

What temptations do you face that seem ridiculous in light of God's omniscience?

With Your Partner...
Discuss this question's answer with your partner.

34

CHAPTER 2
DEEPENING YOUR KNOWLEDGE OF GOD

God is Omnipotent

A Simple Definition

God possesses all power, having the ability to do anything that does not conflict with his own character.

Comment on each of the following verses, summarizing what they teach us about God's omnipotence.

Genesis 18:14

Job 42:2

Jeremiah 32:17

Ephesians 1:19-21

How will a continual and deepening understanding of God's omnipotence change the way you think and live?

Deeper Study...
Ponder the question, "Can God make a rock so big that he cannot move it?" List what the Bible says God "cannot" do (cf. 2Ti.2:13; Hab.1:13, etc.). Think through and attempt to articulate why such limits are important and necessary.

With Your Partner...
Discuss this question's answer with your partner.

PARTNERS:
ONE-ON-ONE DISCIPLESHIP

God is Omnipresent

A Simple Definition

God is everywhere present, being cognizant of all things in every location.

Comment on each of the following verses, summarizing what they teach us about God's omnipresence.

Psalm 139:7-12

Hebrews 4:13

Proverbs 15:3

John 1:48-49

What difference does it make to realize that God is present with you right now and will continue to be no matter where you go today?

With Your Partner...
Discuss this question's answer with your partner.

CHAPTER 2
DEEPENING YOUR KNOWLEDGE OF GOD

God is Eternal

A Simple Definition

God has existed and will exist forever, having no time limits, no beginning and no end.

Comment on each of the following verses, summarizing what they teach us about God's timelessness.

Psalm 90:2

Psalm 93:2

Deeper Study...
Study the implications of a God who exists outside of time. Think through the question of "infinite regression" and God as the "uncaused cause".

Revelation 1:8

John 8:57-58

How does having a relationship with an *eternal* God change your perspective on everyday life and the many things that seem so urgent?

With Your Partner...
Discuss this question's answer with your partner.

37

PARTNERS:
ONE-ON-ONE DISCIPLESHIP

God is Immutable

A Simple Definition

God is unchanging, having no variation, growth, or evolution of his divine character.

Comment on each of the following verses, summarizing what they teach us about God's changelessness.

Malachi 3:6a

Psalm 102:25-27

Deeper Study...
Think through the distinction that exists between God's immutability and God's progressive revelation throughout biblical history, as well as the various economies employed in his dealings with mankind that are recorded in the Bible.

Romans 11:29

Hebrews 13:8

How can your life be impacted, comforted, and challenged by knowing and remembering that God is a God who does not change?

With Your Partner...
Discuss this question's answer with your partner.

38

CHAPTER 2
DEEPENING YOUR KNOWLEDGE OF GOD

God's Shared Attributes

God is Holy

Note...
Remember that the remaining attributes studied in this chapter are said in the Bible to be patterns for how we are to live (i.e. "shared attributes").

A Simple Definition

God is morally perfect, without any defect or error in his actions, attitudes and behavior.

Comment on each of the following verses, summarizing what they teach us about God's holiness.

1 Samuel 2:2

Leviticus 20:7-8

Deeper Study...
Familiarize yourself with the theories of theodicy (i.e., the branch of theology that defends the holiness of God in light of the present evil in the world).

Revelation 4:8

John 6:68-69

How can a deeper understanding and respect for God's holiness change the way you relate to God?

Name a specific area of your life where you need to imitate more of God's holiness.

With Your Partner...
Discuss this question's answer with your partner.

39

PARTNERS:
ONE-ON-ONE DISCIPLESHIP

God is Just

A Simple Definition
God is perfectly equitable, always correct in his compensation of all things.

Comment on each of the following verses, summarizing what they teach us about God's just character.

Psalm 97:2

Job 34:12

Deeper Study...
Study passages such as Romans 3:23-26 and 2 Corinthians 5:21 and be able to articulate how God maintains his justice while forgiving sinners.

Psalm 9:8

Revelation 19:11-13

How does a constant awareness of God's perfect justice (though sometimes delayed and at other times redirected to the cross) change the way you relate and depend on God?

In what area of your life do you need to reflect more of God's equitable nature?

With Your Partner...
Discuss this question's answer with your partner.

40

CHAPTER 2
DEEPENING YOUR KNOWLEDGE OF GOD

God is Love

A Simple Definition

God freely and perfectly acts for the good and well-being of others.

Comment on each of the following verses, summarizing what they teach us about God's love.

1 John 4:8

Romans 5:8

Romans 8:37-39

John 13:34

How is your relationship with God enhanced by knowing and remembering that God is perfectly and consistently loving?

Name a relationship in which you need to imitate God's love. How will you do that?

With Your Partner...
Discuss this question's answer with your partner.

PARTNERS:
ONE-ON-ONE DISCIPLESHIP

God is Faithful

A Simple Definition

God is perfectly reliable, without any deviation in his response to what he has promised.

Comment on each of the following verses, summarizing what they teach us about God's faithfulness.

Psalm 89:1-2

Lamentations 3:22-23

2 Timothy 2:13

Revelation 1:5

What difference does it make that God is a perfectly faithful God?

What specific area of your life needs to reflect more of this kind of faithfulness?

With Your Partner...
Discuss this question's answer with your partner.

CHAPTER 2
DEEPENING YOUR KNOWLEDGE OF GOD

God is Jealous

A Simple Definition

God is inflexible in his expectation of loyalty and rightful recognition.

Comment on each of the following verses, summarizing what they teach us about God's jealousy.

Exodus 34:14

James 4:4-5

Deeper Study...
Be able to distinguish biblically and personally the difference between sinful jealousy (e.g., Gal.5:20; 2Cor.12:20) and godly jealousy (e.g., 2Cor.11:2).

Zechariah 8:2

Matthew 23:37

How is your perspective and attitude adjusted by the thought that God is jealous for us?

In what appropriate and godly way do you need to be jealous for God's sake or over God's people (see Paul's example in 2 Corinthians 11:2).

With Your Partner...
Discuss this question's answer with your partner.

43

PARTNERS:
ONE-ON-ONE DISCIPLESHIP

God is Patient

A Simple Definition
God controls his will with perfect endurance in the face of pain or any other provocation.

Comment on each of the following verses, summarizing what they teach us about God's patience.

Romans 2:4

Exodus 34:6

2 Peter 3:9

1 Timothy 1:16

How does a deeper understanding of God's patience enrich your relationship with him and your worship of him?

In what difficult or uncomfortable situation do you need to demonstrate God's kind of patience?

With Your Partner...
Discuss this question's answer with your partner.

44

CHAPTER 2
DEEPENING YOUR KNOWLEDGE OF GOD

Assessments

How has this study of God and his attributes changed your view of God?

Deeper Study...
Review the fourth passage listed in each of the attributes studied in this chapter. Note that they specifically refer to Jesus Christ. Think through which other divine attributes Jesus perfectly modeled during his earthly ministry, demonstrating that he was God incarnate (cf. Col.1:15; 2:9).

How do you think this study of God and his attributes will enhance your worship?

Write out a prayer that reflects your desire and commitment to know God better.

A. W. Tozer, *Knowledge of the Holy*, p.9

"Those that don't accurately know you Lord, may call upon you as something other than you are, and so not worship you, but rather some creature of their own imagination. Therefore God, enlighten our minds that we may accurately know you and worthily praise you." *(author's paraphrase)*

PARTNERS:
ONE-ON-ONE DISCIPLESHIP

Notes

CHAPTER 2
DEEPENING YOUR KNOWLEDGE OF GOD

Notes

PARTNERS:
ONE-ON-ONE DISCIPLESHIP

Notes

RESOURCES & FURTHER STUDY

Deepening Your Knowledge of God

> Rating Key
> ★ Helpful (four being most)
> ◉ Difficulty (four being hardest)

Devotional Resources on Knowing God Better

★★ ◉ Arthur, Kay. *To Know Him By Name.* Sisters, OR: Multnomah Books, 1995. (This devotional book broadens your understanding of God by expounding on fifteen different names of God in the Old Testament.)

★★★ ◉◉ Packer, J. I. *Knowing God.* Downers Grove, IL: InterVarsity Press, 1973. (This modern classic is a great place to start for a deeper and more accurate view of God.)

★★ ◉◉ Phillips, J.B. *Your God is Too Small.* New York, NY: Macmillan, 1961. (This book addresses some of the common errors we fall into when thinking about God.)

★★★ ◉◉◉ Pink, Arthur W. *The Attributes of God.* Grand Rapids, MI: Baker Book House, 1975. Twenty-ninth printing, 1998. (This uncharacteristically brief book by Pink describes a variety of God's attributes with numerous Scripture references.)

★★★★ ◉◉ Tozer, A. W. *Knowledge of the Holy: The Attributes of God: Their Meaning in the Christian Life.* New York, NY: Harper And Row Publishers, 1961. (A must read that will help you maintain a lofty perspective on our majestic God.)

★★★ ◉◉ _____. *The Pursuit Of God.* Camp Hill, PE: Christian Publications, Inc., 1982. (Another title by Tozer that will inspire you to rightly understand and vigorously pursue God.)

Theological Resources on Understanding the Nature of God

★★ ◉◉◉ Berkhof, Louis *Systematic Theology.* Grand Rapids, MI: Eerdmans Publishing Company, Combined edition with new preface, 1996. (This is a one volume theology textbook with a helpful section on the nature and attributes of God.)

★★★ ◉◉ Bowman, Robert M. Jr. *Why You Should Believe in the Trinity.* Grand Rapids, MI: Baker Book House, 1989. (This book is a brief but helpful response to those who attempt to argue against the biblical understanding of the triune God.)

★★ ◉◉◉ Calvin, John *Institutes of the Christian Religion.* Translated by Henry Beveridge. Grand Rapids, MI: Eerdmans Publishing Company, Reprinted 1993. (This sixteenth century product of the Reformation provides the reader with a majestic and carefully described view of God.)

★★ ◉◉ Chafer, Lewis S. *Systematic Theology.* Vol. 1. Dallas, TX: Dallas Seminary Press, 1947. Tenth printing, 1971. (This first volume concerning God in Chafer's multi-volume set gives a organized and systematic presentation of God's attributes.)

49

★★★ Erickson, Millard J. *Christian Theology*. Grand Rapids, MI: Baker Book House, 1983. Thirteenth
◉◉ printing, 1996. (The section on God is a well written modern theology that does a good job distinguishing a
variety of doctrinal errors from the biblical view of God.)

★★★ _____. *God the Father Almighty: A Contemporary Exploration of the Divine Attributes*. Grand
◉◉◉ Rapids, MI: Baker Book House, 1998. (In this book exclusively about God, Erickson has the
opportunity to expand on many of the themes discussed in his *Christian Theology*.)

★★★ _____. *Making Sense of the Trinity: Three Crucial Questions*. Grand Rapids, MI: Baker Academic,
◉◉◉ 2000. (As the title suggests, Erickson attempts to concisely present the biblical data on the Trinity by addressing
three forthright questions regarding the Father, Son and Holy Spirit.)

★★ Grudem, Wayne *Systematic Theology: An Introduction to Biblical Doctrine*. Grand Rapids, MI:
◉◉ Zondervan, 1994. (This book is probably the most devotional of the systematic theologies, and provide much
to apply to our lives in his section on God.)

★★ Hodge, Charles *Systematic Theology*. Vol. 1. Grand Rapids, MI: Eerdmans Publishing Company,
◉◉◉ Reprinted 1995. (This book is a standard theology textbook which attempts to systematically present God and
his attributes in its appropriate section.)

★★ Strong, Augustus H. *Systematic Theology*. Valley Forge, PA: Judson Press, 1907. Thirty-sixth
◉◉◉ printing, 1996. (This standard theology text also provides a thoughtful and carefully stated discussion on God.)

★★★ Thiessen, Henry C. *Lectures In Systematic Theology*. Grand Rapids, MI: William B. Eerdmans
◉◉ Publishing Company, 1949. (In his concise and well referenced section on God, Thiessen will give you a
helpful overview on the biblical information regarding God and his attributes.)

★★★ Ware, Bruce A. *Father, Son & Holy Spirit: Relationships, Roles & Relevance*. Wheaton, IL: Crossway
◉◉ Books, 2005. (Ware provides a worshipful and practical set of addresses on the importance of the Trinity.)

Resources on Worship

★ Allen, Ronald. *Worship: Rediscovering The Missing Jewel*. Portland, OR: Multnomah Press, 1982.
◉◉ (This book offers a wide variety of directives and suggestions relating to worship..)

★★ MacArthur, John Jr. *The Ultimate Priority*. Chicago, IL: Moody Press, 1983. (This book discusses the
◉ need and the reasons we are called to be worshipping people.)

★★ Tozer, A. W. *Whatever Happened to Worship? A Call to True Worship*. Camp Hill, PA: Christian
◉◉ Publishing, 1985. (This book is filled with urgent motivation for the church to truly worship.)

★★ Wiersbe, Warren. *Real Worship: Playground, Battleground, or Holy Ground. Second Edition*. Grand
◉ Rapids, MI: Baker Books, 2000. (This book will lead you to reexamine your attitude and your life as you
attempt to grow in your worship of God.)

Chapter 3

PARTNERS MEETING #3

Learning to Study the Bible on Your Own

At Partners Meeting #3...

You will discuss a method of inductive Bible study that will help you get the most out of your personal time in God's word. The emphasis will be on accurately understanding and ruthlessly applying the principles you uncover in the Bible. Half the battle is accountability, so you and your partner will take some time to share the goals and methods that will help make the study and application of God's word a regular part of life.

To Prepare for Partners Meeting #3...

- Read chapter 3 carefully and answer the questions.

- Bring to your meeting an example of your personal Bible study (a notebook, study schedule, etc.).

- Be prepared to discuss new Bible study goals.

- If any of the "Deeper Study" topics are of interest to you, prepare to discuss those as well.

- Memorize 2 Timothy 3:16-17.

All Scripture is breathed out by God and profitable for teaching, for reproof, for correction, and for training in righteousness, that the man of God may be complete, equipped for every good work.

– 2 Timothy 3:16-17

PARTNERS:

ONE-ON-ONE DISCIPLESHIP

The Bible is the most important document in the world. God has had his thoughts put down on paper for all time. It can never change nor be altered. It is an enduring record of all that God wants us to know.

> **Isaiah 40:8**
>
> The grass withers, the flower fades, but the word of our God will stand forever.

A Brief History of the Bible

The Bible, being made up of primarily two parts (Old and New Testaments), was originally written in three languages: Hebrew, Aramaic and Koine Greek. The writing of the Bible covers over 1500 years on three continents. It was written by over 40 authors and contains 66 individual books. The writing of the Old Testament began with Moses authoring the Pentateuch (the word Pentateuch represents the first five books of the Old Testament) during the period of the wilderness wanderings after the Jewish exodus from Egypt (approximately 1445 B.C.). This, along with most of the Old Testament, was written in Hebrew and preserved meticulously by Israel as God's written revelation to man. As the "holy writings of Israel" were collected through the years and added to by various other prophets, they were carefully looked after and religiously copied by a special group of Jews called "Scribes" – and this only when needed. The materials on which these books were copied were subject to aging and deterioration through the centuries. When a manuscript was wearing out, it would be copied by a Scribe, checked, double-checked and triple-checked word for word and letter for letter and then the old copy would be destroyed. The Old Testament revelation ended around 430 B.C. in Nehemiah's day with the writing of Malachi.

The New Testament, containing 27 books written entirely in Greek, has a different history. Unlike the Old Testament, there were no Scribes who religiously copied the Text. As Christianity rapidly spread through Asia Minor and the Middle East, the books of the New Testament were copied and recopied by people who were eager to have a record of God's good news concerning Jesus. This resulted in many, many copies of the books in many geographical locations. Like the Old Testament, the New Testament was written on perishable materials which in time simply wore out.

With Your Partner...

Discuss some of the popular misconceptions you have heard about how the Bible came to be.

This situation for both Testaments leaves the church with no original copies from the pens of Peter, Haggai or Samuel. We are left with only copies of the originals. But the good news is that the Bible is the best supported document that we have from antiquity. With the strict copying of the Jewish Scribes and the numerous copies of the New Testament to compare, objectively speaking, a more reliable document than the Bible is not to be found. Like that of the Bible, the original manuscripts of all other writings from antiquity, such as those of Plato,

52

CHAPTER 3

LEARNING TO STUDY THE BIBLE ON YOUR OWN

Socrates, Homer or Aristotle, could not be preserved. All documents from the ancient world were written on perishable materials. When the Bible is compared to these other documents (which rarely are disputed as "authentic"), there is no comparison. Not one scrap of ancient history or literature is better supported by multiple copies or the small gap between the writing and the earliest existing copy than the Bible. There exists very little or no room for distortion or manipulation of the words and message that were originally written by its authors.

The goal of those who study these ancient documents is to examine the many copies of the biblical books and to compare and contrast the minute differences in order to come to a conclusion on exactly what the original manuscript read. This is called the science of textual criticism (also known as "lower criticism").

With the advancement of archeology, we have discovered more ancient copies or manuscripts than were available to some of the early scholars who attempted to translate the Bible into English. Modern translators greatly benefit from the discoveries still being made today. It is always good to have more manuscripts to consider when drawing conclusions on a minor discrepancy in the original Hebrew or Greek manuscripts.

There should be no doubts about the accuracy of the transmission of the Bible. Those who claim that the Bible has been written and rewritten and that the message of the Bible has evolved over time are speaking from ignorance. The facts are that we have a reliable, attested record of God's word. Note the following quotations:

John Warwick Montgomery
***History & Christianity** – p.29*

"to be skeptical of the resultant text of the New Testament books is to allow all of classical antiquity to slip into obscurity, for no documents of the ancient period are as well attested bibliographically as the New Testament"

Sir Frederic G. Kenyon
***The Bible and Modern Scholarship** – p.4*

". . . besides number, the manuscripts of the New Testament differ from those of the classical authors, and this time the difference is clear gain. In no other case is the interval of time between the composition of the book and the date of the earliest extant manuscripts so short as in that of the New Testament."

With Your Partner...
Discuss the importance of archeology in substantiating the accuracy and historicity of the Bible. Discuss any archeological finds that have strengthened your confidence in God's word.

53

PARTNERS:
ONE-ON-ONE DISCIPLESHIP

Nelson Glueck
Rivers in the Desert; History of Negev – **p.31**

"It may be stated categorically that no archaeological discovery has ever controverted a biblical reference."

William F. Albright
The Archaeology of Palestine – **p.127-128**

"The excessive skepticism shown toward the Bible by important historical schools of the eighteenth and nineteenth centuries, certain phases of which still appear periodically, has been progressively discredited. Discovery after discovery has established the accuracy of innumerable details, and has brought increased recognition to the value of the Bible as a source of history."

Millar Burrows
What Mean These Stones? – **p.1**

"On the whole, archaeological work has unquestionably strengthened confidence in the reliability of the Scriptural record. More than one archaeologist has found his respect for the Bible increased by the experience of excavation in Palestine."

Deeper Study...
If you feel you could use some more information on the reliability of the Bible, then be sure to check out the resources on the Resources & Further Study page at the end of this chapter.

Millar Burrows
What Mean These Stones? – **p.278**

"The picture fits the frame; the melody and the accompaniment are harmonious. The force of such evidence is cumulative. The more we find that items in the picture of the past presented by the Bible, even though not directly attested, are compatible with what we know from archaeology, the stronger is our impression of general authenticity. Mere legend or fiction would inevitably betray itself by anachronisms and incongruities."

54

CHAPTER 3

LEARNING TO STUDY THE BIBLE ON YOUR OWN

What does this information about the history and reliability of the Bible do for your attitude toward God's Word? How is that helpful as you think about studying it daily?

Get Ready to Study Your Bible

What would you say if one of your friends told you that he hadn't had anything to eat in days? Imagine him telling you about his good intentions, his busy schedule, and his disappointment that he hadn't gotten around to it. Imagine that person telling you that one trip per weekend with friends to a favorite restaurant was all the time for eating that he had.

I suppose such news would not be well received. You might suggest such a person see a doctor or even consider admitting himself to a special hospital for eating disorders.

Unfortunately, when it comes to our spiritual food we are all too quick to accept this pattern as normal. We find ourselves spiritually malnourished, often blaming it on our busy schedules. This must not be tolerated in our Christian life! It is critically important that we reconsider the importance and the benefits of regular, personal, and daily intake of God's word.

With Your Partner...
Share and discuss candidly your Bible study habits prior to studying this chapter.

> **1 Peter 2:2**
>
> Like newborn infants, long for the pure spiritual milk, that by it you may grow up into salvation--

What are some of the implications found in this verse if we do not regularly ingest God's word?

According to **Hebrews 5:11-14** what are some of the other potential dangers in not having regularly "drunk our milk" and "eaten our solid food"?

With Your Partner...
Discuss some of the negative impacts you have experienced in your Christian life when a regular intake of God's word was neglected.

55

PARTNERS:

ONE-ON-ONE DISCIPLESHIP

Though there is a lot of good spiritual food being served up by gifted Bible teachers, it is important that we don't live on restaurant food—we must learn to fix ourselves a square meal at least once every day!

Lewis Sperry Chafer
Systematic Theology, v.1, p.vi

"No student of the Scriptures should be satisfied to traffic only in the results of the study of other men. The field is inexhaustible and its treasures ever new."

Bible Study is Bible *Study!*

There once sat a well-meaning Christian commencing his daily routine of personal Bible study. His method was haphazard at best and yet it seemed quite sufficient for his needs. He opened his Bible and began to flip through the pages. Intent on obeying the Word of God, his eyes fell upon Matthew 27:5: *"... he departed, and he went and hanged himself."* Unsure of what God was trying to say to him, he quickly thumbed forward several pages and began reading elsewhere. The next verse he read was Luke 10:37: *"...and Jesus said to him, 'You go, and do likewise.'"* Obviously disturbed at the implications of what he had read so far, he quickly fanned the pages of his Bible hoping to come across some verse that would help him make sense of all of this. To his surprise, his eyes locked on to John 13:27 which read, *"...Jesus said to him, 'What you are going to do, do quickly.'"*

The critic of the Bible is often heard saying, "You can make the Bible say whatever you want it to." Unfortunately, many Christians prove this on a daily basis. Without a useful and effective method of Bible study, we can quickly come to false conclusions about what God does and doesn't want for our lives.

Remember that there are not many interpretations of the Bible; there is only one. A passage may have various ways to apply its truth, but as a general rule there is only one truth being communicated. The Bible, like any other written document, including a letter you might write to a friend, is intended to communicate specific concepts and ideas. Just as you would not appreciate your son or daughter making their own sense of a "list of chores," so God does not want you to view the Bible as a free-for-all. To arrive at a proper understanding of each passage of the Bible, you need to learn a workable approach to interpreting the Bible, and then put it to work. That is the ultimate goal of this chapter.

With Your Partner...
Discuss your aversion or attraction to study in general.

This of course will not be as easy as just flipping through the Bible and reading whatever catches our attention. What does **Proverbs 2:1-5** have to say about Bible *"study"*?

56

CHAPTER 3
LEARNING TO STUDY THE BIBLE ON YOUR OWN

> **2 Timothy 2:15**
>
> Do your best to present yourself to God as one approved, a worker who has no need to be ashamed, rightly handling the word of truth.

Respond to this verse. What conviction is felt and what challenges come to mind when you thoughtfully read these words? (Notice the goal.)

God Has Something to Say... To You!

Mirrors are quite an invention. I'm not sure we could live without them these days, though it might be interesting if we tried. If you hadn't used one this morning, you might appear somewhat shocking to your partner, your coworkers, or your classmates who are used to seeing you "well kept." We all see the value in our daily refractive rituals. Notice this insightful comparison:

> **James 1:23-25**
>
> For if anyone is a hearer of the word and not a doer, he is like a man who looks intently at his natural face in a mirror. For he looks at himself and goes away and at once forgets what he was like. But the one who looks into the perfect law, the law of liberty, and perseveres, being no hearer who forgets but a doer who acts, he will be blessed in his doing.

Explain this analogy. What connection have you seen between a disheveled life and personal time spent looking into God's word?

It is important to remember that God wants to encourage, strengthen, challenge, and adjust our lives daily as we spend time studying his word. As Francis Schaeffer said, "He is not silent!" God is a communicator! Our God is a God who has spoken, and he wants to use his eternal word to speak to us each day!

Deeper Study...
Think through the implications of a God who has not communicated. Relate your thoughts to the prevalent views of our relativistic society.

PARTNERS:
ONE-ON-ONE DISCIPLESHIP

Mental Preparation

With Your Partner...
Share an experience when you struggled with accepting the authority of the Bible's clear commands and why.

We must be careful to allow the Bible to speak to us authoritatively. The Bible is not a book of suggestions! God's word serves as the ultimate instruction manual for our lives. It comes directly from the Manufacturer and we must approach it with respect, allowing it to have the final say.

Before you open the Bible to study it be sure to begin with a commitment to do what it says. Remember that you are embarking on a study of God's thoughts, God's values, and God's words.

> **1 Thessalonians 2:13**
>
> And we also thank God constantly for this, that when you received the word of God, which you heard from us, you accepted it not as the word of men but as what it really is, the word of God, which is at work in you believers.

God wants to communicate, but often the process is thwarted when we approach his word critically with skepticism or hesitancy. God is looking for an audience with people who are anxious to hear from him and uncompromisingly obey what he says!

> **D. L. Moody**
>
> "The Bible was not given to increase our knowledge but to change our lives."

God expects this attitude from us, not because he is a tyrant, but because he is the only one who truly knows what is best for us.

Read **Matthew 7:24-27** and describe how you have already found this principle to be true in your life. Give an example from both sides of this analogy.

With Your Partner...
Share your responses to this question and discuss them.

Approaching your personal Bible study with this kind of positive mental attitude is like signing a blank check each day before you begin, and allowing God's word to fill it in. God loves it when his people trust him! Don't approach the word of God by demanding that you first see what it will cost you before you consider signing on. Sign the blank check!

58

CHAPTER 3

LEARNING TO STUDY THE BIBLE ON YOUR OWN

A Daily Bible Study Method

It is important that you take from this chapter a method of Bible study that insures an accurate understanding of each passage as well as an appropriate application for your life, and yet is simple enough to use every day.

On Overview of the Three Steps

Though there are times for a more involved methodology (see page 68) this daily method will call for three simple steps to be applied to a small portion of Scripture. Here are the three steps.

With Your Partner...
Be able to explain these three steps in your own words.

1. THEN (What was being said then?)
The first step will examine the passage with the goal of understanding exactly what was being said to the original audience for which the text was initially intended.

2. ALWAYS (What eternal truth is taught?)
The second step will seek to draw the truth of the passage out of its specific setting in biblical history. In this step you will attempt to articulate what God is teaching in your passage, stating it as a "timeless truth."

3. NOW (How can I apply that truth now?)
The final step will ask you to itemize specific applications of the eternal truth discovered in your passage. The goal here is to give you some specific things to do as a result of what you have learned in your passage.

Where to Start Studying

In seeking an accurate understanding of the passage you are studying each day it is important that you move systematically through a book of the Bible, as opposed to skipping around from place to place. This will keep your mind fixed in the context and flow of thought from day to day.

When learning how to master this method of daily Bible study it is helpful to start in a general and didactic (highly compressed and instructive) book of the New Testament—such as one of the shorter epistles (Ephesians, Colossians, 1 Thessalonians, James, 1 Peter, etc.). These books are the easiest to take through the three steps and lead to a variety of applications along the way. When working your way through one of these books you will often find that just one verse a day is plenty to fill you with new insights and leave you with lots of specific and challenging application.

Slightly more challenging will be the didactic books of the New Testament that are written for a specific purpose, such as Galatians, 1 Timothy, Titus, Philemon, the first half of Romans, etc. The method is not difficult to use in these books, but you will find that the same theme is being addressed from many different angles verse after verse and chapter after chapter. If a book's particular

59

PARTNERS:

ONE-ON-ONE DISCIPLESHIP

theme is of interest to you at this point in your life, then one of these books may prove to be a good choice.

Slightly more challenging still will be New Testament narrative books. These are books that are not written in a highly compacted instructive format. These books include the four gospels (Matthew, Mark, Luke and John) and the book of Acts. Although there are parts of these books that are didactic (i.e., Jesus', Peter's, and Paul's sermons), most of these books are lengthy historical accounts. In these sections you will be forced to take more than just a verse or two to be able to draw out an eternal truth in step two. Sometimes it is necessary to include twelve or fifteen verses to capture the truth that is being expressed in a particular narrative passage.

Old Testament books may prove even more challenging. Though some of these books are very easy to study with highly compacted truths right on the surface (i.e. the book of Proverbs), most are narrative books and need to be carefully understood in light of New Testament principles before they are applied. An Old Testament narrative book is a good choice after you have worked your way through several New Testament books with this daily method.

Most difficult to work through, no matter what the method, are the Old and New Testament apocalyptic books, such as Revelation, Daniel, Zechariah, etc. Apocalyptic literature is highly symbolic, and unless there is a thorough knowledge of the historical settings from which the symbols are taken and a real working knowledge of the rest of Scripture, it is easy to come to the wrong conclusions. Save these books for when you are feeling particularly enterprising.

With Your Partner...
Share with your partner the book you have chosen to study and share why you chose that particular book.

Hopefully just by reading through these categories you have thought of a book that you want to study. If you are still uncertain, you may be able to narrow it down by reading the introductions and summaries that the editors of certain Bibles often provide at the beginning of each individual book. If you can't decide, let me recommend the book of James. It is concise, practical, and extremely challenging. It is a great place to start!

What to Expect

You should get a spiral bound or a three hole punched notebook to be used for your daily Bible study. Depending on the size of your notebook and how big you write, you probably will only need one or two pages for each day's entry.

Be sure to schedule from 20 to 40 minutes each day for this Bible study method. This works very well if you have blocked out an hour each day for spiritual disciplines like Bible study, prayer, and Bible reading. I would suggest that if you only have an hour, an ideal breakdown might include 30 minutes of Bible study, 20 minutes of prayer and 10 minutes of Bible reading. Of course, the more time the better, but at a minimum most Christians should at least be able to carve out an hour in their daily schedule to focus on God and his word!

CHAPTER 3
LEARNING TO STUDY THE BIBLE ON YOUR OWN

This is how a page from your Bible study notebook can be laid out:

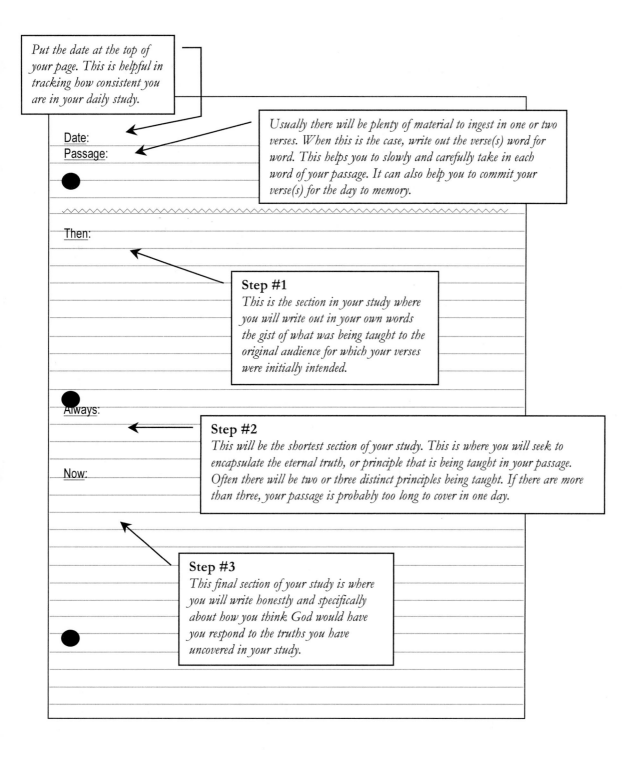

As I mentioned, you may not be able to get all of this on one page, but be careful not to spend too much of your allotted Bible study time on the first couple of steps. It is important that each day you get all the way to step #3. If you don't then you risk not becoming the "doer of the word" that God wants.

PARTNERS:
ONE-ON-ONE DISCIPLESHIP

Now that you know what you are shooting for, let's take a closer look at each of the three steps.

Step #1: <u>THEN</u>

Starting here will save you a ton of mistakes. So often anxious Bible students dive into a passage of Scripture seeking to discover what it "means to me". This is a huge mistake, not because it won't have meaning to you, but because any proper understanding of any message must first be understood in its historic context.

The Bible contains 66 books that were written at particular points in history, to particular audiences, that lived in particular cultures. Though the Bible is full of eternal principles, we cannot be sure we rightly understand those principles unless we arrive at them by taking the "THEN" into account.

Reading a bit of the historical background to the book you have chosen to study will help immensely at putting you into the sandals of the original audience. This will allow you to understand the specific problems that the writer was addressing in that time, the illustrations and examples that were utilized in the book, and perhaps even some of the specific application called for. Here are a few places to look for historical background on the book you are going to study.

1. **The Book Introduction in a Study Bible**. If you have not yet invested in a good study Bible (a Bible with extra notes, comments, and maps designed to help you study) you might want to do so. The brevity and concise nature of the historic settings found at the beginning of each book are invaluable for a quick overview of what was going on in that day.

2. **A Good Commentary**. For a more thorough explanation of the historical setting and helpful comments on each particular passage you will encounter, you may want to purchase a commentary. The best commentaries are generally those which are written to assist in understanding one particular book of the Bible. Single commentaries that try to tackle the entire Bible or even the entire New Testament are usually not as thorough, and therefore not as helpful. Since this daily Bible study method moves you slowly through each verse of a Bible book, you may find that it is worth purchasing one good commentary at the outset of each new book you study.

3. **A Bible Dictionary**. Though it might sound like a Bible "dictionary" simply defines words found in the Bible, in reality a good Bible dictionary addresses themes and concepts as well as specific words. A Bible dictionary will have an entry for each individual book of the Bible usually containing important historical background as well as a simple outline of each book's content.

4. **A Bible Handbook**. Bible handbooks are notorious for answering a wide range of historical and cultural questions in a brief manner. A popular Bible handbook may give you just the help you need to understand the message of your book in the sandals of its recipients.

Remember that it is not only the historical context that is important; it is also the immediate context that helps you rightly understand your passage. Be sure to take note of the verses that precede and follow the verses you will be studying.

FYI...
For help on choosing specific authors or titles that are sound and reliable be sure to ask your pastor or your local Christian bookstore for help.

With Your Partner...
Share a list of titles that you have in your personal library of Christian books.

CHAPTER 3
LEARNING TO STUDY THE BIBLE ON YOUR OWN

Often they give important clues as to what exactly was being said in the verse(s) you are studying.

If you run into words in your passage that confuse you try using an English dictionary, as well as consulting a different Bible translation if you have one available. A commentary and Bible dictionary will also prove helpful.

That may sound like a lot, but remember not to get bogged down in this first step. These resources are important, but you will not need them every day. It is helpful to have them on hand the days when your passage presents you with particular questions.

Remember that when you are writing out this step you should be using a lot of words like "them," "they," and "then," as opposed to words like "we," "us", and "I."

Step #2: **ALWAYS**

In this part of your daily study you will seek to extract the principle or principles that are true for all time. You will seek to state the teaching of your passage in a way that is timeless. It may be a statement that is directed toward Christians (i.e. *"Christians should make evangelism a priority over personal comfort."*) or it may be directed toward people in general (i.e. *"A person cannot be made acceptable before God by doing good things."*).

This is a very important step so don't rush through it. Carefully word a sentence or two that communicates what you think is being taught, but is not specific to the original audience. To do this you must distinguish between what is being taught and what is not!

Consider a passage like Acts 24:25. In this narrative passage verse 25 tells us that Paul *"reasoned about righteousness and self-control and the coming judgment, Felix was alarmed and said, 'Go away for the present. When I get an opportunity I will summon you.'"* If you were studying this text you might be tempted to state a principle like: *"People do not respond positively when Christians talk about righteousness, self-control and the judgment to come."* But this is not always true. Though this is what happened in Acts 24, it is not what happens elsewhere in the book of Acts. This narrative passage explains one historical situation, but is obviously not teaching that these topics will always bring that response. A better "ALWAYS" sentence might be: *"Christians shouldn't always expect a positive response when explaining to others the truth of the Bible."*

Narrative passages are particularly prone to this mistake, as are Old Testament passages. Suppose you were studying Psalm 51:10-11 in which David is confessing his sins and says *"Create in me a clean heart, O God, and renew a right spirit within me. Cast me not away from your presence and take not your Holy Spirit from me."* An "ALWAYS" principle one might suggest from this passage is: *"When a Christian confesses his sins he should ask God not to remove the Holy Spirit from his life."* In light of the New Testament teaching about the permanent indwelling of the Holy Spirit in the Christian's life during the New Covenant Age this principle would not be accurate. This Old Testament concern of King David (which related to the Spirit's special indwelling that kings and prophets often enjoyed allowing them to lead the

63

PARTNERS:
ONE-ON-ONE DISCIPLESHIP

people righteously) would have to be governed in our minds by the New Testament promises for Christians. A better principle derived from this passage that encompasses both Testaments might be: *"When God's people confess their sins they ought to recognize the offense that has been caused to the Holy Spirit."*

A growing knowledge of the New Testament in general is a great help in avoiding errors in this step. Always bounce your "ALWAYS" sentences off of the rest of the knowledge you have acquired of the entire Bible. Looking up cross-references (often in the margins of your study Bible) is helpful during this step as well. A book of cross-references like R. A. Torrey's *Treasury of Scripture Knowledge* can also be a great resource in double-checking the principles you have written.

Good "ALWAYS" statements should be brief, to the point, and should include words like "People," "Christians," or "God's people" and should be absent of words like "them," "then," "they," as well as "we," "us," and "I."

Step #3: <u>NOW</u>

In this third and final section of your daily Bible study you will attempt to draw up some very practical plans to put the truth you have spelled out in step #2 to work in your own life.

With Your Partner...
Discuss any major life events or concerns that you are currently facing that you think will be a recurring theme in your application.

It is essential that you craft your application from the timeless truths that you have written in section two and not the statements from section one. We can only accurately know what the Bible is saying to us once we have carefully determined what is being taught in the passage and what is not.

It should be relatively easy to see the kinds of things that we should do if we are looking intently at the principles that we have gathered from our passage. The question for you in this part of your daily Bible study is what would God have you do? Be as specific as possible. Name names, and spell out a plan of attack. How would God have you put those "ALWAYS" statements to work in the "NOW"?

Avoid long-term items and try to focus on how God would have you respond today or this week—remember you plan to come back to the Bible for more tomorrow.

Often honest and heartfelt statements in this section will turn into written prayers directed to God. Go ahead and word some, if not all, of your comments in this section to God. Make commitments to him, reaffirm beliefs that he wants to see in your life, and communicate with your written words your resolve to put his word to work in very specific and practical ways.

As you might imagine, good "NOW" comments are filled with words like "I," "me," and "my." They are also punctuated with names, people, and places that you interact with every day.

CHAPTER 3

LEARNING TO STUDY THE BIBLE ON YOUR OWN

An Example

Below is a sample of what a typical day in God's word might yield as you use this method.

With Your Partner...
Discuss this sample entry.

Date: November 9th

Passage: James 3:9-10 With it (the tongue) we bless our Lord and Father, and with it we curse people who are made in the likeness of God. From the same mouth come blessing and cursing. My brothers, these things ought not to be so.

Then: In the last 8 verses James has been hammering away at the problems that this first century group of Christians can have when they don't control their words. In these two verses he brings up the inconsistency that exists when these first century Christians praised God one minute and then turned around to criticize and slam people the next. He tries to get these Christians to see that the people that they slammed were people that God had made. It is clear from the previous verses that people can obviously do bad things, and apparently there is a time to confront those things, but he really drives home the point here that it doesn't give them the permission to go around "cursing" each other. James tells these people that from their mouths that praise and worship God should not come cutting language that demeans people made in God's image.

Always: • Christians should restrain their cutting remarks toward people because people are made in God's image.

• It is inconsistent for Christians to worship God with their mouth and then curse people with their mouth.

Now: I can see the way that my remarks about Tom have offended God, especially when God listens to me sing those words from the worship songs on Sunday morning and then listens to my mean comments about Tom throughout the week. Forgive me God for this inconsistency! I notice that I am tempted to talk most about those that frustrate me when I spend time with Jim. He brings out the worst comments in me. I am going to spend less time with Jim this week. Instead of eating lunch with him today, I think I will eat lunch with Tom and actually try to encourage him with the words I say. When Jim starts going off on the "idiots" in the office, I am going to change the subject, walk away, or even say something to him about it if he won't stop. Jesus, help me to see the best in people like Tom, I know that he is made in your image even though he is not a Christian. I want to say kind things to him for the sake of consistency, as well as to honor the fact that you created him!

Now that you have an idea of what you are shooting for go ahead and get started. Choose a book that you will study and jump in right now. Prepare a sample to discuss with your partner and then keep going in your study each day from this point on.

Even if you already utilize a different Bible study method, put this one to work throughout your time in the Partners program so that you can become well acquainted with this method and be able to effectively pass it on to the people you take through the Partner's program.

With Your Partner...
Bring in your Bible study notebook and be prepared to discuss your progress in using this method. Don't worry if you have only had enough time for one or two daily entries, it will be helpful to discuss whatever you have completed to date.

65

PARTNERS:
ONE-ON-ONE DISCIPLESHIP

How to Keep It Going

Have a Specific Time to Study

Scheduling a regular time slot in your daily schedule does not make Bible study impersonal; it makes it possible. Time for Bible study will slip right through your fingers unless you nail down a specified time to do your daily study. Decide right now when in your day you will do your Bible study. Be specific. Will it be before breakfast? Will it be after you shower? Will it be during your lunch hour? Make sure it is a good time of the day for you mentally. Don't give God the leftovers!

With Your Partner...

Share your answers to each of these questions in this section. Continue to make these three items points of accountability in your Partners appointments. Update these plans if needed.

Have a Specific Place to Study

Pick a place that you know will be a convenient yet quiet place to do your study every day. Again, be specific. Will it be at your desk at home? Will it be at the library on the way home from work? Will it be at the kitchen table? Wherever you choose to do your study, be sure it is conducive to quiet, uninterrupted thinking. Where will you do your personal Bible study?

Have an Accountability Partner

During your participation in the Partners program, your partner will be the obvious choice for someone to keep you accountable for this. Make sure he or she asks you each week! Think through and write down who you hope will keep you accountable for your daily study once Partners ends. Don't underestimate the power of the question: *"Hey, how many times did you do your personal Bible study this week?"* Sharing what you are learning with your accountability partner can make this more than just "checking in." Who will your accountability partner be?

Other Ways to Get More Bible

Read the Bible

Bible reading is an indispensable supplement to your Bible study regimen. Reading through the Bible provides you with the big picture. It gives you insights almost every day into the section you are studying.

Don't get slowed down studying what you are reading, just keep reading. A star or a question mark in the margin can take you back to a curious passage at another time when you are intending to dig deeper.

66

CHAPTER 3

LEARNING TO STUDY THE BIBLE ON YOUR OWN

You might be surprised at how little time it actually takes to read through the Bible. If you were to read it aloud, it would only take 78 hours to read the Bible from cover to cover. If you read it silently it should take somewhere between 50 and 60 hours to finish reading all 66 books of the Bible. Or to look at it another way, there are 1189 chapters in the Bible. Reading just three and a half chapters per day will get you through the Bible in less than one year.

Though there are many Bible reading schedules, and even Bibles that are broken down into daily portions to be read each day, I have found that the best method is simply a bookmark and some scheduled time. I have personally benefited from two bookmarks (one in the Old Testament and one in the New Testament) and equal time allotted to reading both.

Even if you were to give five minutes to both Testaments you will easily gather the big picture of the entire Bible a time or two each year. I suggested earlier that if you only have an hour you might want to study for 30 minutes, pray for 20 minutes, and read for 10 minutes.

What are your Bible reading goals?

With Your Partner...
Discuss the advantages and the challenges you face in reading through the Bible and acquiring the big picture.

Listen to the Bible

Though it is not quite as fruitful as actually reading it, listening to the Bible being read is a great way to keep your mind entrenched in the Scriptures. It is relatively inexpensive these days to purchase the Bible on audio CD. You can even find web sites that have all the books of the Bible available in an audio format.

Go to Church

This may seem obvious, but don't forget that God places teachers in his church to help you understand his word. Your pastor's preaching can be a terrific supplement to your personal Bible study and vice versa. Other opportunities at your local church like medium and small group studies are also important ways to establish you in the knowledge and application of the Bible.

What teaching programs are you committed to regularly attending at your church?

Listen to the Radio

If available to you, take advantage of the sermons that are broadcast on your local Christian radio station (but keep in mind that all Christian radio lineups are not created equal). If the sermons are sound and biblically based, listening to gifted pastors preach from God's word can assist your growing knowledge of Scripture.

With Your Partner...
Discuss the preaching lineup on your local Christian radio station. Your partner may help you avoid the sloppy teaching and hone in on the better teaching in your area.

67

PARTNERS:
ONE-ON-ONE DISCIPLESHIP

Do an In-depth Study

With Your Partner...
Share any experience you might have in doing in-depth biblical studies.

At least once a month it is a great idea to dedicate a Saturday afternoon to an in-depth study of a passage that has piqued your interest. It might be something you marked during your reading, or a passage you studied but felt you really didn't get. Pull out all the study tools you have available to you, roll up your sleeves, and have at it.

What monthly time slot could you dedicate to this kind of in-depth study?

Memorize the Bible

Writing out your verse or verses for the day in your Bible study notebook can be the first step in committing them to memory. After spending a half an hour examining them you may find that you are more than half way there. To get you the rest of the way there, write out your verse(s) for the day on the back of a business card and keep it in your shirt pocket, or place it on the dash of your car. Spend a few minutes at each meal trying to say your verse without looking at the card.

What does Psalm 119:11 say about the importance of this practice?

Meditate on the Bible

Try to make a point of bringing your thoughts back to your passage throughout the day. Ponder the truth of your passage during the spare moments of your day and you will find a rich benefit in keeping your mind stayed on God's word.

What does Psalm 1:2-3 promise for this kind of habit?

None of these other methods of biblical intake are designed to replace your daily Bible study, they only serve to augment and supplement your diet of God's words.

CHAPTER 3
LEARNING TO STUDY THE BIBLE ON YOUR OWN

Notes

PARTNERS:
ONE-ON-ONE DISCIPLESHIP

Notes

RESOURCES & FURTHER STUDY

3 Learning to Study the Bible on Your Own

Rating Key
* Helpful (four being most)
⊙ Difficulty (four being hardest)

Resources on the Reliability of the Bible

*** ⊙⊙⊙ Aland, Kurt and Barbara Aland. *The Text of the New Testament: An Introduction to the Critical Editions and to the Theory and Practice of Modern Textual Criticism.* Grand Rapids, MI: Eerdmans Publishing, 1989. (This is an excellent yet challenging work that, like Metzger's contribution with the same title, will give you an insightful overview of how the modern Greek New Testament editions have come to be.)

** ⊙ Belcher, Richard P. *A Layman's Guide To The Inerrancy Debate.* Chicago, IL: Moody Press, 1980. (This brief work will familiarize you with the importance of the doctrine of inerrancy – the teaching that the Bible was inspired by God without error in the original documents.)

*** ⊙⊙ Carson, D. A., *The King James Version Debate: A Plea for Realism.* Grand Rapids, MI: Baker Book House, 1979. (This book is an excellent response to those who would attempt to promote the King James Version of the Bible as the most accurate or preferred version.)

*** ⊙ Ewert, David. *From Ancient Tablets to Modern Translations.* Grand Rapids, MI: Zondervan Publishing House, 1983. (This is a readable overview of the history of the Bible touching on broad variety of related topics.)

**** ⊙ Geisler, Norman L. *From God To Us – How We Got Our Bible.* Chicago, IL: Moody Press, 1974. (This is a must if you want to have an easy to read overview of the history of the Bible from God's act of revealing his thoughts to the prophets to the modern translations we possess today.)

** ⊙ MacArthur, John F. Jr. *Why I Trust The Bible.* Illinois: Victor Books, SP Publications, 1983. (This book highlights some basic reasons to believe in reliable of the Bible.)

*** ⊙ McDowell, Josh. *Evidence That Demands A Verdict.* San Bernardino, CA: Here's Life Publishers, 1972. (This modern classic has a helpful section on the reliability of the Bible.)

** ⊙⊙⊙ _____. *More Evidence That Demands A Verdict.* San Bernardino, CA: Here's Life Publishers, 1975. (This is a more involved treatment of the problems with a variety of high critical and liberal views of the biblical texts.)

*** ⊙⊙⊙ Metzger, Bruce M. *The Text Of The New Testament: Its Transmission, Corruption, and Restoration.* New York, NY: Oxford University Press, 1968. (Like the Aland's book of the same name, this work explains many of the details of how modern Greek New Testament editions have been assembled.)

** ⊙⊙ Pache, Rene. *The Inspiration and Authority of Scripture.* Chicago, IL: Moody Press, 1969. (This book expounds on the importance and implications of having a Bible that was given by Divine inspiration.)

*** ⊙⊙⊙ Schaeffer, Francis A. *He is There and He is Not Silent.* Illinois: Tyndale House Publishers, Inc. 1972. (This book deals with the broader aspects and implications of a God who has spoken.)

** ⊙ Thomas, Griffith W. H. *How We Got Our Bible.* Dallas, TX: Dallas Seminary Press, 1984. (This is

71

an easy to read and concise work that overviews how we got our Bible.)

Resources on the Study and Interpretation of the Bible

★★★ Fee, Gordon D. and Stuart, Douglas. *How To Read The Bible For All Its Worth*. Grand Rapids, MI:
◉◉   Academie Books, Zondervan Publishing House, 1982. (This book gives helpful information on everything from picking a Bible translation to basic Bible study methods.)

★★ Kaiser, Walter C. Jr. *Toward an Exegetical Theology: Biblical Exegesis for Preaching and Teaching*. Grand
◉◉◉   Rapids, MI: Baker Book House, 1981. (This book is intended to help teachers properly understand how to approach the Bible in message preparation describing a variety of governing principles of exegesis.)

★★★★ Klein, William W., Craig L. Blomberg and Robert L. Hubbard. *Introduction to Biblical Interpretation*.
◉◉   Dallas, TX: Word Publishing, 1993. (This is a readable and thorough overview of biblical hermeneutics.)

★★ Leigh, Ronald W. *Direct Bible Discovery*. Nashville, TN: Broadman Press, 1982. (This book suggests
◉◉   and describes an inductive Bible study method.)

★★★ Ramm, Bernard. *Protestant Biblical Interpretation: A Textbook of Hermenutics*, Third Revised Edition.
◉◉◉   Grand Rapids, MI: Baker Book House, 1970. (This textbook provides a widely accepted set of principles for interpreting the Bible.)

★★★ Sire, James W. *Scripture Twisting*. Downers Grove, IL: InterVarsity Press, 1980. (This book points out a
◉◉   variety of mistakes made in interpreting the Bible that lead to heretical conclusions.)

★★★ Virkler, Henry A. *Hermeneutics. Principles and Processes of Biblical Interpretation*. Grand Rapids, MI:
◉◉   Baker Book House, 1981. (This is a readable and fairly concise hermeneutics textbook.)

Resources Used to Study the Bible

★★★ Archer, Gleason L. *Encyclopedia of Bible Difficulties*. Grand Rapids, MI: Zondervan Publishing
◉◉   House, 1982. (This book covers apparent discrepancies and problem passages in canonical order.)

★★★ Douglas, J. D. ed. *The New Bible Dictionary*. Downers Grove, IL: InterVarsity Press. 1996. (This is
◉◉   one of the many available Bible dictionaries that addresses biblical topics, names and themes, not primarily words.)

★★★ Elwell, Walter A. *Topical Analysis of the Bible*. Grand Rapids, MI: Baker Book House. 1995. (This is
◉   a helpful reference work that topically and logically arranges Bible texts of the NIV.)

★★★ Gaebelein, Frank E. ed. *The Expositor's Bible Commentary (12 volumes)*. Grand Rapids, MI:
◉◉   Zondervan Publishing House, 1984. (This is a valuable and doctrinally reliable commentary set.)

★★★ Kohlenberger, John R. III, Edward Goodrick, and James Swanson, eds.. *The Greek-English*
◉◉   *Concordance to the New Testament*. Grand Rapids, MI: Zondervan Publishing House, 1997. (This is a very helpful reference tool that helps you work with the original languages which underlie the English.)

★★★ _____. *The Hebrew-English Concordance to the Old Testament*. Grand Rapids MI: Zondervan
◉◉   Publishing House, 1998. (This is the Old Testament companion volume to the work listed above.)

★★★★ Logos Research Systems Inc. *Logos Library System Software*. 1999. (This is very powerful, expandable, and
◉◉   extremely helpful Bible study tool. Information on Logos software is available at www.logos.com .)

★★★ Mounce, William D. *The Crossway Comprehensive Concordance of the Holy Bible, English Standard Version*.
◉   Wheaton, IL: Crossway Books, 2002. (This is a must have unless you are using Bible software.)

★★ Walvoord John F. and Roy B. Zuck, eds. *The Bible Knowledge Commentary (2 volumes)*. Wheaton, IL:
◉   Victor Books, 1985. (This is a very understandable two volume commentary set.)

Chapter 4

PARTNERS MEETING #4

Developing an Effective Prayer Life

At Partners Meeting #4...

You will work with your partner to improve your prayer life. Almost every Christian senses the need to give more effort and attention to the art of praying, but we often fail to give the time to analyze what is happening and what needs to happen when we talk to God. This chapter is intended to be the catalyst to get your prayer life up to speed. You will learn more about the conceptual and the practical elements that are essential in having an effective prayer life.

To Prepare for Partners Meeting #4...

- Read chapter 4 and answer the questions about prayer.

- Bring to the meeting a list containing the names of people and issues that are important to you. Be prepared to decide on a prayer system if you don't already have one.

- If any of the "Deeper Study" topics are of interest to you, prepare to discuss them.

- Memorize the books of the New Testament in order.

- Memorize Philippians 4:6

Do not be anxious about anything, but in everything, by prayer and supplication, with thanksgiving, let your requests be made known to God.

– Philippians 4:6

73

PARTNERS:
ONE-ON-ONE DISCIPLESHIP

Prayer is arguably the most underutilized and anemic part of the Christian life for most Christians. And this is a tragedy considering that God has called us to a life of prayer that is promised to be one of the most significant and powerful opportunities for deepening our intimacy with God and maximizing our usefulness in this world for Christ.

The Privilege of Prayer
Consider the following passages, noting the powerful way God's word is beckoning us to spend more time devoted to prayer. List the privilege that each text is holding out to us as a motivation, and briefly state why those might encourage you to spend more time praying to God this week.

With Your Partner...
Honestly evaluate the time you have actually spent in undistracted prayer over the past few weeks. Discuss the obstacles that have made your prayer time a challenge.

- Deuteronomy 4:7

- Psalm 86:5

- Jeremiah 33:2-3

- Matthew 7:7-11

If prayer has not been what it should be in your life, now is the time to seek God's empowerment to make prayer a central priority in your daily life. Your participation in a meaningful and life-changing prayer life begins with a clarified understanding of what prayer actually is.

What is Prayer?

It is important that we know what it means to pray. Ponder this question for a minute and attempt to define prayer in the most basic way. What is the bare minimum required to say that one has actually prayed? Do you have to bow your head or fold your hands? Do you have to speak audibly? Can a prayer be written out instead of verbalized? Write a barebones definition of prayer. What must be done to say that someone has just prayed?

CHAPTER 4

DEVELOPING AN EFFECTIVE PRAYER LIFE

Defining Prayer

Beyond using synonyms to define prayer, if we understand that a particular posture or procedure is not required and if we understand that there is biblical precedent for a variety of people praying in a variety of different settings, with varied durations, both audibly and inaudibly, we eventually discover that prayer, in its most basic form is:

"A mental activity by which a person
directs and offers his thoughts to God."

This definition does not exclude the reality that prayer also engages our emotions and feelings – sometimes in a profound way – but the intent to express the content of one's thoughts is at the core of the act of communication. Keep in mind that when it comes to prayer these thoughts may or may not be expressed verbally. They might be written out or directed silently, they might be sung or read, but in one way or another they are an expression of one's thoughts to God. Remember also that these expressed thoughts cover a wide range of categories and subjects. They may be requests, confessions, praise, or concerns.

What Prayer is Not

Jesus said…

Matthew 6:7

"And when you pray, do not heap up empty phrases as the Gentiles do, for they think that they will be heard for their many words."

Depending on your background, you may have grown up in a church in which they taught you to memorize and recite certain prayers. Many people learn to articulate a set of words from a scripted prayer. These words, at their inception were meaningful statements directed toward God, but all too often they become nothing more than a ritual of parroted words that are disconnected from the participants' thoughts. Someone may recite words without ever engaging their minds and willingly directing those thoughts to God. When this happens the person may say that they have prayed, but of course they have not.

This tragic mistake doesn't just happen in church. Many people have grown accustomed to reciting rote slogans and phrases before a meal, or with their children before bed, and unfortunately, while the bowed head and closed eyes may give the appearance of prayer, when the mind is not engaged and the heart is not directing these thoughts to God there is no prayer taking place.

Take a moment to think through some of the slogans, phrases or words that undoubtedly have had meaning at one time or another, but are sometimes

Deeper Study…
Explore the history and background of some of the more prominent Christians prayers that have traditionally been recited in church services throughout the centuries.

PARTNERS:
ONE-ON-ONE DISCIPLESHIP

recited by you or your family without clearly thinking about what they mean. Make a list of a sampling of these phrases that have become prayer clichés.

With Your Partner...
Discuss the origin and original intent of some of the phrases and words that have crept into our prayer lives that no longer engage our brains. Seek to discover why these words became our habit. See which words and phrases can and should be salvaged and which ones we would be better off to drop altogether.

Remember that we have two choices when it comes to words that have become "meaningless" in our praying.

1) Learn what the words and phrases mean and continue to use them with a thoughtful understanding of what we are trying to communicate to God.

or

2) Exchange the old words with new words that will more readily activate our minds with the intended meaning and with less confusion.

Make a chart of updated and more meaningful expressions below

Deeper Study...
In ancient Corinth there was a lot passing for "prayer" that was not actually prayer. Emotionalism had become the goal for many and some had advocated "turning off your mind" when approaching God in prayer. Read God's corrective in 1 Corinthians 14:15 and explore the biblical problems associated with defining prayer as emotional and unintelligible outbursts.

Old clichés that my mind often glosses over	→	New phrases which will more likely keep my mind engaged
"Lord, please bless them"	→	
"grant us traveling mercies"	→	
"to the nourishment of our bodies"	→	
	→	
	→	
	→	
	→	

Group Prayer Problems

With Your Partner...
Discuss the weekly opportunities you have to pray in groups or in pairs with other Christians. Consider whether you are taking advantage of praying together with brothers and sisters in Christ.

A lot of praying that takes place in the Christian life will rightly be group praying, where one person is "leading in prayer" and the others are to "join the leader in prayer." This always takes place in the weekly church service. It also takes place at Bible studies, small group meetings, prayer meetings and even during a Partners appointment.

CHAPTER 4
DEVELOPING AN EFFECTIVE PRAYER LIFE

It is important that we don't miss the opportunity to really pray in these settings. Unfortunately, it can be more difficult than one would think!

Group Prayer... Not a Spectator Sport

The number one problem for Christians during group prayer sessions is that one person is praying while all the other people are just listening to one person praying. All too often we find ourselves thinking about what the person is praying, maybe evaluating what the person is praying, sometimes critiquing what the person is praying, but we ourselves are not praying!

Remember, prayer is not taking place unless our minds are engaged and directing our own praise-filled, or request-filled thoughts to God. If we are only thinking about the prayer and not grabbing on to those same thoughts for ourselves and volitionally directing them to God, then we have missed out on an opportunity for prayer.

Review and analyze your thought process during some recent times of group prayer. How often would you say that group prayer time fails to be genuine prayer for you? What are the reasons you sometimes miss out on truly praying when someone else is "leading" in prayer?

With Your Partner...
Discuss the distractions that occur during your prayer times with other Christians. Exchange ideas that have helped you keep your mind active during prayer.

Group Prayer... More than Whispering "Yes"

Sometimes when someone is leading in prayer he or she says something that truly resonates with us, something with which we are in full agreement, and we find ourselves concurring emotively. Often you'll hear yourself or others say softly (sometimes loudly) "yes!" or "amen." While this agreement is essential, it should be clear by now that it does not mean that we have actually "joined in" in actually praying. More than just agreement, real prayer necessitates that I direct that thought to God as well. If I am only mindful of the person praying, or the statement that has been prayed, and I am not mindful of the true audience, again I may go away thinking I have prayed, when in reality I have not.

Group prayer takes as much mental effort as praying individually; arguably more! Knowing what real prayer is and seeking to actually engage in it every time someone invites you to pray with them can make even the most routine prayer, like one before a meal, a meaningful and life-changing activity.

What can you do to keep your mind engaged in prayer and not just affirmation the next time you pray in a group?

77

PARTNERS:
ONE-ON-ONE DISCIPLESHIP

Group Prayer... The Perils of Leading Others in Prayer
There are probably times when you are asked to lead in prayer—maybe before a large group meeting at church, perhaps in a small group Bible study, or possibly at a gathering before a meal. Be careful.

What applicable warnings did God give to those who relished this experience in Matthew 6:5?

How should that affect our attitude when we lead in prayer publicly?

With Your Partner...
Consider together the goal of praying before a meal. Discuss why praying "for the food" or "blessing the meal" is not the point. Carefully read Christ's example in Matthew 14:19 and reaffirm the goal and the object of Jesus' "blessing" or "thanksgiving."

When you are leading in group prayer don't forget the One you are supposed to be addressing. Of course, care should be given so that your words are adequate prompts for the others you hope to have join you in praying, but your goal is to sincerely talk to God. Avoid ostentatious language and showy displays of your biblical knowledge. Give careful thought to your words, ensuring that your sentences aren't constructed to impress people, but crafted to communicate with God.

What are some of the temptations you face when you are asked to lead others in prayer?

The Purpose of Prayer

Deeper Study...
Consider the assumptions about prayer in the "name it and claim it" circles that see God as an avenue to get what I want. What are some subtle ways we can drift into this kind of error if we are not careful?

One of the biggest misunderstandings about prayer relates to the reason God calls us to pray. A survey of popular discussions about prayer may lead us to believe that prayer is all about getting God to do what we want. But this is clearly not the case. There are two primary biblical reasons God calls us to pray.

Personally Relating to God

God is not a force, a principle or a rule to live by. God is a person. He created us to glorify him as we praise him, serve him and personally relate to him. While sin created a serious barrier in a perfect relationship that will not be completely rectified until his people are personally in his presence with glorified bodies, there is a foretaste of our personally relating to our God when we engage in prayer.

CHAPTER 4
DEVELOPING AN EFFECTIVE PRAYER LIFE

Note the intimate words of David in **Psalm 62:5-8**. Note especially verse eight that calls for a personal and heartfelt expression to God. Describe the kind of content that might be included in "pouring out" one's heart to God (v.8).

What would it be like for you if a family member or a friend only spoke to you in the form of requests when he or she wanted something from you and never personally expressed to you his or her thoughts, feelings, joys and hurts?

With Your Partner...
Discuss with your partner strategies to ensure that your prayer time isn't just a list of "prayer requests" but that you sincerely share your thoughts and feelings with God when you pray.

Being A Part of What God Wants to Accomplish

Prayer is not a "me-centered" mechanism to get more of what I want. Instead it is God's gracious opportunity for us to be a part of what he is accomplishing in our lives and in the world. This is made clear in the way Jesus taught us to pray.

Deeper Study...
Explore the conundrum related to God's sovereignty and our praying. Map out the options in understanding the apparent tension between a sovereign divine plan and the "power and effectiveness" spoken of in James 5:16b.

Praying in Jesus' Name

Jesus' repeatedly emphasized the essential ingredient to our praying—asking in his name. If this condition is met, it appears that Jesus is granting a kind of carte blanche for our prayers.

> **John 14:13-14**
>
> "Whatever you ask in my name, this I will do, that the Father may be glorified in the Son. If you ask me anything in my name, I will do it."

> **John 15:16**
>
> "You did not choose me, but I chose you and appointed you that you should go and bear fruit and that your fruit should abide, so that whatever you ask the Father in my name, he may give it to you."

But what does this mean? Is this some magical phrase we tack on to the end of our prayers and "presto" they all come true? Do we have to say "in Jesus' name, Amen" for our prayers to be heard? What is the stipulation all about?

To rightly understand the admonition to "pray in Jesus' name" we must recall how important the concept of one's "name" was in God's word. Remember

79

PARTNERS:

ONE-ON-ONE DISCIPLESHIP

that God put a special emphasis on the illuminating and revelatory nature of "names" in the Scripture. He sought to teach us about himself through his own names. He told us his name was to be revered as holy. This was not because the combination of letters or sounds was magical or supernatural; it was because the name was a representation of the Person. God was so transcendent and majestic that one name did not suffice. We learned about the many facets of God's character by his revealed names. The same is true in the New Testament regarding his Son.

According to Hebrews 1:3, God's Son "is the radiance of the glory of God and the exact imprint of his nature." Jesus (the New Testament form of the Old Testament name "Joshua" meaning "Salvation") is the embodiment and revelation of all the perfection of God. So when we are asked to "pray in his name" we are asking for something in accordance with all that he is and all that he stands for. In other words, we are to be asking for those things that are in keeping with the perfection of God's character as we see it demonstrated in Christ.

This use of "in the name of" is not completely foreign in our culture. We have retained some uses of this phrase, like the one you might hear as a police officer yells at a fleeing bank robber to "Stop in the name of the law!"

Just a little contemplation and we begin to see how this will limit and reshape our prayer requests. Consider what a police officer could not say "in the name of the law." He could not tell you to wash his car or pay for his lunch "in the name of the law." But he could certainly tell you to "pull over" your speeding car, or stop destroying someone else's property "in the name of the law." He is justified in saying those things because they are in keeping with what "the law" says and what the law stands for.

List some of the prayer requests that clearly could not be prayed "in the name of Jesus" because they are in no way consistent with who Jesus is or what Jesus stands for.

List some of the obvious requests that would be in keeping with Christ's character and would relate to the issues that face your life this week.

With Your Partner...
Take a few minutes to pray through this list with your partner.

Always be mindful in your praying (whether you conclude your prayers with the words or not) that your petitions and requests need to be in keeping with the character, desires and purposes of Christ.

80

CHAPTER 4

DEVELOPING AN EFFECTIVE PRAYER LIFE

Jesus as our Mediator

There is another biblical reminder that we derive from the command to pray in Jesus' name. It is the emphasis on the grace we have received in Christ before God. Jesus repeatedly made his role clear as it related to our access to God the Father.

John 14:6

Jesus said to him, "I am the way, and the truth, and the life. No one comes to the Father except through me."

Read **1 Timothy 2:5**. Based on what you have learned about the Gospel, why is it that we need a mediator and why is the incarnate Christ the only one available?

Seeing Jesus as our mediator is fundamental to understanding the redemptive work of Christ that grants us (and our prayers) access to a holy God. This is what it means when the writer of Hebrews tells us that Jesus is our great High Priest.

Hebrews 4:14-16

Since then we have a great high priest who has passed through the heavens, Jesus, the Son of God, let us hold fast our confession. For we do not have a high priest who is unable to sympathize with our weaknesses, but one who in every respect has been tempted as we are, yet without sin. Let us then with confidence draw near to the throne of grace, that we may receive mercy and find grace to help in time of need.

When you pray be mindful that you approach God and bring your requests to him in the "right standing" or the righteousness you have been granted through Christ. How could you verbally acknowledge this truth as you pray, beyond just including the words "in Jesus name"?

PARTNERS:

ONE-ON-ONE DISCIPLESHIP

Praying to the Triune God

While we should always be mindful of the theological truth that Jesus grants us access to the Father, there may be times when it is appropriate to direct our prayers to other Persons of the Godhead. To whom specifically does Stephen direct his prayer in **Acts 7:59-60**? Why do you think this might have been the choice for Stephen as he was being martyred?

Hebrews 4:15 emphasized Christ's sympathy for our weakness. How does a knowledge that Jesus experienced the same kinds of temptations and frustrations that you encounter motivate you to periodically direct your prayers to the Son of God?

In **John 14:16** the Holy Spirit is described as our "Comforter," "Counselor" or "Helper." In what circumstances might you directly address the Holy Spirit in prayer?

With Your Partner...
Discuss your response to the idea of periodically praying to Jesus and the Holy Spirit.

A Pattern for Prayer

We should not only want to pray more, we should want to pray better. Thankfully Jesus addressed the question of "how" to pray. While the following section of Scripture is often referred to as "The Lord's Prayer" it really is more accurately seen as a template for the disciple's praying. It is a model for praying as we ought.

Jesus' Model Prayer

After pointing out a number of problems to avoid when praying, Jesus offered a template or pattern for our communication with God. This brief teaching from Christ can guide us to pray for the right things in the right way.

82

CHAPTER 4
DEVELOPING AN EFFECTIVE PRAYER LIFE

Jesus said:

> **Matthew 6:9-13**
>
> "Pray then like this:
>
> 'Our Father in heaven, hallowed be your name, your kingdom come, your will be done on earth as it is in heaven. Give us this day our daily bread, and forgive us our debts, as we also have forgiven our debtors. And lead us not into temptation, but deliver us from evil.'"

Some have made their praying a mere repetition of Christ's words. Others have rightly understood this prayer as a guide and have sought to reflect the component parts of Christ's prayer instead of just reciting the words verbatim. To utilize this model prayer we have to decipher its various parts. Here is a breakdown of the elements Christ included for us.

Worship & Praise – "Our Father in heaven, hallowed be your name…"

Spend time in your praying expressing praise to God. Credit him with the honor and gratitude he deserves for all the good things he has done. Put an emphasis on his majesty and tell him that you personally affirm his greatness.

Hope in Christ's Return – "…your kingdom come,"

An important part of your prayer life should be fixing your hope on the coming kingdom of God. There ought to be a focus on the consummation of God's plan for us. As 1 John 3:2-3 tell us, when our heart is fixed on Christ's return we cannot help but have the entirety of our Christian life affected.

Adjust Your Requests – "your will be done on earth as it is in heaven."

This phrase concerning God's will being done on earth is similar to the directive to pray in Jesus' name. If we are engaged in prayer that is guided by an interest in God's desires then it cannot help but shape the kinds of petitions and requests we bring to God. We should focus on adjusting our "wants" to match the "wants" of God, praying for those kinds of requests to be realized here on earth, like they are in God's realm of heaven.

Bring Your Requests – "Give us this day our daily bread…"

Here is the subject heading that prompts us to bring our godly and appropriate petitions to God. This is clearly a significant part of our praying (see Psalm 5:1-3).

Further Study...
Realize that the model prayer of Matthew 6 is one of several inspired examples of godly praying. Take, for instance, the way that Colossians 1:10b-12 gives us a template for praying for others (1) Praying for others to produce more good deeds; (2) Praying for others to understand God better; (3) Praying for others to be empowered by God; (4) Praying for others to give more thanksgiving to God. Find other New Testament examples of prayer and outline their content.

PARTNERS:
ONE-ON-ONE DISCIPLESHIP

Confessing Your Sins – "Forgive us our debts…"

As we come to prayer, our relationship with God should be unhindered by unconfessed sins. Give time to the prayer of Psalm 139:23-24.

Ask for a Forgiving Heart – "…as we also have forgiven our debtors."

With Your Partner
Look up and discuss the following verses: Ephesians 4:32 and 1 Peter 3:7.

One of the indicators of a regenerate heart is the divine ability to forgive those who have sinned against you. Make sure your prayers include an affirmation of this virtue, expressing your dependence on him for the ability to do so.

Pray for a Holy Life – "And lead us not into temptation…"

Your prayer life should include a concern for living a godly and righteous life. Few things are more in line with Jesus' purposes than Christlikeness.

Seek God's Protection – "…but deliver us from evil."

Being godly cannot be achieved without the empowerment and protection of God himself. We should pray specifically that God would grant us protection as we seek to bring him glory in our daily lives.

Looking back through these components of Christ's model prayer, which of them would you say you most often neglect in your prayer life? Why do you think that is the case?

Which components are the "easiest" to include in your praying? Why is that?

84

CHAPTER 4
DEVELOPING AN EFFECTIVE PRAYER LIFE

Focused Prayer Times

It is not easy to pray well. Focused times of prayer can be an intense battle. The struggle of real, heartfelt prayer is illustrated by Christ as he prayed in the Garden of Gethsemane. A more basic struggle for a focused time of prayer is illustrated by the disciples' failure to stay awake. Read **Matthew 26:36-45**. Describe the contrasted prayer lives of Christ and the disciples. How does Jesus respond to the disciples' failure to pray?

How would you describe the quality, quantity and frequency of your times of focused praying? What are the obstacles to you praying more often and with more focused attention?

With Your Partner

Tell your partner about the season of your Christian life when your prayer life was best. Why do you think that was so?

Jesus made prayer his priority. To stay alert and focused in prayer he had to regularly carve out undistracted times in quiet places. Note the following testimonies regarding Christ's prayer life.

Luke 5:16

But he would withdraw to desolate places and pray.

Mark 1:35

And rising very early in the morning, while it was still dark, he departed and went out to a desolate place, and there he prayed.

Matthew 14:23a

After he dismissed the crowds, he went up on the mountain by himself to pray.

PARTNERS:
ONE-ON-ONE DISCIPLESHIP

What is the best time in your schedule to give to focused prayer?

List two or three quiet places where you can pray without distraction?

E. M. Bounds

"There is neither encouragement nor room in the Christian life for feeble desires, listless efforts, and lazy attitudes."

Martin Luther

"If I should neglect prayer but a single day, I should lose a great deal of the fire of faith."

E. M. Bounds

"The little estimate we put on prayer is evident from the little time we give to it. Not infrequently the Christian's only praying is by his bedside in his night clothes, ready for bed and soon in it, with perchance, the addition of a few hasty snatches of prayer before he is dressed in the morning. How feeble, vain and little is such praying compared with the time and energy devoted to praying by holy men in and out of the Bible! How poor and mean our petty, childish praying is beside the habits of the true men of God in all ages."

With Your Partner
Discuss a prayer plan that includes a specified and measured amount of time given to this important task. Discuss where and how you will do this.

Read **Colossians 4:2** and write out some specific goals to increase the time and attention you invest in focused times of prayer.

86

CHAPTER 4

DEVELOPING AN EFFECTIVE PRAYER LIFE

Praying All the Time

Focused times of scheduled prayer are critically important in the Christian life, but the Bible also speaks of an additional kind of ongoing communication with God that we must never neglect.

> **1 Thessalonians 5:17**
>
> pray without ceasing

The Bible calls us to live our lives with a continual awareness and an incessant communication with the One who has promised to "never leave us or forsake us" (Hebrews 13:5).

This kind of prayerful communication throughout the day can be compared to the intermittent statements that might punctuate a long ride in a car with a family member. You might not talk every minute of every hour, but you will never forget that your loved one is present, and there will be a continual interaction throughout the journey. So it should be with God. We should always be mindful of his presence and we should make it our intention to express to him our thoughts, our feelings and our thanksgiving.

What practical steps can you take to be mindful of God's presence throughout the day? What creative reminders can be utilized to prompt you to keep expressing your thoughts to God hour by hour?

With Your Partner
Share your ideas with your partner about how you can "pray without ceasing."

Keeping a Prayer List

In the Bible we often find Christians sharing their "prayer requests." After Paul exhorts the Colossians to devote themselves to prayer, he asks them to pray for a few things in his life.

> **Colossians 4:3-4**
>
> At the same time, pray also for us, that God may open to us a door for the word, to declare the mystery of Christ, on account of which I am in prison— that I may make it clear, which is how I ought to speak.

87

PARTNERS:

ONE-ON-ONE DISCIPLESHIP

How often do people ask you to pray for them? What are some of the requests that you have been asked to pray for lately?

As you become more consistent and effective in your praying, from whom would you like to acquire more prayer requests? What do you think their reaction would be to your desire to pray more specifically for them?

There are several ways to keep track of prayer requests, God's answers and your progress in praying. Here are a few suggestions.

Journaling Your Prayers

Writing out your prayers in paragraph form is one way to effectively chronicle your prayer life. Writing your prayers can be helpful as you slow down and organize your thoughts through the process of writing or typing. Journaling your prayers also provides you with the ability to read back over the prayers you have been presenting to God and reflect on the way he has responded. You can note his answers in the margins or electronically annotate the document with the way God has creatively responded to your petitions.

As prayer requests come your way, with your prayer journal handy, you can quickly itemize the requests at the top of a new page and later spend time writing out your prayers prompted by those specific requests.

A Split Page Prayer List

One of the simplest ways to track your prayer life is with a simple "T" chart. In one column, bearing the heading "Requests," you can list the items for which you are called to pray. The other column heading simply reads "Answers," under which you record God's responses as they happen. This simple method can be utilized on a computer, a digital assistant or even an electronic file on a cell phone. The goal is to itemize specific requests on a readily available list that has a space to record God's answers.

CHAPTER 4
DEVELOPING AN EFFECTIVE PRAYER LIFE

A Weekly Prayer Calendar

The more you work to become effective in prayer, the more you will realize there is an abundance of things for which you can be praying. You may discover that a prayer calendar helps you to cover a large variety of categories or recurring topics at least once a week as you pray.

You can make a prayer calendar by vertically folding one sheet of paper two times to create eight columns (four on one side of the page and four on the other). The first column is used for items you will pray for every day. The other seven columns can be filled in with lists that correspond to each day of the week. Each day may have the same recurring categories (e.g., "my church leaders," "my extended family," "national leaders," "fellow employees," etc.), but each day the names or items listed are different. This is an efficient way to insure that you are praying for a large number of people and issues at least once per week.

With Your Partner
Discuss the pros and cons of prayer lists and prayer systems that you have utilized.

This same method can be applied in a notebook form. With one divider labeled "every day" and seven others labeled for each day of the week, you can fill each section with subject headings and specific requests that cover all of the items for which you want to pray.

Card File of Prayer Requests

Another way to keep a large number of prayer items organized and systematically before your eyes is with a three-by-five card file system. Any office supply store will present you with a variety of card file box options that can prove to be a perfect solution for keeping your prayer requests handy and up to date.

Three-by-five cards are an ideal size to carry with you throughout the day. You can strategically place them on your car's dashboard, by your keyboard at work, in the kitchen, or by your nightstand. Color-coded cards can also help to distinguish various groups or topics. You might have one card for each person you are praying for, with requests on the front and God's answers recorded on the back.

Computer Options

Many Bible software programs are now including prayer list modules that can creatively track and organize your prayer requests and answers. This may be a perfect solution if you are already using such software packages to study God's word each day.

A lot of church websites and other Christian internet sites have pages that allow you to post, read and update various prayer requests online. Email and blogging can also be effective tools to communicate and organize your prayer requests.

89

PARTNERS:
ONE-ON-ONE DISCIPLESHIP

Whatever method you use, it should be helpful and adaptable to your life and prayer patterns. Choose a system that works for you so that when it is time to pray you are not left wondering what you should be praying for.

Take a moment to write out the commitments you are making regarding your prayer life as a result of this chapter.

CHAPTER 4
DEVELOPING AN EFFECTIVE PRAYER LIFE

Notes

PARTNERS:
ONE-ON-ONE DISCIPLESHIP

Notes

RESOURCES & FURTHER STUDY

Developing an Effective Prayer Life

> Rating Key
> ★ Helpful (four being most)
> ◉ Difficulty (four being hardest)

Resources on Prayer

★★★ Bennett, Arthur. **The Valley of Vision: A Collection of Puritan Prayers and Devotions.** Edinburgh,
◉◉ Scottland: The Banner of Truth, 1975. (This is highly devotional read, taking you into the heart of how the Puritans prayed.)

★★★★ Bounds, E. M. **The Complete Works of E. M. Bounds on Prayer.** Grand Rapids: Baker Books,
◉◉ 1990. (Bounds will rarely fail to motivate you to spend more time in prayer. The "Complete Works" is a collection of a number of smaller titles that Bounds produced on prayer.)

★★★ Brother Lawrence. **The Practice of the Presence of God.** Whitaker House, 1982. (Though dated, this
◉◉ work by a seventeenth century monk is helpful in aiding our attempts to "pray continually." It can also be found in updated English versions.)

★★★ Carson, D. A. **A Call to Spiritual Reformation: Priorities from Paul and His Prayers.** Grand
◉◉◉ Rapids, Baker Books, 1992. (This is an insightful work that highlights the heart of the Apostle Paul as seen through the recorded prayers in his epistles.)

★★ Eastman, Dick. **No Easy Road: Inspirational Thoughts on Prayer.** Grand Rapids: Baker Books,
◉ 1971. (This is an easy read that biblically illustrates that effective prayer of a righteous man accomplishes much.)

★★★ Hiebert, D. Edmond. **Working with God Through Intercessory Prayer.** Greenville, SC: BJU Press,
◉◉ 1991. (Hiebert is a Bible commentator who thematically addresses ten biblical examples of intercessory prayer.)

★★★ Hybels, Bill. **Too Busy Not to Pray: Slowing Down to Be With God.** Downers Grove, IL:
◉ InterVarsity Press, 1998. (This easy to read book gives a number of practical helps in making daily prayer a top priority.)

★★ Jarrell, Jane. **50 Ways to a Thankful Heart.** Eugene, OR: Harvest House, 2000. (This is a book for
◉ children that directs elementary-age children to learn to be grateful.)

★★ Jeremiah, David. **Prayer: The Great Adventure.** Sisters, OR: Multnomah Publishers, 1997. (The
◉◉ author offers insights from the Lord's model prayer of Matthew 6 and Christ's "high priestly prayer" of John 17.)

★★★ Lockyer, Herbert. **All the Prayers of the Bible.** Grand Rapids: Zondervan Publishing House, 1959.
◉◉ (This volume chronicles all the prayers found in the Bible with brief explanation and commentary.)

★★★ MacArthur, John. **Jesus' Pattern of Prayer.** Chicago: Moody Press, 1981. (The author draws from the
◉◉ biblical template of Jesus' model prayer in Matthew 6 and provides practical directives for our prayer life.)

★★ Moody, D. L. **Prevailing Prayer.** Chicago: Moody Press, 1987. (This book on prayer passionately calls us to
◉ persevere in our prayers in a classic Dwight Moody style.)

93

★★★ Mueller, George. **Answers to Prayer: From George Muller's Narratives.** Chicago: Moody Press,
◉◉ 1984. (Mueller, who demonstrated great dependence on God, offers testimonials on the power of prayer.)

★★★ Murray, Andrew. **The Best of Andrew Murray on Prayer.** Uhrichsville, OH: Barbour Publishing,
◉◉ 1997. (Popular devotional writer of the early 1900's motivates Christians to invest more time in prayer.)

★★★ Piper, John. **A Hunger for God: Desiring God Through Fasting & Prayer.** Crossway Books, 1997.
◉◉◉ (Piper delivers biblical insight on the act of fasting and its relationship to seeking God in prayer.)

★★ Ryken, Philip Graham. **When You Pray: Making the Lord's Prayer Your Own.** Wheaton: Crossway
◉◉ Books, 2000. (Ryken examines the context and content of Christ's model prayer in Matthew 6.)

★★ Ryle, J. C. **A Call to Prayer.** Laurel, MS: Audubon Press, 2002. (In this short booklet, Ryle, a Puritan pastor,
◉◉◉ addresses the need to return to a more ardent prayer life.)

★★★ Spurgeon, C. H. **The Power of Prayer in a Believer's Life.** Reprint. Lynnwood, WA: Emerald Books,
◉◉ 1996. (In his classic style, Spurgeon calls Christians to prayer in these collected sermons on the subject.)

★★ Strauss, Lehman. **Sense and Nonsense About Prayer.** Chicago: Moody Press, 1974. (In this book,
◉ Strauss pastorally compares the role of prayer to several aspects of the Christian life.)

★★★ Tada, Joni Eareckson. **Seeking God: My Journey of Prayer and Praise.** Brentwood, TN:
◉◉ Wolgemuth & Hyatt Publishers, Inc. (As a quadriplegic, Tada communicates with power and integrity the
role of prayer and praise in our daily lives.)

★★ Taylor, Hudson. **Hudson Taylor's Spiritual Secret.** Chicago: Moody Press, 1987. (This classic work
◉◉ biographically demonstrates the prayerful dependence of this pioneering missionary to China.)

★★ Torrey, R. A. **How to Pray.** New Kensington, PN: Whitaker House, 1983. (This brief book, written in 1900
◉◉ explores the importance and role of prayer in the Christian life.)

★★★ Torrey, R. A., C. H. Spurgeon, et al. **A Closer Walk with God: Prayer as a Way of Life.** Reprint.
◉◉ Lynnwood, WA: Emerald House Group, 1997. (This is a compilation of classic Christian authors
addressing the topic of prayer.)

★★★ Thrasher, Bill. **A Journey to Victorious Praying: Finding Discipline and Delight in Your Prayer
◉◉ Life.** Chicago, IL: Moody Press, 2003. (The author provides practical insight and compassionate
motivation to help us approach God with dependency and joy.)

Chapter 5

PARTNERS MEETING #5

Living a Life Led by the Holy Spirit

At Partners Meeting #5...

You will explore the biblical data on the current ministry of the Holy Spirit as well as God's instructions about our proper response to his indwelling presence. You will seek to better understand and identify the work of the Holy Spirit in your life and clarify your expectations about his leading and conviction.

To Prepare for Partners Meeting #5...

• Read chapter 5 and answer the questions about the Holy Spirit's ministry.

• Prepare to discuss any "Deeper Study" topics that are of interest to you.

• Memorize the first half of the Old Testament books in order (Genesis through Song of Solomon).

• Memorize Galatians 5:16 and 25.

> But I say, walk by the Spirit, and you will not gratify the desires of the flesh.
>
> – Galatians 5:16
>
> If we live by the Spirit, let us also walk by the Spirit.
>
> – Galatians 5:25

PARTNERS:
ONE-ON-ONE DISCIPLESHIP

Unfortunately, the topic of the Holy Spirit is often fraught with confusion and dread in the minds of many Christians. Because modern teaching on the Holy Spirit has resulted in a myriad of unbiblical views and diverse opinions, many Christians have failed to personally examine the biblical data on the Holy Spirit and have settled for an unsatisfactory understanding of the third person of the Triune God. This is unacceptable for those who are called to daily walk in step with God's Spirit. We cannot afford the confusion. It is crucial that each of us understand his assigned ministry in us, to us and through us.

Who is the Holy Spirit

As discussed in chapter 2, God is a unique triune Being who is one essence, yet exists in three distinct persons. The Bible describes the Holy Spirit as a "person" of the Godhead. How does Acts 5:1-4 equate the person of the Holy Spirit as co-equal with God?

With Your Partner...

Describe how your understanding of the tri-unity of God has improved, been clarified or challenged since you started your study through the Partners program.

Notice how the following passages list and equate the persons of the triune God. What broad observations can you make about the Holy Spirit in these two verses?

• Matthew 28:19

• 2 Corinthians 13:14

The "Personhood" of the Holy Spirit

There have been, and now are, several groups that do not believe that the Holy Spirit is a person. But as we concluded in chapter two, the traits of intellect, emotion and will are all attributed to the person of the Holy Spirit. Identify how intellect (i.e., the capacity to think and reason), emotion (i.e., the ability to have

96

CHAPTER 5

LIVING A LIFE LED BY THE HOLY SPIRIT

and express feelings as a sentient being) and will (i.e., the volitional capacity to decide and act) are demonstrated in the following passages.

- Ephesians 4:30

- Romans 8:27

- 1 Corinthians 12:11

With Your Partner...

Discuss with your partner why it makes a difference that the Holy Spirit is a person and not a force or a principle.

Deeper Study...

Research the historical doctrinal errors related to the non-personhood of the Holy Spirit. Note the forms this teaching has taken in certain periods of early church history.

The "personhood" of the Holy Spirit is more than a theological discussion; it is also a practical consideration. We should be mindful as we interact with the Holy Spirit that we are not dealing with a principle, a standard, or a force. We are being prompted by a person. Our relationship with the Holy Spirit is personal. We are responding to a person—a perfectly "holy" person, but a person, nonetheless. And the person of the Holy Spirit is very concerned with how we live as children of God.

With Your Partner...

What are some other implications of the Holy Spirit being a person and not something less?

The Holy Spirit: Our Personal Connection with God

It is comforting, inviting and convicting to realize that God has not left us without his personal presence in our everyday life. And yet, that may be exactly what we picture without an understanding of the biblical teaching regarding the Holy Spirit. Consider the following biblical statements

...about God the Father

"Our God is in the heavens;" (Psalm 115:3)

"For thus says the One who is high and lifted up, who inhabits eternity, whose name is Holy: 'I dwell in the high and holy place,'" (Isaiah 57:15)

"he who is the blessed and only Sovereign, the King of kings and Lord of lords, who alone has immortality, who dwells in unapproachable light," (1 Timothy 6:15-16)

97

PARTNERS:
ONE-ON-ONE DISCIPLESHIP

…about Jesus Christ

Jesus said to her, "Do not cling to me, for I have not yet ascended to the Father;" (John 20:17)

"While he [Jesus] blessed them, he parted from them and was carried up into heaven." (Luke 24:51)

"He is the radiance of the glory of God and the exact imprint of his nature, and he upholds the universe by the word of his power. After making purification for sins, he sat down at the right hand of the Majesty on high,." (Hebrews 1:3)

Deeper Study...
Look up and list the few biblical passages that speak of Christ being "with" his followers after his ascension, without a specific reference to the Holy Spirit. Consider also how Christ was called "Emmanuel" ("God with us") and be able to articulate how certain passages summarize God's presence with his people without describing how or in what sense he is personally present with us. See how you can make possible distinctions between God's omnipresence, his omniscience and God's focalized presence.

Even so, the Bible tells us that in one very important respect the Father and the Son have not retreated to some distant heaven to watch our lives from afar. Instead the Godhead is present with us in the person of the Holy Spirit.

Carefully read **John 14:16-17** and answer the following questions:

• Who is making the request regarding the Holy Spirit?

• Who is said to be giving the Holy Spirit?

• How is the One being sent referred to? List all the ways he is described.

• What is the final relationship that is promised between the disciples and the "sent One"?

Deeper Study...
Do a word study on the word in John 14:16 translated "Helper" in the ESV.

98

CHAPTER 5

LIVING A LIFE LED BY THE HOLY SPIRIT

Your Relationship with the Holy Spirit

The Bible says several things about the Christian's relationship with the Holy Spirit. The better we understand what the Scripture teaches about our relationship with the Holy Spirit, the better we will be at relating to him as we ought.

Your Relationship with the Holy Spirit is a New Covenant Relationship

A New Testament follower of Christ is promised a new kind of relationship with the Holy Spirit. This is hinted at by the wording of John 14:17 as we have already seen. Notice the "in" as opposed to "with" relationship that is promised to Christ's disciples. This distinctive arrangement is predicted in the promise of the New Covenant in Ezekiel and Jeremiah.

• How is the "in you" of John 14:17 described in **Ezekiel 36:26-27**?

The Old Testament describes the "with you" ministry of the Holy Spirit as more general and more transient. Broadly speaking, the Holy Spirit was said to be with God's people. Notice this kind of Old Covenant description in **Haggai 2:4-5**. The Holy Spirit "came upon" and even temporarily "indwelt" some in the Old Testament to empower them for ministry or leadership. See **Genesis 41:38**, **Exodus 31:1-3** and **Numbers 11:17**.

This Old Testament reality regarding the Holy Spirit prompted leaders to make statements like the one in Psalm 51 which some have attempted to misapply to New Covenant followers of Christ. Read **Psalm 51:11** and state in your own words why this is not a legitimate concern for New Testament Christians in light of promises like **John 14:16** and **Ephesians 4:30**.

Your Relationship with the Holy Spirit is a Permanent Relationship

Because our relationship with the Holy Spirit is a New Covenant relationship we can quickly deduce that it is then a permanent relationship—the permanent indwelling of the Holy Spirit is the distinctive mark of New Covenant Christ-followers.

99

PARTNERS:
ONE-ON-ONE DISCIPLESHIP

How does **2 Corinthians 1:22** logically describe the permanence of the indwelling of the Holy Spirit in the lives of Christ's followers?

How does **Ephesians 1:13-14** speak to the permanence of the presence of the Holy Spirit and therefore our relationship with God?

After a lengthy discussion about the presence of the Holy Spirit in our lives throughout Romans 8, Paul concludes the chapter with these words:

> **Romans 8:35-39**
>
> Who shall separate us from the love of Christ? Shall tribulation, or distress, or persecution, or famine, or nakedness, or danger, or sword? As it is written, "For your sake we are being killed all the day long; we are regarded as sheep to be slaughtered." No, in all these things we are more than conquerors through him who loved us. For I am sure that neither death nor life, nor angels nor rulers, nor things present nor things to come, nor powers, nor height nor depth, nor anything else in all creation, will be able to separate us from the love of God in Christ Jesus our Lord.

What difference does it make in your thinking and your feelings knowing that God's Holy Spirit is a permanent resident in your life and that nothing can separate you from the triune God?

Your Relationship with the Holy Spirit is an Internal Relationship

Again, it is because our relationship with the Holy Spirit is a New Covenant relationship that it is a permanent *internal* relationship. The shift from "with you" to "in you" in John 14:17 and the explanation of Ezekiel 36:26-27 that God's Holy Spirit prompts New Covenant followers from "within" helps us to understand the "closeness" and "intimacy" of the Spirit's work in our lives. The Holy Spirit is not a foreign, external constraint on our spirit (or heart). He dwells within us and works with our regenerate, remade, converted spirit to prompt us and influence our behavior.

100

CHAPTER 5
LIVING A LIFE LED BY THE HOLY SPIRIT

How does **Romans 8:15-16** describe the closeness we have with the Holy Spirit?

Deeper Study...

Explore the Bible's use of spatial terms like "with" and "in" to relate degrees of relationship. Obviously, the Holy Spirit as a spirit takes up no space, and concepts like "indwelling" are not meant to be understood as filling a void in a cavern of one's body. How does **Romans 8:15-16** *describe the closeness we have with the Holy Spirit?*

The Bible often spells out implications related to the presence of the Holy Spirit in our lives. Take note of the context of **1 Corinthians 6:19** and list some of the implications Paul makes regarding the presence of the Holy Spirit in the Christian's life?

What are some other logical implications of having the third person of the Godhead resident in your life?

Your Relationship with the Holy Spirit Begins Prior to Conversion

Though many people generalize our relationship with the Holy Spirit as beginning when we become Christians, the reality is that we cannot become Christians without the Holy Spirit's work that leads us to repentance and faith in Christ. If you are a Christian you can be sure that the Holy Spirit was actively involved in convicting you of all that was necessary to turn from sin and put your trust in Christ.

In your own words, summarize the aspects of the "convicting" role of the Holy Spirit as seen in **John 16:7-11**, now that Christ has ascended and the Spirit has been sent into the world.

With Your Partner...

As you look back on the time when you became a Christian, how can you see the threefold activity of the Holy Spirit in your life leading up to your conversion?

How does Paul describe the "power" of his evangelistic preaching among the Thessalonians in **1 Thessalonians 1:5**?

How does this biblical understanding of the Holy Spirit's "pre-conversion" ministry change the way you view your efforts in evangelism?

101

PARTNERS:
ONE-ON-ONE DISCIPLESHIP

Your Relationship with the Holy Spirit is Formally Established at Conversion

The Holy Spirit was at work to convict you prior to your conversion to Christ, but then at the moment of your regeneration the Holy Spirit invaded your life to formally place you into a permanent relationship with Jesus Christ.

The old Greek word for "placed into" is *baptizo*, which unfortunately has been left untranslated in English Bibles and has simply been transliterated "baptize." This leads to a lot of unnecessary confusion. To help clarify the intent of any passage of Scripture, when you come across the word "baptize," "baptized" or "baptism" you must think "place into" or "placed into." There are two primary uses related to the word "baptism" in the Bible. The first has to do with being "placed into Christ" and second has to do with "being placed into water" (as a external expression of being placed into Christ). While a lot of extrabiblical doctrines have grown up around the words "baptism of the Holy Spirit," the concept is quite simple. When you are brought to the point of repentance and faith the Holy Spirit "places you into" Christ and his family (or his body) and then the same Holy Spirit takes up residence in your life.

> **1 Corinthians 12:13a**
>
> For in one Spirit we were all baptized into one body--

How does **Galatians 3:26-27** describe this transaction? What is the resulting picture?

Deeper Study...
Study the grammar of Acts 1:5 more closely, especially the use of the Greek preposition "en" which can be translated "in," "with" or "by."

Understanding the "baptism of the Holy Spirit" as something that God does to us at the point of conversion, instead of something that we seek to achieve or need to pursue after our conversion, helps us avoid a myriad of misconceptions and potential dangers related to this biblical phrase. A right understanding will also help us speak more accurately about our daily and ongoing interaction with the Holy Spirit throughout our Christian life.

What are the activities of the Holy Spirit mentioned in **Titus 3:5** and when do they take place according to this passage?

102

CHAPTER 5

LIVING A LIFE LED BY THE HOLY SPIRIT

What are some of the changes we can expect in a person's life when God does what **Titus 3:5** says?

There are some who teach that the Holy Spirit is not present or in some cases not "active" in the Christian life until some point months or years after one becomes a Christian. They teach that Christians must seek a subsequent point in their Christian experience wherein they receive the Holy Spirit. This kind of teaching is sometimes called "second-blessing" theology. How does **Romans 8:9-11** make it clear that such a theology cannot be true?

Deeper Study...
Discover the hermeneutical considerations related to the validation of the Gospel and the work of the Holy Spirit through the transitional stages recorded in the book of Acts. Deal specifically with the exceptional events related to the Apostles in Acts 8:14-17.

The Role of the Holy Spirit

The ministry and activity of the Holy Spirit in the universe is vast, from his role in creating the world (Gen.1:2), and his work in converting countless individuals to Christ (Tit.3:5), to the inspiration of the Scriptures (2Pet.1:21). But when it comes to our daily lives perhaps one biblical title given to the Holy Spirit best summarizes his ongoing ministry:

> **John 14:16**
>
> "And I will ask the Father, and he will give you another *Helper* to be with you forever,"

The word translated "Helper" in John 14:16 is the rich and thoughtful Greek word, *parakletos*. A *parakletos* is someone who is "called alongside of" to help (*para* = alongside; *kletos* = called). The word can refer to a lawyer "called alongside" to defend one in trouble; thus the translation "Advocate" is used in some translations. Obviously the use of the word is broader than that and can refer to any kind of assistant being called in to bring needed aid; thus some translators use the word "Counselor" in translating the word *parakletos*.

The focus of Christ's teaching on the eve of his crucifixion in the upper room with his disciples regarding the coming of the Holy Spirit depicts the Spirit as a "replacement" of sorts for the kind of standard, guidance and conviction Jesus had been personally providing during his earthly face-to-face ministry. Jesus

103

PARTNERS:
ONE-ON-ONE DISCIPLESHIP

said he would not "orphan" them by his departure but that the Spirit would guide them and provide them with all that his absence would necessitate (Jn.14:17-18).

His ministry to us is not altogether different. Though we have the written product of what appears to be in view throughout the upper room discourse to the apostles (i.e., the New Testament Scriptures; see John 15:26-27; 16:12-14), which does indeed give us Christ's standard, guidance and conviction, the Holy Spirit's ministry continues throughout the church age to confirm, highlight and underscore his written words.

The New Testament epistles tell us that the "help" the Holy Spirit provides is primarily aimed at empowering us and directing us to live holy lives. Part of this empowerment is his work in enabling us and equipping us to serve the church (i.e., "spiritual gifts of the Holy Spirit" – more on that in Partners chapter 8). When the Holy Spirit invades our lives he works to make us holy. Our job is to respond rightly to his ministry in our hearts.

Deeper Study...
Some are concerned that Bible teaching churches do not put enough attention on the Holy Spirit. But according to the Bible's description of the Holy Spirit's ministry (e.g., Jn.15:26; Jn.16:13-14; Rom.1:4; et al.) his role in our lives and in our churches is not to bring glory to himself but rather to put the attention on Christ and therefore bring glory to God the Father (Phil.2:11). Explore the various passages that clarify the focal point of our attention and teaching and note the varied roles of the persons of the Godhead.

How do the following passages add to our understanding of the Holy Spirit's desire to make us holy?

• Galatians 5:16-25

• Romans 8:4-14

• Ephesians 5:15-19

104

CHAPTER 5

LIVING A LIFE LED BY THE HOLY SPIRIT

Responding Rightly to the Holy Spirit

As the Holy Spirit desires to make us more holy, it is our responsibility to respond rightly to his work in our lives. There are three basic biblical responses to the Holy Spirit's work that will aid in our spiritual growth and sanctification.

Obey the Spirit's Inspired Words

We can be sure that the Holy Spirit would want, as a top priority, for us to respond rightly to what he has directed as recorded in the Scriptures. We would be foolish to ask for the Holy Spirit's direction and blessing if we are not being directed by the words he has already recorded for us in the pages of the Bible. It should be remembered that one of the primary works of the Holy Spirit was the revelation and inspiration of the eternal words of God. He has left us a Book that is packed with his instructions for daily living.

Consider the Holy Spirit's work in and through the human authors of Scripture.

> **2 Peter 1:20-21**
>
> Knowing this first of all, that no prophecy of Scripture comes from someone's own interpretation. For no prophecy was ever produced by the will of man, but men spoke from God as they were carried along by the Holy Spirit.

By way of example, describe the Spirit's role in each of these passages as it relates to the recording of God's words through David who penned a significant amount of the Old Testament.

• 2 Samuel 23:2

• Acts 1:16

105

PARTNERS:
ONE-ON-ONE DISCIPLESHIP

• Acts 4:25

• Matthew 22:43

With Your Partner...
Discuss a situation early in your Christian life when you felt some inner prompting to do what you thought was godly, only to later discover that the prompting could not have originated with the Holy Spirit because it, in fact, contradicted God's word.

As we think about our daily interaction with the Holy Spirit it is critical we remember that the Holy Spirit will never convict us or prompt us to do anything that contradicts his inspired Word. The same immutable Spirit that moved the apostles and prophets to write God's thoughts on paper is the same Spirit that lives in us today. He is perfectly consistent and unaffected by changing cultural mores and values.

Before we blame our impulses or aversions on the Holy Spirit we must be careful students of his written word. We must not assign divine authority to the experiential or environmental conditioning of our minds or consciences. Keep in mind the historical context of **Romans 14**, specifically how the ceremonial laws had been fulfilled and set aside by Christ (cf. Hebrews 9 – 10) including the passé ceremonial Jewish laws regarding a specific diet and a specific day for worship.

Now read **Romans 14:1-6** and comment on how the problem of condemning each other over matters of conscience was likely fueled by wrongly assigning inner impulses and aversions to the Holy Spirit.

Deeper Study...
Explore the biblical distinctions between eternally binding moral laws (expressed throughout the Old and New Testaments), the Jewish ceremonial laws that have been set aside because of their fulfillment in Christ (cf. Col.2:16-17) and the Old Testament civil laws delivered to run the government of the theocracy and monarchy of Israel. How does one carefully and accurately distinguish between the three?

Read **Acts 6:2-4** and **Ephesians 4:11-13**. Based on these verses, why are your pastors a logical resource for helping you make sure that you are not mistakenly assigning a personal preference to divine authority?

106

CHAPTER 5

LIVING A LIFE LED BY THE HOLY SPIRIT

Respond to the Spirit's Conviction

We have already seen that the Holy Spirit's work of conviction begins even before our conversion to Christ. The conviction of sin allows us to see our guilt and our need for Christ. But beyond that initial ministry, once we repent of our sins and place our trust in Christ, the Holy Spirit takes up residence in our lives to begin a life-long relationship of guiding our hearts. He guides us away from and out of sin each time we are confronted with a temptation or a potential compromise which violates the instructions laid out for us in his written word. Even as a brand new Christian we can testify to the way his conviction grips our hearts over sins that we have yet to read about in his word.

With Your Partner...
Describe a situation when God's Spirit convicted you with feelings of guilt over something you later discovered was either commanded or prohibited by Scripture. Notice how the ministry of the Holy Spirit goes beyond the ministry of your conscience.

From birth we are wired by God with a conscience that reflects the basic precepts of God's truth. What do we learn about the human conscience in **Romans 2:1, 14-15**?

Obviously the conscience is not an exhaustive guide to God's precepts. And it can easily be damaged as we stubbornly oppose it. Even from childhood our rebellion against its conviction can leave us without all but its strongest impulses. The subtleties of our conscience can easily be eroded to the point where most of what our consciences were initially designed to detect is no longer felt, and where our ability to justify and rationalize sin becomes second nature (see **Tit.1:15; 1Tim.4:2** and **2Pet.2:12**).

Deeper Study...
Explore the New Testament's teaching on the conscience (Gk.: suneidesis). Note how easily it is damaged and how Christians are to treat it with great care and deference, yet without assigning our consciences' convictions to the level of divine authority for others.

But when the Holy Spirit invades our lives, at the moment of conversion, our weakened and distorted consciences are no longer alone. We have the Spirit of Truth indwelling our lives. His conviction is unavoidable.

Describe some of the obvious convictions the Holy Spirit has brought to your heart throughout your Christian life.

107

PARTNERS:

ONE-ON-ONE DISCIPLESHIP

Carefully examine the following passage of Scripture.

> **Ephesians 4:25-31**
>
> 25 Therefore having put away falsehood, let each one of you speak the truth with his neighbor, for we are members one of another. 26 Be angry and do not sin: Do not let the sun go down on your anger, 27 and give no opportunity to the devil. 28 Let the thief no longer steal, but rather let him labor, doing honest work with his own hands, so that he may have something to share with anyone in need. 29 Let no corrupting talk come out of your mouths, but only such as is good for building up, as fits the occasion, that it may give grace to those who hear. 30 And do not grieve the Holy Spirit of God, by whom you were sealed for the day of redemption. 31 Let all bitterness and wrath and anger and clamor and slander be put away from you, along with all malice.

Verse 30 tells us that we can "grieve" the Holy Spirit by our acts of sin. Notice, in the context, how the sins listed in the paragraph move beyond the obvious violations of the Scripture's straightforward prohibitions such as telling lies and distorting the truth (v.25). Take note of how the Holy Spirit's expectations move from not "stealing" (v.28a) and no "corrupting talk" (v.29a) to the implications and righteous reactions like "honest work" (v.28b) and words that are "good for building up" (v.29b). This is an important observation and something to which all Christians can attest. The Holy Spirit's conviction extends beyond the minimum written rules, to the application, implication and full expression of those rules. The Holy Spirit does not appear to be content with a minimalistic, wooden or rote adherence to his revealed instructions. The Author of God's Word wants us to own them, and to live them out with a fullness and integrity that is described in this passage. Note the varied expressions in verse 31 of the topic of anger that was initially mentioned in verse 26. After a variety of inclusive descriptive terms the text then adds "along with *all* malice." This is certainly the arena of the Spirit's conviction. He is convicting us of all forms and types of sin that are often far-reaching implications of a written command. Likewise, the grief we bring the Holy Spirit results when we resist and rebel against what he is driving us to do, or not do.

Give some examples of the way the Holy Spirit has convicted you about a specific implication of a biblical prohibition.

CHAPTER 5
LIVING A LIFE LED BY THE HOLY SPIRIT

Describe what it is like for you when you recognize that your actions have "grieved the Holy Spirit."

Because of Christ, even when we grieve the all-knowing and all-powerful Holy Spirit there is immediate forgiveness available.

---

1 John 1:8-9

If we say we have no sin, we deceive ourselves, and the truth is not in us. If we confess our sins, he is faithful and just to forgive us our sins and cleanse us from all unrighteousness.

Deeper Study...
Research the context and setting of Matthew 12:31-32 and explain why the "blasphemy against the Spirit" is a unique historical transgression that is not available to sinners today.

To restore a harmonious fellowship with the Holy Spirit it is required that we "confess" our sins. Confession consists of agreeing with God that our sin really is sin and as such that we are turning from it (cf. 2Cor.7:11). Just as confession is required to begin our relationship with the Holy Spirit, it is also required to restore a harmonious fellowship with him when an act of sin or compromise has been committed in our daily life.

Write out the kind of prayer you ought to pray when you realize your words, actions or attitudes have grieved the Holy Spirit.

Carefully Follow the Spirit's Leadership

We all know the reality of grieving the Holy Spirit when we do what he does not want us to do, but it is also important to realize that we can "quench" the work of the Holy Spirit in our lives when we do not move forward in doing what he wants us to do.

---

1 Thessalonians 5:19

Do not quench the Spirit.

PARTNERS:
ONE-ON-ONE DISCIPLESHIP

Just as the Holy Spirit convicts us when we violate the implications of his written prohibitions, it is also true that he prompts us to apply a variety of implications regarding his written directives. For instance, the Bible commands us to be ambassadors of Christ and his gospel (2Cor.5:18-20), and in certain situations we can attest to the Spirit's prompting to open our mouths and obey that command.

While we cannot infallibly identify his promptings (just as we are susceptible to wrongly assigning a personal aversion to the Holy Spirit), we should be open to the godly ways the Holy Spirit would want us to apply his written instructions.

How do the following passages refer to the Holy Spirit's promptings?

- Matthew 4:1

- Mark 1:12

- Luke 2:27

- Romans 8:5

- Romans 8:6-9

- Romans 8:13-14

- Romans 8:16

- Romans 8:26

- Romans 9:1

- Galatians 5:25

110

CHAPTER 5

LIVING A LIFE LED BY THE HOLY SPIRIT

Again, it is important to stress that every internal prompting cannot be assumed to be the Holy Spirit. The Spirit's desire to make us holy must, of course, correspond to his written word. It will also be in keeping with a healthy and intact conscience. But recognize that the Holy Spirit's prompting to apply biblical instructions will grate against several aspects of our human desires. Consider the following insight from Paul's discussion about the Holy Spirit's leading in the lives of the Galatian Christians.

Galatians 5:16-17

But I say, walk by the Spirit, and you will not gratify the desires of the flesh. For the desires of the flesh are against the Spirit, and the desires of the Spirit are against the flesh, for these are opposed to each other, to keep you from doing the things you want to do.

The Holy Spirit is working against an entire set of human, fallen (i.e., "fleshly") desires in our lives. And living daily with such a contrasted variety of desires we can see why many misguided Christians blame a lot of sinful actions on the prompting of the Holy Spirit. Just because they have a strong impulse or desire to do something they are tempted to say, "the Spirit led me" to do it, even when it clearly contradicts God's word. Obviously then, we must let the objective word of God be our guide in knowing how to sort through the various promptings, impulses, and desires in our lives.

With that said, the Holy Spirit is our Counselor and Helper, sent to guide us into an increasing life of righteous and fruitful words and actions. And we are commanded to "keep in step" with him in our lives (Gal.5:25). "Keeping in step" with him will always involve a deference to his desires and a priority given to his will over and above the dictates of our fallen humanity (i.e., our "flesh"). Understanding God's written word helps us to identify the Spirit's promptings and impulses in our hearts. Take a moment to compare the list of "fleshly" desires and the Holy Spirit's desires as they are manifested in our daily lives.

111

PARTNERS:
ONE-ON-ONE DISCIPLESHIP

Use the lists from **Galatians 5:19-23** to fill in the following chart.

The Desires of the Flesh	*The Desires of the Spirit*
v.19a	v.22a
v.19b	
v.19c	v.22b
v.20a	v.22c
v.20b	
v.20c	v.22d
v.20d	v.22e
v.20e	
v.20f	v.22f
v.20g	v.22g
v.20h	
v.20i	v.23a
v.21a	v.23b
v.21b	
v.21c	

We could extend this list (as is suggested by "...and the like" and "such things" in vv.21, 23) almost indefinitely as we consider the clash of desires in our lives. The goal though, according to Galatians 5, is that we choose to follow the desires of the Holy Spirit and deny the desires of our sinful flesh.

Galatians 5:24-25

And those who belong to Christ Jesus have crucified the flesh with its passions and desires. If we live by the Spirit, let us also walk by the Spirit.

With Your Partner...
Share an example of the contrasting and conflicting desires of the "flesh" and the Holy Spirit in your life.

112

CHAPTER 5

LIVING A LIFE LED BY THE HOLY SPIRIT

Paul illustrates the quest of following the Spirit's desires with a thought provoking illustration.

Ephesians 5:17-18

Therefore do not be foolish, but understand what the will of the Lord is. And do not get drunk with wine, for that is debauchery, but be filled with the Spirit.

Intoxication with alcohol diminishes righteous inhibitions and drunk people do as their sinful impulses desire. Scripture makes an antithetical parallel of being "filled with the Spirit" so that the sinful barriers that inhibit are overcome and the desires of God's Spirit prevail in our lives. For example, instead of being "filled with anger" (cf. Gal.5:20) so that our words and actions are prompted by anger, God would have us be "filled with the Spirit" so that our words and actions are prompted by him. So then, in all areas of life we must be resolved to allow the Holy Spirit's desires to overrule any fleshly encumbrances to doing what is right and to do what leads to increasing holiness.

Because of this illustration some like to use the word "control" to describe the Holy Spirit's leadership in our lives. But the fullness of the Bible's instructions regarding the Holy Spirit does not lead us to conclude that we are to engage in some kind of personal passivity, expecting the Holy Spirit to "take over." The Bible always advocates that Christians maintain mental and spiritual control of their faculties (cf. 1Cor.14:15; Rom.6:12-17). The goal is to be resolute in offering ourselves to the will of the Holy Spirit, rightly denying ourselves fleshly desires and impulses, and always seeking to do what the Spirit has commanded and is leading us to do. We are not passively "letting go and letting God," instead we are actively following him and his will for our lives.

Consider the biblical concept of "following" God. How is the idea expressed in the following passages?

• Deuteronomy 13:4

• Psalm 31:3-5

• Matthew 16:24

113

PARTNERS:
ONE-ON-ONE DISCIPLESHIP

Just as God's Spirit will sometimes orchestrate circumstances to direct us into or out of a path he desires for us (cp. the "open door" language regarding specific opportunities for advancing the Gospel in 1Cor.16:9; 2Cor.2:12; Col.4:3), sometimes God prompts our sanctified desires or godly apprehensions to direct us into or out of a path he desires for us. How is this observed or implied in the following passages of Scripture?

• 2 Corinthians 2:12-14

• Romans 9:1-2

• Acts 16:6-7

• Acts 20:22

With Your Partner...
Discuss some of the ways the Holy Spirit has prompted you to apply his written word...

• 1 Thessalonians 3:1-2, 5

Whenever possible, wise Christians are careful to crosscheck what they understand the Holy Spirit's prompting to be regarding the application of his written instructions by seeking the prayerful counsel of mature Christians.

What does **James 1:5** add to our understanding of how to know the Holy Spirit's direction as to the decisions of our lives?

How do you, should you, and will you go about doing what **Proverbs 15:21-22, 11:14** and **20:18** direct you to do? Who are your wise and godly advisors?

With Your Partner...
Discuss at least one decision you are facing and ask for godly counsel.

Read **2 Chronicles 10:1-11**. How does Rehoboam's approach to "seeking counsel" actually invalidate the process?

114

CHAPTER 5
LIVING A LIFE LED BY THE HOLY SPIRIT

Notes

PARTNERS:
ONE-ON-ONE DISCIPLESHIP

Notes

RESOURCES & FURTHER STUDY

5 *Living a Life Led by the Holy Spirit*

Resources on Understanding the Holy Spirit

Rating Key
★ Helpful (four being most)
◉ Difficulty (four being hardest)

★★★
◉◉◉
Chantry, Walter. *Signs of the Apostles: Observations on Pentecostalism Old & New*. Banner of Truth, 1973. (While this book's topic is broad, it is helpful in identifying aberrant responses and expectations regarding the Holy Spirit.)

★★
◉◉◉◉
Conant, Thomas Jefferson. *The Meaning and Use of BAPTIZEIN*. Reprint. Kregel, 1977. (This is an in depth book that addresses the biblical uses of the transliterated word "baptism".)

★
◉◉
Dallimore, Arnold. *Forerunner of the Charismatic Movement: The Life of Edward Irving*. Moody Press, 1983. (This is an interesting read regarding the theological trends that led to several misunderstandings regarding the Holy Spirit.)

★★★
◉◉
Edgar, Thomas. *Satisfied by the Promise of the Spirit*. Kregel, 1996. (This work specifically addresses the expectations we should have as church-age followers of Christ.)

★★★
◉◉◉
Ewert, David. *The Holy Spirit in the New Testament*. Wipf and Stock, 2005. (This is a thorough biblical theology of the Holy Spirit which takes the reader canonically through each section of the New Testament and its teaching on the Holy Spirit.)

★★
◉◉◉
Ferguson, Sinclair. *The Holy Spirit (Contours of Christian Theology)*. InterVarsity Press, 1997. (This fairly recent volume of the Contours series focuses on the person of the Holy Spirit and seeks to summarize orthodox pneumatology against various competing views.)

★★★
◉◉
Guinness, Os. *The Call: Finding and Fulfilling The Central Purpose of Your Life*. Word Publishing, 1998. (This work is included here because it may be helpful in thinking through one's vocation as a decision in keeping with the Spirit's work in the world.)

★★★
◉◉
Johnson, Arthur. *Faith Misguided: Exposing the Dangers of Mysticism*. Moody Press, 1998. (Johnson warns of the expressions of subjectivism and mysticism present in the modern church often existing under the guise of the Holy Spirit's direction.)

★★★
◉◉
Lloyd-Jones, Martyn. *God the Holy Spirit*. Crossway Books, 1997. (This classic reprint from a pastor's heart seeks to champion a proper understanding and application of the doctrine of the Holy Spirit.)

117

★★★ MacArthur, John F. *The Charismatics: A Doctrinal Perspective.* Zondervan, 1978. (This book chronicles
◉ much of the extreme Scriptural abuse that takes place in the name of the Holy Spirit.)

★★ Masters, Peter and John C. Whitcomb. *The Charismatic Phenomenon.* Wakeman Trust, 1982. (Sections
◉◉ of this book also help to govern expectations regarding the Holy Spirit's promised activity in our lives.)

★★ Needham, David. *Alive for the First Time: A Fresh Look at the New Birth Miracle.* Multnomah Press,
◉ 1995. (This work is listed because it adds something to our understanding of our spirit's interface with the Holy
Spirit.)

★★★ Pache, Rene. *The Person and Work of the Holy Spirit.* Moody Press, 1954. (Pache summarizes in an
◉◉ accessible manner the theological teaching regarding the Holy Spirit.)

★★ Packer, J. I. *A Quest for Godliness.* Crossway Books, 1994. (Packer takes a look at the Puritan era and the
◉◉◉ Puritans views of practical holiness.)

★★★ Pentecost, Dwight. *The Divine Comforter.* Moody Press, 1963. (This is a helpful, straightforward treatment of
◉ the Bible's teaching on the Holy Spirit with a view to correcting modern doctrinal error.)

★★ Pettegrew, Larry D. *The New Covenant Ministry of the Holy Spirit.* Kregel, 2001. (This book tackles the Old
◉◉ and New Covenant distinctions as they relate the ministry of the Holy Spirit.)

★★★ Ryrie, Charles. *The Holy Spirit. Revised and Expanded.* Moody Press, 1997. (This is a standard and readable
◉ evangelical treatment of the doctrine of the Holy Spirit.)

★★★ Sproul, R.C. *The Mystery of the Holy Spirit: Discover the Work of the Living Spirit of the Living God.*
◉◉ Tyndale House, 1990. (This is a broad yet concise examination of the person and work of the Holy Spirit with
a helpful and substantive opening section on the Trinity.)

★★ Spurgeon, Charles. *A Passion for Holiness in a Believer's Life.* YWAM Publishing, 1996. (This book
◉◉ pastorally exhorts readers to share the Holy Spirit's sanctifying goal for our lives.)

★ Tozer, A. W. *Man: The Dwelling Place of God.* Christian Publications, 1966. (While not a doctrinal treatise,
◉ Tozer, as usual, zealously motivates us to consider the presence of God's spirit in our lives.)

★★ Unger, Merrill F. *The Baptism & Gifts of the Holy Spirit.* Moody Press, 1974. (This book is helpful in
◉◉ exploring the "baptism of the Holy Spirit" and its doctrinal context especially in the Gospels and the book of Acts.)

★★★ Walvoord, John F. *The Holy Spirit: A Comprehensive Study of the Person and Work of the Holy Spirit.*
◉◉ Zondervan, 1991. (Walvoord codifies his seminary teaching on pneumatology and systematically presents a
thorough treatment of the subject.)

PARTNERS MEETING #6

The Importance of a Good Church

At Partners Meeting #6...

In this chapter you will explore the important role of the church in a Christian's spiritual growth and development. You will study God's plan for the church and your connection to it. You will review the biblical structure of the church and some of the ways it is worked out in today's world. You will also think through your basic responsibilities as a part of your church and rekindle your love and appreciation for this special institution commissioned by God's word.

To Prepare for Partners Meeting #6...

- Read chapter 6 and answer the questions.

- If any of the "Deeper Study" topics are of interest to you, prepare to discuss them.

- Memorize the second half of the books of the Old Testament in order (Isaiah through Malachi).

- Memorize 1 Timothy 3:14-15

> I hope to come to you soon, but I am writing these things to you so that, if I delay, you may know how one ought to behave in the household of God, which is the church of the living God, a pillar and buttress of the truth.
>
> – 1 Timothy 3:14-15

PARTNERS:

ONE-ON-ONE DISCIPLESHIP

FYI...

Of all the words the New Testament uses to describe the followers of Christ, "brother" is number one at 277 occurrences (not counting references to biological brothers). Compare that to the 240 references to "disciple", or the 45 occurrences of the word "saint", or the only 3 uses of the word "Christian".

The church is of utmost importance for the growth and development of every Christian. The Christian life was never designed to be lived alone. God purposed his followers to live as brothers and sisters as a committed and organized team.

Read **Proverbs 27:17** and **Ecclesiastes 4:9-12**. What does the Bible say is the problem with Christians who want to "go it alone" and attempt to follow God in isolation?

With Your Partner...

Discuss how we can, for all practical purposes, live our lives in isolation while faithfully attending a church. Consider why we are tempted to do this and discuss how we can avoid these isolating strategies as we interface with our church family.

Hebrews 10:23 describes our fundamental calling to hold on to our hope in Christ without wavering or compromise. The next two verses follow up with an important ingredient in doing so effectively. Read **Hebrews 10:23-25**. God designed the church to be the New Testament environment for meeting this important need in the Christian life.

Describe your commitment to being involved in your church. How specific is your commitment to regular attendance and participation in the various events in your church?

Deeper Study...

Research the rise of monasticism in the fourth and fifth century. Discover why Athanasius' book The Life of Antony *was such an important work in the rise of the monastic movement. Be able to articulate why eremitical monasticism was an unbiblical way of life. Be able to explain why the communal form of monasticism also fell short of God's plan for the Christian life.*

Defining Church

Today people use the word "church" in at least four ways. First, we might say "the church has new carpet," meaning the building where we meet for worship. Second, we might also say "we had church tonight," meaning we attended a worship or preaching service. Third, we might say "our church has a new pastor," meaning a defined group of Christians who worship and serve together. Fourth, we also might say "the Church has been advanced by generations of missionaries," meaning all of God's people since New Testament times.

With Your Partner...

Discuss how you can maximize your involvement at each meeting or activity at your church. How can you prepare, participate and follow up on the events you attend at church?

The Bible utilizes the word "church" in the last two of the above four ways. Most often in the New Testament we find the word "church" employed to describe defined groups of Christians who worship and serve together in specific geographical locations. This common biblical use of the word is often designated as the "local church." The other way the Bible employs the word "church" is to describe all of God's people since New Testament times, or at least from the indwelling of God's Spirit in Acts 2. This broad use of the word "church" is often distinguished as the "universal church."

120

CHAPTER 6

THE IMPORTANCE OF A GOOD CHURCH

The Universal Church

The word in the Greek New Testament translated "church" is the word *ekklesia* which means "called out" or "assembled." It makes sense then that Scripture would from time to time utilize this term in a broad sense for the entire group that God has called out and redeemed from all the nations throughout the centuries. Passages which use the word *ekklesia* in this way refer to realities that apply to Christians regardless of who they are, where they are or when they lived. Consider a passage like **Ephesians 5:23-27**, for instance. List some of the truths in this passage that can be claimed as true for your local church as well as for a church in any city and in any period of church history.

While we learn much about God's care of and commands for our individual churches from studying passages that refer to the universal church, it is important to note that the Bible expects every Christian to be actively involved in a local or geographically specific church. We know this because a church or *ekklesia* in a specific sense is a group that is "called out" and actually "assembles." Every specific or local church assembles regularly for worship, Bible study and fellowship. Unfortunately, until we reach heaven, we cannot assemble with the universal church. Not only can we not presently meet with the universal church, we cannot give to the universal church or utilize our spiritual gifts in the universal church. In other words, while as a Christian you are a part of the universal church, God requires that you also be a part of a local church.

How might you biblically reason with a person who professes to be a Christian but insists that he did not need to attend any church because he was already a part of the universal church?

Specific Local Churches

The emphasis throughout the New Testament is on the Christian's relationship to a specific or local church, which meets in a particular location. This is evidenced in part by the fact that of the 114 times the word *ekklesia* appears in the New Testament almost 80% of the occurrences refer to specific churches. It may be appealing to stay focused on the broad biblical truths related to the universal church, but the reality is that God calls us all to live out our Christian lives in the context of a specific church, which gathers in a specific place. One of the reasons people balk at that calling is because real churches will always have real problems. Consider the churches described in Revelation chapters 2 and 3. Take a few

Deeper Study...
Distinguish for yourself the local or universal usage of each New Testament occurrence of the word ekklesia. *You can do this by utilizing a concordance or a Bible software program and examining each use in context.*

121

PARTNERS:

ONE-ON-ONE DISCIPLESHIP

With Your Partner...

Discuss how we can continue to enthusiastically embrace God's institution of the church even though every church will eventually encounter problems and imperfections. Explore the parallels of how you want others to accept and embrace you with your associated problems and imperfections.

minutes to skim through those chapters and note the very real problems associated with real and specific churches. How does the picture presented in those two chapters differ from the idyllic experience of pondering **Ephesians 5:23-27?**

Your Church

With Your Partner...

Discuss the importance of praying for your church and identify a few pertinent prayer requests based on the points in this section of the chapter.

Before we take a look at God's instructions regarding your relationship with your church, it is important to consider some basic biblical criteria which should be met by your church.

We would be wise to thoughtfully evaluate the strengths and potential weaknesses of a particular church before we choose to settle in as an active participant. The following points provide us with a good prayer list to pray regularly for the health of our church.

Biblical Purpose

The church of Jesus Christ was designed by God to be much more than a social club or support group. Ultimately, each individual church is commissioned to be a disciple-making organization. Read carefully what has come to be known as the "Great Commission" of the Church in **Matthew 28.**

> **Matthew 28:18-20**
>
> And Jesus came and said to them, "All authority in heaven and on earth has been given to me. Go therefore and make disciples of all nations, baptizing them in the name of the Father and of the Son and of the Holy Spirit, teaching them to observe all that I have commanded you. And behold I am with you always, to the end of the age."

In the Greek language in which this command was originally recorded, there is actually one imperative verb and three supporting participles. The central command is to "make disciples" and the three supporting participles are translated "go," "baptizing" and "teaching".

122

CHAPTER 6
THE IMPORTANCE OF A GOOD CHURCH

A church which "makes disciples" is a church that is purposefully cultivating and developing "learners," "pupils," or "followers" of Christ. That is the meaning of the word "disciple." Take a minute to describe how your church, its programs, meetings, and services have recently helped you to become a better follower of Jesus Christ.

The three supporting participles in the Great Commission (translated "go," "baptizing" and "teaching") describe aspects or stages that disciples go through, and should in some way govern the kinds of ministries and programs a church provides. Let's consider these three participles.

With Your Partner...
Discuss the difference one can expect when involved in a church which is governed and directed by a passion to make, educate and equip disciples for service.

1. A church should strategically seek to bring people to the place of initial repentance and faith, which culminates in the external expression of "baptizing" them.

2. A church should strategically seek to bring followers of Christ into a life of obedience in everything Jesus commanded, which is accomplished primarily through "teaching" them.

3. A church should strategically seek to develop followers of Christ so that they are enabled to "go" and participate in making disciples.

Churches may express these aspects of disciple-making in a variety of ways. A church may say that it exists to see as many people as possible come to "know him" (conversion to Christ), "love him" (obedience to Christ) and "serve him" (service in the cause of Christ). Other churches may express these strategies by stating that they exist to "reach people for Christ," "teach people to be like Christ" and "train people to serve Christ." Other churches may crystallize these participles from the Great Commission with single words by saying we exist for the "evangelism," "edification" and "equipping" of God's people.

However they are expressed or communicated, a church's focus and efforts should be directed by a core biblical purpose that involves making new disciples, instructing those disciples to be obedient to Christ and preparing those disciples to make more disciples.

123

PARTNERS:
ONE-ON-ONE DISCIPLESHIP

Biblical Doctrine

Every church and its leaders should be rightly concerned with upholding and maintaining "sound doctrine" as the Bible puts it. Sound doctrine is literally "healthy teaching," an uncompromised theology or an accurate understanding of the truths of Scripture. How does the imagery in our memory verses (**1 Timothy 3:14-15)**, particularly **v.15**, powerfully underscore this priority?

What is the concern of **2 Timothy 4:3-4** and how relevant is this concern in light of the menu of organizations listed in the "church" section of your local phone book?

What is Paul's solution surrounding vv.3-4 (i.e., **2 Timothy 4:1-2, 5)**? What are some of the implications of these verses if your church and its leaders take this job seriously?

Below is an abbreviated list of the fundamental aspects of biblical doctrine that should be carefully researched, articulated and defended by your church and its leaders. A statement of your church's understanding of these eight points and some elaboration on each of them should be posted, printed or readily made available to all who would consider making your church their church family.

Deeper Study...

Locate the doctrinal statement of your church along with any expanded doctrinal statements from your pastoral leadership. Most pastors have had to write and defend a personal doctrinal statement during their ordination process. Carefully review these doctrinal statements looking up all listed supporting passages.

1. The Bible or "Bibliology"

Your church should uphold the biblical assertion that the written word of God has been given by the inspiration of the Holy Spirit and is not the product of human creativity or ingenuity. See **2 Peter 1:20-21; 2 Timothy 3:16; Matthew 5:18; John 17:17; Psalm 19:7**). Why is it logical to conclude that a church's doctrine of the Bible will affect every other doctrine in the church?

124

CHAPTER 6
THE IMPORTANCE OF A GOOD CHURCH

2. God or "Theology Proper"

Your church should affirm that there is only one true, eternal and living God who exists in three persons – the Father, Son and Holy Spirit. See **Deuteronomy 6:4; Isaiah 45:5-6; 1 Corinthians 8:4; Matthew 28:19; 2 Corinthians 13:14**. How does a church's doctrine of God affect the church's approach to worship and expectation of obedience?

3. Jesus Christ or "Christology"

Your church should unashamedly proclaim that Jesus is God incarnate, who died for our sins, rose from the dead and will return one day for his Church. See **John 8:57-58; Philippians 2:5-8; John 10:15; Romans 5:8; 1 Peter 2:24; Romans 1:4; 1 Corinthians 15:16-20; Acts 1:9-11; 1 Thessalonians 4:13-17**. Why is a church's doctrine of Christ so important in light of **1 John 4:1-2**?

4. The Holy Spirit or "Pneumatology"

Your church should affirm the biblical teaching that the Holy Spirit is God, who indwells Christians, leading and enabling them as they follow his written word and respond to his conviction. See **Acts 5:3-4; 28:25-26; Galatians 5:16-25; Ephesians 5:18; Romans 8:14**). Why is it important for a church to be clear about its understanding of the doctrine of the Holy Spirit?

5. People or "Anthropology"

Your church should uphold the biblical teaching that people were created by God to enjoy God and honor God, but forfeited their intended fellowship with God because of sin, becoming subject to God's punishment. See **Genesis 1:26-27; Isaiah 43:7; 59:2; Genesis 2:16-17; Romans 5:6-12; John 3:36; Romans 3:10-18**. How might an unbiblical view of "people" change a church's understanding and presentation of the gospel?

125

PARTNERS:
ONE-ON-ONE DISCIPLESHIP

6. Salvation or "Soteriology"

With Your Partner...
Discuss why a church's view of soteriology is so important? Why does Galatians 1:6-9 make this topic a top priority on deciding which church to call home?

Your church should boldly proclaim that Christians are saved from the penalty of their sin when they are drawn to the place of repentance and exclusive faith in Christ's perfect life and substitutionary death on their behalf. See **Mark 1:15**; **Luke 24:46-47**; **Acts 3:19**; **11:18**; **20:21**; **1 Peter 3:18**; **2 Corinthians 5:21**; **Romans 3:21-22**; **8:33**. What is at stake when factions arise within a church that have differing views on the doctrine of salvation?

7. The Church or "Ecclesiology"

Your church should affirm that it is God's will for Christians to fellowship, serve and spiritually grow through their participation in local churches that are faithful to teach the Bible. See **1 Corinthians 1:2**; **Galatians 1:2**; **1 Thessalonians 1:1**; **Acts 2:42-47**; **Hebrews 10:24-25**. What are some of the obvious reasons a church should have a firm understanding of the biblical doctrine of the church?

8. The Last Things or "Eschatology"

Deeper Study...
While there is usually some grace and latitude granted in matters of eschatology, learn the position of your pastors on the millennial Kingdom, their understanding of the rapture, the timing and nature of the resurrection, etc. Unless your pastor is new, he likely has a series of recorded messages available, which contain his understanding of these future events.

Your church should uphold Christ's promise that God will establish an eternal kingdom in which resurrected Christians will graciously participate, but that those without Christ will be resurrected to incur the penalty of their sins. See **Acts 24:14-15**; **1 Corinthians 15:22-23**; **2 Corinthians 4:14**; **Revelation 20:13-15**; **Daniel 12:2**; **Revelation 20:1-9**; **21:1—22:5**. What deficiencies may arise in a church that never expounds the biblical doctrine of the end times?

Biblical Values

Beyond your church's statement of core doctrine there is likely a set of biblical values that govern much of what the church does and which end up affecting how the church "feels." These values and the resultant church culture are shaped by the leadership's sense of discerned threats, challenges and opportunities. Some churches articulate these kinds of values in writing while others don't. Even without a written statement, most people can discern a church's values after faithfully participating for six to twelve months.

CHAPTER 6
THE IMPORTANCE OF A GOOD CHURCH

Listed below is a set of important church values that are broad enough to be applicable for most churches in today's world.

1. Good Churches Keep the Bible Central

In a society where feelings and subjective impressions are king, we need more churches where the Bible continues to be the final arbiter of life, doctrine and church conduct. Healthy churches may express this in a variety of ways, but especially in our day, if a church does not resolutely value the Bible as the ultimate source of authority, there will be negative, ungodly and far-reaching consequences. See **Psalm 43:3; 119:105; John 17:17; 1 Timothy 3:15.**

With Your Partner...
Especially if your church does not have a written set of values, take some time with your partner to sketch out some of the values your church exudes by the way it functions. What are the discernable values based on its preaching, programming and events?

2. Good Churches Showcase Biblical Preaching

With the current trend to downplay biblical preaching, it is important for good churches to purposefully endorse God's ordained method for the spiritual health of God's people. Bible-based preaching is more than the preacher quoting a few Bible verses. Instead of the preacher using the Bible to preach his messages, the Bible should be utilizing the preacher to preach its message. Nothing can or should replace church meetings that highlight strong, meaty and relevant biblical preaching. See **Hebrews 4:12; 2 Timothy 4:2-4; 1 Corinthians 1:21-23; Colossians 1:28.**

3. Good Churches Maintain a High View of God

In response to the declining reverence for God and as the line distinguishing the church from the world is increasingly blurred, it is important that a healthy church purpose to maintain a high view of God. When God becomes one's "buddy," "the Man upstairs" or the self-help therapist, the church will inevitably suffer God's judgment. See **Malachi 1:6-11; Isaiah 6:1-5; Revelation 1:12-18; 4:7-11.**

With Your Partner...
Share your thoughts about the importance of a high view of God and how this value's presence or absence is detected in a church.

4. Good Churches Proclaim a Biblical Gospel

It is essential that clarity about what the gospel is and isn't be a conscious and vigilant concern of a healthy church. The Book of 1 John and the Book of Galatians should be adequate reason for a church in any era to consciously and zealously value the accurate presentation of the gospel. A weak or compromised gospel will be impotent to save. And when the church fails to proclaim a saving gospel there is no hope of having a healthy church. See **Romans 1:16; Galatians 1:6-9; 3:1-14; 1 John 1:5-6; 3:2-15.**

Deeper Study...
Explore and define the heretical aspects of the false gospels described in Galatians and 1 John. Note the contrasting errors in both books, especially those articulated in 1 John 3 and Galatians 3.

127

PARTNERS:

ONE-ON-ONE DISCIPLESHIP

5. Good Churches are Reliant on Prayer

Because "God opposes the proud, but gives grace to the humble" (James 4:6) it is important that individual churches never fall into feeling self-sufficient or self-important. Churches are utterly dependent on God and cannot afford to neglect their humble reliance on him. Notice the self-deception of a church that failed to be a prayerful, dependent church in **Revelation 3:17-20**. Consider the imagery of Christ standing outside of this church knocking to garner this prideful church's attention. A church filled with participants who invest time in prayer will be a strong and resilient church. See **John 15:4-5**; **Colossians 4:2-4, 12**; **Matthew 6:6**; **26:41**; **Luke 5:16**; **9:28**; **Mark 1:35**; **Ephesians 6:18**.

6. Good Churches Have Highly Committed Participants

Much like the goal of this chapter and the next chapter of Partners, a healthy church will always seek to move people from passivity to productive activity for the glory of God. In a day when many think that "being a part of a church" is nothing more than sitting through one church service a week, good churches will work to recapture the church-centered lives that made such a difference in the pages of the Book of Acts. See **Ephesians 4:11-16**; **Acts 4:34-35**; **1 Corinthians 12:12-27**.

7. Good Churches Have Authentic and Sacrificial Leaders

With Your Partner...

Discuss the importance of praying for your church leaders and discuss a plan to pray more specifically and more frequently for them.

Healthy churches obviously must have gifted and godly leaders. Godly leadership is always honest, upfront, forthright and truthful. It is also hardworking, disciplined, diligent and sacrificial. In a societal culture that is increasingly fixated on comfort and convenience, today's churches should be strategic in underscoring the biblical standards of church leadership. See **2 Corinthians 6:3-11**; **Titus 1:6-9**; **1 Thessalonians 2:8-9**; **1 Timothy 3:1-13**.

8. Good Churches are Always Working to Plant New Churches

A church cannot truly be healthy until it participates in Christ's work to expand and reproduce his church. God's heartbeat is to make disciples and establish churches nearby and far away. Seeing that accomplished in your "Jerusalem, Judea, and Samaria" as well as the "ends of the earth" requires a purposeful focus and effort from biblical churches. See **Acts 1:8**; **Matthew 9:37-38**; **28:19-20**; **2 Corinthians 5:18-20**.

CHAPTER 6
THE IMPORTANCE OF A GOOD CHURCH

Biblical Leadership

While there are a variety of ways churches today are structured and many titles for a church's leaders, in the New Testament God has specifically prescribed only two essential levels of leadership for churches. One level is commissioned with the decision-making and preaching, while the other level is entrusted with the key ministry responsibilities. Your church may choose to add boards, committees and councils to its structure, but it is important to recognize that those entities are not commissioned or required by God or the precepts of the Scripture.

1. Pastors

There are three New Testament words used as descriptive titles for the administrative and preaching leaders of a church. It is important to note, as we will see, that the following three titles are used synonymously throughout the New Testament.

- *"Episkopos"*

    The word *episkopos* is one of the three titles given to the top level of leadership in a church and is usually translated "overseer" or "bishop" in older translations. The word contains the sense of responsibility to superintend, provide oversight, and serve as a spiritual guardian for the congregation. It is a word that is often overlooked, but obviously gives us a clear description of the important commission of the pastors.

    Look up the following verses, which all utilize the word *episkopos* (overseer, bishop, guardian) and describe some of the aspects of church leadership implied or expressed.

    - **Acts 20:28**

    - **1 Timothy 3:1-2**

    - **Titus 1:7**

129

PARTNERS:
ONE-ON-ONE DISCIPLESHIP

- *"Poimen"*

The word *poimen* is the second of three titles given to the administrative leaders in the church. *Poimen* is usually translated "shepherd" or "pastor" and describes the leading and feeding functions of church leaders. The picture of a shepherd caring for a flock is a common biblical motif and one that depicts the pace-setting and teaching function of church leaders. The New Testament utilizes the verbal form of this word for leaders and it is translated "to tend," "to feed," "to rule" and "to care for" the sheep or people of God.

Look up the following verses, which all utilize a form of the word *poimen* (pastor, shepherd) and describe some of the aspects of church leadership implied or expressed.

- **1 Peter 5:2**

- **Ephesians 4:11-12**

- **John 10:1-11**

- *"Presbuteros"*

The word *presbuteros* is the third word utilized to describe those who feed and care for the church. It is a word borrowed from the Old Testament as well as the intertestamental period for the leaders, judges, teachers and administrators of the synagogues in Israel. The word *presbuteros* is usually translated "elder" unless it is used in a common, non-leadership context in which it is simply translated "old man" or "elderly man." The word *presbuteros* was logically connected with leaders because of the wisdom and insight that usually came with living and learning for many years. Of course, not all church leaders were elderly. Timothy, for instance, was young and yet was able to aptly lead the church (see 1 Timothy 4:12). But Scripture makes it clear that it takes a lot of study and preparation to show competence to teach and administrate in the church (see 2 Timothy 2:15 and Titus 1:9).

130

CHAPTER 6
THE IMPORTANCE OF A GOOD CHURCH

Look up the following verses, which all utilize the word *presbuteros* (elder or elders) and describe some of the aspects of church leadership implied or expressed.

• **Titus 1:6**

Deeper Study...
What do we learn about church leadership and age from comparing 1 Timothy 4:12; 1 Timothy 3:6 and 2 Timothy 2:15. Why do you think Scripture does not give a specific age requirement for a presbuteros?

• **James 5:14**

• **1 Timothy 5:19**

Again it is critical that we understand that all three of these titles (*episkopos, poimen and presbuteros*) are used interchangeably in the New Testament for one class of leaders in the church. When, as some tend to do, one title is used to denote a "board member" and another is used for a "preacher," unbiblical distinctions are being made which are not made in the New Testament. Pastors are elders and overseers. If the leaders of a church find superfluous structures such as committees, boards or councils helpful, they of course have the freedom to put them in place, but one cannot claim that those added structures have a biblical mandate or biblical precedent.

Note carefully the synonymous use of these three terms and their derivatives in the following passages.

Acts 20:17, 28

Now from Miletus he sent to Ephesus and called the elders (*presbuteros*) of the church to come to him.... Pay careful attention to yourselves and to all the flock (*poimnion*), in which the Holy Spirit has made you overseers (*episkopos*), to care (*poimaino*) for the church of God, which he obtained with his own blood.

131

PARTNERS:
ONE-ON-ONE DISCIPLESHIP

> ### 1 Peter 5:1-2
>
> So I exhort the elders (*presbuteros*) among you, as a fellow elder (*presbuteros*) and a witness of the sufferings of Christ, as well as a partaker in the glory that is going to be revealed: shepherd (*poimaino*) the flock (*poimnion*) of God that is among you, exercising oversight (*episkopos*), not under compulsion, but willingly, as God would have you; not for shameful gain, but eagerly;

FYI...

While the biblical basics on church leaders presented in this section raise a variety of questions regarding church governance and church polity, it is important to be gracious and adaptable when interfacing with your own church and its chosen form of governance. It is easy to see when the various forms of church structure are put head to head that God has intended a degree of freedom in working out the specifics of how an individual church will function given the limited parameters detailed in the New Testament. See for instance, Perspectives on Church Government: Five Views of Church Polity, edited by Chad Owen Brand and R. Stanton Norman (Broadman & Holman, 2004).

How does clarity about the synonymous nature of these terms help you dispel some of the confusion that pervades so much of the modern church? How can these streamlined biblical definitions help you reevaluate some of the traditional and cultural baggage that often clutters modern definitions of words like "pastor", "elder" and "bishop"?

Further Study...

Identify the twenty-one requirements for the episkopos / poimen / presbuteros *which were given to Timothy and Titus as they were filling these important leadership positions. Study each requirement so that you are able to provide a simple explanatory definition for each of them.*

The New Testament does allow and even commands that there be certain distinctions among the pastors of a church. Just as Timothy was a leader among the leaders in Ephesus, Paul commanded that certain leaders be granted more "honor" than others. Read the context of this Scriptural command in **1 Timothy 5:17** and list the criteria and kind of distinctions described in this passage.

FYI...

The biblical concept of pastors appointing pastors gave rise to the widely-utilized process of "ordination" for pastors – especially senior pastors or lead preaching pastors. The procedures relating to ordination vary in different kinds of churches, but most include a careful screening process by other pastors focusing in on the life, doctrine, gifts and education of a pastoral candidate.

It is important to recognize in Scripture that pastors are appointed by other pastors. Notice the pattern in **1 Timothy 4:14**. Just as in **Ephesians 4:7-8, 11**, the "office" of pastor-teacher is spoken of here as a "gift"—one endowed, not by self-appointment, but by the confirmation of other qualified and gifted pastors. This is a helpful biblical observation, especially when we encounter those claiming to be "self-appointed" pastors, or small group participants who say their leader is their "pastor."

CHAPTER 6
THE IMPORTANCE OF A GOOD CHURCH

2. Ministry Leaders

The second tier of leadership in a church is described by the New Testament word *diakonos.* This word is used as a masculine noun and feminine noun referring to men and women who served the church. The word *diakonos* is the noun form of the verb we translate in the Bible "to minister" or "to serve." Those who serve in important positions of trust, under the direction and oversight of the pastors are called *diakonos,* that is "servants" or "ministers." Because these are prominent positions of responsibility, the "ministry leaders," like the pastors of a church, must meet a set of biblical requirements itemized in 1 Timothy 3 and Titus 1.

Whether your church uses the transliterated Greek word "deacon" and "deaconess" or some other descriptive title, these "ministry leaders" should be godly, gifted and hard-working examples in the church. Notice in **Hebrews 6:10** how the Scripture says it would be "unjust" if God were to "overlook" or not recognize and reward the work that Christians exert in "serving" (*diakoneo*) the people of God. If it would be "unjust" of God, it is certainly not right for us to "overlook" such work. How can you recognize, appreciate or reward those who serve faithfully in your church?

What are some of the instructions given to us in **Hebrews 13:17** regarding our church leaders? How might you specifically "Let them do this with joy and not with groaning"?

Deeper Study...
Study the use of diakonos *in reference to a female named Pheobe in Romans 16:1. Also study the repeated and systematic use of the word "likewise" or "in the same way" (*hosautos*) in 1 Timothy 3 as the ministry requirements for different groups are listed. Note especially the third group (the second use of* hosautos*) in reference to women (*gune*) in verse 11. You can see why this syntactical pattern leads many to assume that these additional requirements apply to female* diakonos. *While there is debate concerning this passage, it is clear throughout the New Testament that there are many women who are exemplary servants or* diakonos *in the church (e.g., Priscilla, Junias, Nympha, Euodia, Syntyche. See Romans 16:3-5, 7; 1 Corinthians 16:19; Colossians 4:15; Philippians 4:2-3).*

Fully Participating in Your Church

Committed to Your Church

We live in an age of unprecedented consumerism. And unfortunately, Christians often view the churches in their community the way they view the local restaurants. All too often they bounce from church to church sampling from the menu of preaching, programs and worship. They will go to this church for a sermon series, that church for a retreat, and still another church for a weekly Bible study. These kinds of "church consumers" rationalize their church hopping by seeing churches as spiritual commodities in God's marketplace. But of course, this is not how God sees it. The only "church hoppers" we find in the Scriptures were missionaries and preachers going from city to city to establish churches and feed young flocks in need of spiritual direction. That mentality is antithetical to the motives of today's church consumers.

133

PARTNERS:
ONE-ON-ONE DISCIPLESHIP

FYI...
Some church leaders have decided to formalize the attendee's commitment to their specific church through a process of "church membership." Other churches have "church covenants" or "annual church agreements" which codify or express an individual Christian's association with that particular church. Still other churches do not add this layer of formalization. Whatever the decision of your church leaders (especially in light of Hebrews 13:17) be sure to discover and participate in any expressions of church commitment which your leaders have established.

In the New Testament a Christian is portrayed as being committed to one local fellowship, serving and worshipping together under the direction of one group of pastors and ministry leaders. Individual Christians are described and commanded to have a cohesion, dedication and solidarity with a local church.

Just as it is difficult to be an effective member of two biological families, so it is hard, if not impossible, to be a functioning and contributing member of two Christian congregations. How do the descriptive and directive words of **Hebrews 13:7 & 17** make a commitment to one local body of disciples an obvious necessity?

How do the principles of **1 Corinthians 12:12-18** show us that there is no place for a "consumer" mindset when it comes to the churches in our community? (Keep in mind that 1 Corinthians and the words of chapter 12 were intended to be understood in the context of a local church, not the universal church.)

Participating in Baptism

An ordinance is a specific commanded practice given for churches to repeat until the return of Christ. While many goals commissioned to the church in the New Testament can be accomplished in a variety of ways, biblical ordinances are "ordained" to be carried out in a specific manner. The two biblical ordinances of the church are baptism and the Lord's Supper. We must be thoughtful and intentional about our participation in both.

Baptism, as opposed to the Lord's Supper, is ordained by Christ as a "one-time" act of obedience, given that the "one-time" is after our conversion to Christ and in the proper context and mode.

The word "baptism" is "transliterated" into the English language from the common Greek word *baptizo*. I point out that it is "transliterated," as opposed to "translated". Were the word actually "translated" there would likely be a lot less confusion about this ordinance. The word *baptizo* means to "immerse," "submerge," "dip" or "place into." This is precisely what the word means, although in two very distinct contexts.

134

CHAPTER 6
THE IMPORTANCE OF A GOOD CHURCH

The most important use of the word *baptizo* expresses our new relationship with Christ, when we repent of our sins and put our trust in him. The Bible says that we are "placed into" Christ (*baptizo*) by faith and that we now receive all the benefits of his death and his life. The second use of the word *baptizo* describes the ceremonial practice ordained by God to have converted disciples "placed into" or "immersed in" water. Read the following passages and carefully consider which "baptism" is being described.

• **Acts 8:36-39** =

• **Colossians 2:12** =

• **Romans 6:3-5** =

• **Acts 10:47-48** =

• **1 Corinthians 1:16** =

• **Mark 1:7-8** =

Notice how **1 Peter 3:21** clarifies that the "baptism" that saves is not the baptism that "removes dirt from the body" but the baptism that corresponds with our "appeal to God." There is a baptism that takes place externally in water. And there is also a preceding baptism which takes place internally when we are "placed into Christ" at the moment of our repentance and faith (Ac.20:21).

The mode of water baptism is expressed in the word *baptizo,* which means to "place into" or "immerse" (see the "Resources & Further Study" list at the end of this chapter for more on the mode of baptism).

The timing of baptism is clearly seen in Matthew 28:19. Reread this passage and note that the ordinance of baptism was to be applied to "them" (i.e., the "disciples" that have been made). The ceremony of water baptism should only come *after* a person has become a disciple.

With Your Partner...
Because one baptism saves you (i.e. being placed into Christ by the Holy Spirit) and one baptism only memorializes the other (i.e., the ceremony of water baptism), some people say they do not need to be baptized in water. After all, they say, there are those like the thief on the cross who got saved without water baptism. Why would you still advise Christians to be baptized?

Matthew 28:19

"Go therefore and **make disciples** of all nations, **baptizing _them_** in the name of the Father and of the Son and of the Holy Spirit."

135

PARTNERS:
ONE-ON-ONE DISCIPLESHIP

With Your Partner...
If you have not been baptized by church leaders after your conversion to Christ, talk to your partner about how to sign up for the next baptism at your church.

With Your Partner...
Discuss what you would say to someone who tells you that he or she is too afraid or embarrassed to be baptized.

FYI...
The Bible does not command church leaders how often the Lord's Supper should be observed. Many churches choose to practice the Lord's Supper once a month, others every week and still others once a year (following the pattern of the Passover). Whatever the frequency for your church, it is important that you thoughtfully and prayerfully participate each time the Lord's Supper is observed in your church.

Deeper Study...
Notice in Luke 22:18 and in Mark 14:25 that Christ calls the contents of the cup "the fruit of the vine". Note carefully this comes after the statement that "this is my blood of the covenant" (Mk.14:24). Clearly the statement equating the cup to his blood is to be considered symbolic, not actual. Also see Paul's description in 1 Corinthians 11:26 (i.e., "bread") of what was previously associated with Christ's "body" in v.23. Compare these observations to the religious groups which view the contents of the cup and the bread as being mystically or actually changed to Christ's blood and body. Why is this an important clarification?

With Your Partner...
Discuss the importance of how to spiritually prepare for and participate in the Lord's Supper.

Since this command is given to the church as an external sign of association with the people of God it should be done by pastors or other church leaders in a setting that is appropriate to such a proclamation. A private "baptism" by a Christian friend is not the intent or the context for this church ordinance.

Have you been baptized or immersed in water, by church leaders, after you became a disciple by repentance and faith, as a sign to others that you are a follower of Christ? If so, you have been obedient to this ordinance of Christ and there is no need to repeat it. Briefly describe that experience (or write down your intention to be obedient to this ordinance).

Participating in the Lord's Supper

The Lord's Supper was ordained by Christ for the Church as a modified and simplified form of the Old Testament Passover Meal. He commanded the assembled church to continue to periodically practice this ordinance until his second coming.

Read **Luke 22:14-20**. What do you learn in this passage about the focus and meaning of this ordinance?

Read **1 Corinthians 11:23-32**. What does this passage add to your understanding of how we should approach this ceremonial act?

136

CHAPTER 6
THE IMPORTANCE OF A GOOD CHURCH

Submitting to Church Discipline

As we have seen, the word "pastor" is the word for "shepherd." The spiritual "shepherds" of the flock are given a special responsibility to look out for the people of God. How critical is that role as described in **Acts 20:28-31**?

What instructions are given to a "flock" regarding their pastors in the following verses?

• **1 Thessalonians 5:12-13**

• **1 Corinthians 16:15-16**

• **Hebrews 13:7**

• **Hebrews 13:17**

There are times when pastors must confront, correct and even impose restrictions and limitations on those who participate with, serve in, or attend the church. These can be difficult times, but those who attend church are considered by God to be under the care, leadership and accountability of their pastors. Therefore it is important to be responsive to these kinds of expressions of biblical leadership.

There are times when you need to inform your pastors regarding situations that need their attention. Read **Matthew 18:15-20** and write down the preliminary steps that are your responsibility as an individual Christian before you report the matter to your pastors. List the progressive steps and consider what kinds of sinful behavior might be in view in this passage.

FYI...
Sadly, there are occasions when pastors abuse their positions of authority and seek to impose unbiblical restrictions or directions on God's people. When confronting these issues does not bring about reform, Christians are rightly forced to seek another church where the pastors are faithfully discharging their duties as spiritual leaders.

137

PARTNERS:
ONE-ON-ONE DISCIPLESHIP

Giving

The Bible clearly teaches that when you are part of a church, you are responsible to support your church financially. God grants the right to pastors to make a living leading, serving and teaching in his church. Read **1 Corinthians 9:7-14** and **Galatians 6:6** and note how Scripture makes this point.

Beyond the living expenses of the pastors and ministry leaders, your church of course, has to pay the bills related to the ministries, missions, outreach, facilities, furnishings, supplies, utilities and a variety of other operating expenses. All of this requires that God's people are faithful to give as God instructs. In many ways, the health of the church depends on the obedience of God's people to this fundamental command. Read **2 Corinthians 8:1-9** and **2 Corinthians 9:6-15** and write down some of the additional motivation that God utilizes in these passages.

The Bible tells us that we should give regularly (**1 Corinthians 16:1-2**) and "off the top" (**Proverbs 3:9-10**). Some would say they cannot afford to give because they fail to follow these two basic instructions. New Testament giving does not require a certain amount or percentage, it does though require that each person give. How do Jesus' observations and words in **Luke 21:1-4** motivate you in this regard?

With Your Partner...
Discuss the topic of giving and how God works for our good and the good of the church when we are generous to give as we are commanded.

God wants you to see these gifts as an act of worship. He wants you to see these financial gifts as gifts to him. Note in **Nehemiah 10:37-39** and **Malachi 3:6-12** the contrast between the practical use of the gifts, and the way God sees these gifts as gifts to him. How does this personal connection motivate you, especially in light of verses like **2 Corinthians 9:7**?

Connecting & Serving

The next two chapters of *Partners* will address the issues of connecting and serving. These, of course, are essential aspects of fully participating in your church.

138

CHAPTER 6
THE IMPORTANCE OF A GOOD CHURCH

Notes

PARTNERS:
ONE-ON-ONE DISCIPLESHIP

Notes

RESOURCES & FURTHER STUDY

6

The Importance of a Good Church

> Rating Key
> ★ Helpful (four being most)
> ◉ Difficulty (four being hardest)

Resources on the Church

★★★
◉◉
Adams, Jay. *Handbook of Church Discipline.* Grand Rapids, MI: Zondervan Publishing House, 1986. (This practical book describes the process of church discipline and the hope of restoration, when professing Christians persist in sinful behaviors.)

★★★
◉◉
_____. *Preaching with Purpose.* Grand Rapids, MI: Zondervan Publishing House, 1990. (This forthright book on preaching can help all Christians understand the important role of good preaching in a healthy church.)

★★★
◉◉◉
Blaising, Craig A. and Darrel Bock, eds. *Dispensationalism, Israel and the Church.* Grand Rapids, MI: Zondervan Publishing House, 1992. (This helpful book, with contributions by several authors, presents thoughtful arguments as to the importance of maintaining certain distinctions between Israel and the Church.)

★★★
◉◉
Carson, D. A. *Becoming Conversant with the Emerging Church: Understanding a Movement and Its Implications.* Zondervan Publishing House, 2005. (In his careful manner, Carson sheds some important light on the meaning and impact of the "Emergent Movement" on church life.)

★★★
◉◉
Eby, David. *Power Preaching for Church Growth: The Role of Preaching in Growing Churches.* Great Britain: Christian Focus Publications, 1997. (Eby strongly argues for the indispensable role of a strong pulpit in a healthy, advancing church.)

★★★
◉◉
Fabarez, Mike. *Preaching that Changes Lives.* Eugene, OR: Wipf and Stock, 2002. (This is my offering on the role of preaching and how effective proclamation of God's truth should transform the congregation.)

★★
◉
_____. *Praying for Sunday.* Aliso Viejo, CA: Focal Point, 2008. (This short work is my plea for every congregant to actively, ardently and regularly pray for the effectiveness of the preaching in his or her church.)

★★
◉◉
Frazee, Randy. *The Connecting Church.* Grand Rapids, MI: Zondervan, 2001. (Frazee's book can prove to be helpful in challenging the residual individualism and consumerism often found in church programs.)

★★
◉◉
Gangel, Kenneth O. *Building Leaders for Church Education.* Chicago, IL: Moody Press, 1970. (This somewhat dated offering can be helpful as one applies its observations and principles to finding and training leaders for church ministries.)

★★★
◉◉
Getz, Gene A. *Sharpening The Focus Of The Church.* Wheaton, IL: Victor Books, 1984. (Getz offers many good insights into how to form and evaluate the effectiveness of a church ministry strategy.)

★★★
◉◉
_____. *The Measure Of A Church.* Glendale, CA: Regal Books, 1973. (Though this book was written many years ago, it can powerfully challenge a church's self-evaluation regarding its health and effectiveness.)

★★
◉
Hull, Bill. *The Disciple-Making Church.* Grand Rapids, MI: Fleming H. Revell Co., 1977. (This book is an effective call to look past the programs of the church to the goal of making disciples.)

★★
◉
Larson, Knute. *The ABF Book: Growing Adults on Sunday Morning.* Wheaton, IL: Victor Books, 1991. (This book can help a church to structure and set up the management for adult ministry.)

141

★★★ MacArthur, John. *Book on Leadership.* Nashville, TN: Thomas Nelson Publishers, 2004. (In this
◉ book MacArthur systematically describes and explains the biblical traits of godly leadership.)

★★ Montgomery, John Warwick. *Damned Through the Church.* Minneapolis, MN: Dimension Books,
◉ 1970. (This challenging and forthright little book can raise awareness of the need not to neglect evangelism within
the walls of the church.)

★★★ Sanders, Oswald. *Spiritual Leadership.* Chicago, IL: Moody Press, 1980. (This classic work by Sanders is a
◉◉ devotional challenge to any who aspire to leadership within the Church of Jesus Christ.)

★★★ Saucy, Robert L. *The Church in God's Program.* Chicago, IL: Moody Press, 1972. (This helpful resource
◉◉ is a systematic outline of the biblical doctrine of the Church in the Scriptures.)

★★★ Schaeffer, Francis A. *The Church at The End of the 20th Century.* Downers Grove, IL: InterVarsity
◉◉◉ Press, 1970. (In Schaeffer's thoughtful and probing way, he surveys the threats, problems and solutions to
keeping our churches faithful to Christ.)

★★ Shaw, Mark. *10 Great Ideas from Church History.* Downers Grove, IL: InterVarsity Press, 1997. (In
◉ this creative little book, Shaw draws from a variety of specific leaders throughout church history to challenge the
modern church in ten important aspects of church life.)

★★ Spader, Dan. *Growing a Healthy Church.* Chicago, IL: Moody Press, 1991. (This book can give some
◉ direction and help to a church forming or rethinking the investment of their efforts in their church.)

★★★ Whitney, Donald. *Spiritual Disciplines Within the Church: Participating Fully in the Body of Christ.*
◉◉ Chicago, IL: Moody Press, 1996. (Whitney covers a number of practical and important aspects of being
an active and contributing part of one's church.)

★★ Woodbridge, John D. *Great Leaders of the Christian Church.* Chicago, IL: Moody Press, 1988. (This
◉◉ motivating book surveys a number of important and influential leaders throughout Church history.)

Resources on Baptism

★★★ Carson, Alexander. *Baptism: Its Mode and Subjects.* Reprint. Kregel, 1981. (This book, originally rewritten in
◉◉◉◉ the early 19th century, carefully examines the data regarding the mode and timing of water baptism.)

★★★ Conant, Thomas Jefferson. *The Meaning and Use of BAPTIZEIN.* Reprint. Kregel, 1977. (This
◉◉◉◉ somewhat tedious book takes you into the longstanding debate over water baptism.)

★★★ Dyer, Larry E. Baptism: *The Believer's First Obedience.* Kregel Publications, 2000. (Dyer provides a
◉ straightforward and helpful primer on what water baptism is and is not.)

★★★ Jewett, Paul K. *Infant Baptism & the Covenant of Grace: An Appraisal of the Argument.* Wipf & Stock,
◉◉◉ 1978. (In a more updated manner, Jewett tackles and analyzes much of the data from Carson and Conant.)

★★ Malone, Fred A. *A String of Pearls Unstrung: A Theological Journey Into Believers' Baptism.* Founders
◉◉ Press, 1998. (Malone personally writes of his thoughtful journey from infant baptism to believer's baptism.)

★★★★ Schreiner, Thomas, ed. *Believer's Baptism: Sign of the New Covenant in Christ.* B & H Academic, 2006.
◉◉ (This book with several contributors effectively presents the case for believer's baptism.)

★★★ Watson, T. E. *Should Babies Be Baptized?* Grace Publications, 1995. (This book analyzes and refutes the
◉ practice of baptizing babies.)

★★★ Waymeyer, Matt. *A Biblical Critique of Infant Baptism.* Kress Christian Publications, 2008. (Waymeyer
◉◉ takes a close look at Scripture to reevaluate the baptism of infants.)

Chapter 7

PARTNERS MEETING #7

Being Intentional About Biblical Fellowship

At Partners Meeting #7...

You will be discussing the importance of being thoughtful and intentional about biblical fellowship. You will explore and discuss what the Bible has to say about your need for healthy, godly and loving relationships within your church. You will be challenged to create and deepen relationships with other Christians, which are centered on Christ. It is intended that you will discover the joy and fulfillment of mutually edifying Christian relationships.

To Prepare for Partners Meeting #7...

- Read chapter 7 and answer the questions.

- If any of the "Deeper Study" topics are of interest to you, prepare to discuss them.

- Be able to recite all the books of the Old Testament in order.

- Memorize John 13:34-35

A new commandment I give to you, that you love one another: just as I have loved you, you also are to love one another. By this all people will know that you are my disciples, if you have love for one another.

– John 13:34-35

143

PARTNERS:

ONE-ON-ONE DISCIPLESHIP

As Christians we need each other. God designed the Christian life to be lived with a distinct sense of community and interrelatedness. It is God's plan that as we follow Christ, we do so with the help and encouragement of other followers of Christ. Isolation is a major enemy of the Christian life. Without consistent, intentional and meaningful Christian fellowship our relationship with Christ will suffer and our choices to "go it alone" will be in direct disobedience to Scripture's clear command.

> ### Hebrews 10:24-25
>
> And let us consider how to stir up one another to love and good works, not neglecting to meet together, as is the habit of some, but encouraging one another, and all the more as you see the Day drawing near.

With Your Partner...

Some people naturally seek time with others. Other people gravitate toward "alone time" and isolation. Talk to your partner about your tendencies and discuss how this might impact your response to God's call for biblical fellowship.

The Word "Fellowship"

The word "fellowship" translates the Greek word *koinonia* and means "to share together" or "have a common participation." The word "fellowship" is used in both a passive and an active sense in the New Testament. In a passive sense the word "fellowship" describes *the experience we share as Christians*. In an active sense the word describes *the sharing we Christians do* as a part of God's family. We will take a look at both of these aspects of "fellowship" in this chapter.

Deeper Study...

Do a word study on the nineteen occurrences of the word koinonia in the New Testament. Note the various ways it is translated and how it is utilized in the Scriptures. Discuss your findings with your partner.

The Foundation of Biblical Fellowship

Before we examine the "shared experience" (passive) and "sharing of our lives" (active) aspects of fellowship, let's consider the biblical assumptions regarding Christian fellowship. First, true Christian fellowship involves true Christians. The kind of fellowship the Bible prescribes is not just a call for us to be more outgoing people or to be more social. God is directing us to be selectively involved as regenerate people with other regenerate people.

144

CHAPTER 7

BEING INTENTIONAL ABOUT BIBLICAL FELLOWSHIP

What do we learn in the following verses about the importance of building relationships with people who share a similar devotion to God and his truth?

• 1 Corinthians 15:33

• Psalm 1:1

• Proverbs 13:20

With Your Partner...

Discuss with your partner the negative effects that have come into your Christian life from choosing to closely associate and ally yourself with those who do not share your commitment to follow Christ.

Some reject this kind of discrimination regarding their choice of friends and social alliances. They often resort to quoting passages like Matthew 9:11, Luke 15:2, and Matthew 11:19, which depict Christ's critics describing him as a "friend of tax collectors and sinners." While they imagine Jesus comfortably "hanging out" with the sordid elements of society, it is important to note that Christ's interface with the notorious sinners of his day was purposeful and focused on evangelism. How do **Luke 5:32** and **Matthew 4:17** capture the intention of Christ in his connections with "sinners"?

With Your Partner...

Discuss the rationale of some single churchgoers who "missionary date" (i.e., professing Christians getting romantically involved with an avowed non-Christian under the stated hope of trying to "save them"). Why is this an unwise decision even if there are those who testify that "it worked"?

What does **Ephesians 5:6-14** teach us about our strategic connections with people who do not share our commitment to Christ?

145

PARTNERS:
ONE-ON-ONE DISCIPLESHIP

How does this kind of evangelistic endeavor differ from the New Testament's teaching on biblical fellowship as described in **2 Corinthians 6:14-18**?

Of course God is not directing us to withdraw from society, or to build monasteries or communes as some Christians have historically done. Not only would our call to evangelize be thwarted, but our lives would also fail to fulfill the directives found in **Matthew 5**.

Matthew 5:13-16

You are the salt of the earth, but if salt has lost its taste, how shall its saltiness be restored? It is no longer good for anything except to be thrown out and trampled under people's feet. You are the light of the world. A city set on a hill cannot be hidden. Nor do people light a lamp and put it under a basket, but on a stand, and it gives light to all in the house. In the same way, let your light shine before others, so that they may see your good works and give glory to your Father who is in heaven.

Read **1 Corinthians 5:9-10** (and its context) and describe the differences between the kind of daily relationships we have by necessity with the people of the world and the selective and more intimate relationships God calls us to have with those who are following Jesus Christ.

Further Study...
Questions related to Christian fellowship arise when one considers Christians who are married to non-Christians. Study 1 Corinthians 7:10-16 and 1 Peter 3:1-6, then trace the biblical logic of why a Christian should seek to honor their marital covenant even if their spouse does not share a commitment to Jesus Christ.

Another foundational New Testament assumption regarding Christian fellowship is that our fellowship should primarily be with those who are a part of the same local assembly of Christians. In the previous chapter of Partners we studied that the church is God's specially designed organization of which he expects us to be a highly committed participant. On occasion we obviously enjoy some meaningful times of fellowship with those from other churches, but the instructions regarding Christian fellowship in the New Testament are directed to participants of the same local congregation.

146

CHAPTER 7

BEING INTENTIONAL ABOUT BIBLICAL FELLOWSHIP

In light of **1 Corinthians 1:10** and **Hebrew 13:7, 17**, what are some advantages to developing your closest Christian relationships with those in your own congregation?

Sometimes Christians choose to avoid engaging in close relationships with those of their own church and say that they find their fellowship elsewhere. At best, this is a misguided decision, or more likely, it is indicative of other problems in that person's Christian life. What do you suppose are some of the reasons a person might choose this strategy? What are some of the reasons you are tempted to withdraw from fellowship with those in your church?

Further Study...

Think of those you know who have withdrawn from fellowship in your church. Consider how you might reach out to them in order to see them restored to active participation in the life of your church.

Fellowship by "Shared Experience"

The passive sense of the concept of fellowship in the New Testament requires that we are purposefully sharing certain experiences together as brothers and sisters in Christ. In this set of experiences, picture us living our Christian lives "side-by-side". Later we will see how fellowship also includes a very important "face-to-face" component.

1. Worshipping Together

At the core of Christian fellowship are the shared times of corporate worship and the experience of learning together under the preaching of God's word. Note this fundamental aspect of Christian fellowship in the following Acts 2 description of the early church.

147

PARTNERS:
ONE-ON-ONE DISCIPLESHIP

> **Acts 2:42-47**
>
> And they devoted themselves to the apostles' teaching and the fellowship, to the breaking of bread and the prayers. And awe came upon every soul, and many wonders and signs were being done through the apostles. And all who believed were together and had all things in common. And they were selling their possessions and belongings and distributing the proceeds to all, as any had need. And day by day, attending the temple together and breaking bread in their homes, they received their food with glad and generous hearts, praising God and having favor with all the people. And the Lord added to their number day by day those who were being saved.

With Your Partner...
Discuss your commitment and pattern of church attendance. Talk about the obstacles you sometimes face in personally and physically attending church services and how you can best and most consistently overcome these obstacles.

With Your Partner...
Who you sit with during the worship services can be an important part of deepening and enriching your relationship with other Christians. Discuss why and how this is so with your partner.

As the Christians in Acts 2 sat under the same preaching, attended the same meetings, and praised God together, their relationships were enriched and deepened. This is a kind of shared experience that requires your personal presence. It is one thing to sing praises by yourself in your car, or to watch your church's worship services on the internet. But it is an altogether different reality when you are physically present with others, learning and praising God together. Remember **Hebrew 10:25** and the call to "meet together."

What indications regarding the advantage of being physically present in Christian fellowship do you gather from a reading of **1 Thessalonians 3:1-13**?

Deeper Study...
Research the ways the Gospel writers describe the relational characteristics of the twelve apostles. Consider the ways these men were bound together through their mission and ministry.

2. Serving Together

Another aspect of Christian fellowship that deepens our relationships and strengthens our spiritual lives is when we serve Christ together in ministry. Serving side-by-side to advance the gospel or build up the church draws disciples of Christ together in a profound way.

CHAPTER 7
BEING INTENTIONAL ABOUT BIBLICAL FELLOWSHIP

In the following passages, list and define the illustrative terms Paul uses to describe his brothers and sisters in Christ with whom he ministers.

• Philippians 2:25

• Philippians 4:3

With Your Partner...
Discuss the way your relationships with others have been deepened and enhanced through serving in ministry together.

Throughout Paul's New Testament letters we see names like Silas, Timothy and Epaphras appear again and again. Paul is clearly not out doing ministry by himself. He is continually setting an example of teaming up with others as he serves the body of Christ. As we saw in the passages above, the spiritual bond that forms between Christians when they serve side-by-side is significant.

In what way have you experienced this kind of connection as you have served in ministry?

3. Being Refreshed Together

To be a part of the church of Jerusalem in the early chapters of the Book of Acts was more than simply showing up for a weekend church service and participating in a weeknight ministry project. Reread **Acts 2:44-47** and envision the "down time" these Christians spent together between Sundays.

With Your Partner...
If you have been on church retreats, talk about how your connection with other Christians has been enriched through the "recreational" or "leisure" aspects of the church retreats you have attended.

Read **Mark 6:30-32**. Why do you think Jesus didn't just send the apostles away individually to spend solitary time recuperating? What is the advantage of getting away to rest and being refreshed together as a team?

149

PARTNERS:
ONE-ON-ONE DISCIPLESHIP

Fellowship by "Sharing"

The passive use of the word fellowship is important and helpful, but at the heart of New Testament fellowship is the active fellowship of sharing ourselves. Picture the orientation of our lives moving from "side-by-side" (in corporate worship, serving together and times of refreshment) to "face-to-face." It is strengthening to our walk with Christ when we share common experiences with other Christians, but there is something profoundly enriching added to our faith when we begin to actually give of ourselves for Jesus' sake.

1. Sharing Our Meals

With Your Partner...
Discuss how you can purposefully schedule more of your meals with fellow Christians. Talk about how to make the conversations that take place in those settings the most spiritually profitable.

The Bible gives us many examples of people, who share a common faith and devotion to God, taking their meals together. Christ himself took many, if not most of his meals together with his disciples. This practice extended well beyond the inner circle of "the Twelve." Recall the following scenes from the life of Christ: his feeding the five thousand (Mt.14:16-21), requesting to dine with Zacchaeus (Lk.19:5-7; Mk.2:16), and having a meal with the two on the Road to Emmaus (Lk.24:30-35).

Read **John 21:12-15**. How does the setting of this scene, with Jesus fixing breakfast for Peter, change the way one might otherwise view the exchange that starts in verse 15?

Describe some of the differences between a conversation that takes place over a meal as opposed to one that does not.

2. Sharing Our Homes

With Your Partner...
Note how in Acts 2:46-47 there was a "God-focused" aspect to the fellowship. Remembering that "praising God" (v.47) is not just accomplished through singing, describe how "in homes" and around meals "with glad and sincere hearts" (v.46) you might make sure praise is given to God?

A lot of true Christian fellowship can take place around a table at a restaurant, but there is another level of interpersonal connection that takes place between Christians when they have those meals in their homes. Not only does that experience place our chairs face-to-face around a dining room table, but also the time before and after the meal in the living room or family room, provides us with a great opportunity for heartfelt conversation and personal interaction.

150

CHAPTER 7
BEING INTENTIONAL ABOUT BIBLICAL FELLOWSHIP

Read **Acts 2:46-47**. How often would you say that you host meals for other Christians in your home? Why is it not more often? What are some of the risks and vulnerabilities involved in having Christians over to your home and how do you think God would have you respond to those concerns?

1 Peter 5:3 tells us that the pastors of the church should be an example to all in the church. **Titus 1:8** requires that all pastors be "hospitable." It follows then that we all should be striving to be more hospitable as we purposefully open our homes more often for fellowship with other Christians.

What is the next practical step for you in being more hospitable?

FYI...
While there is some debate about whether the "breaking of bread" in Acts 2:46 refers to our everyday meals or whether it refers to the Lord's Supper, it seems likely that the setting (especially in v.46, in contrast to v.42) points to our everyday meals. This is in contrast to the corporate nature of the Lord's Supper elsewhere in Scripture (cf. 1Cor.11:17-22).

Describe how your relationships have been enriched by spending time with other Christians in their homes talking about biblical truths or sharing your spiritual struggles or victories?

Deeper Study...
Study the word "philoxenos" and "philoxenia" that is translated "hospitable" and "hospitality" in the New Testament. Explore the concentric ways this term can be understood.

3. Sharing Our Prayers

Praying can often feel like a very intimate and personal expression of our heart to God, but clearly the Bible teaches us that it should not always be private. Look again to **Acts 2:42** which describes true Christian fellowship including a commitment to prayer.

151

PARTNERS:
ONE-ON-ONE DISCIPLESHIP

Read **Acts 12:12** and describe what this must have looked like.

With Your Partner...
Discuss the opportunities your church provides for small group fellowship that include times of prayer together. Discuss how and when you can experience this with some from your church family.

> **James 5:16a**
>
> Confess your sins to one another and pray for each other.

It may feel quite vulnerable to lead prayer aloud with a group of our Christian brothers and sisters in our living rooms, but it is a kind of bonding, spiritual fellowship that is unlike any other. When we join our hearts together in prayer for the common good of the church, the advancement of the gospel, or for the temporal needs of others, true fellowship results. We genuinely get to know one another on a spiritual level, when we "pour out our hearts to God" together in prayer (cf. Ps.62:8).

Describe some of the best, most unifying experiences you have had praying in a small group with other Christians?

4. Sharing Our Knowledge of Christ

One way to ensure our attempts at Christian fellowship are actually more than just "social time" is to regularly bring the conversation back to Christ. This includes discussing and explaining the things we are learning in our Christian life, especially the new insights and truths we have discovered in God's word. Talking about effective ways that we have implemented God's truth and applied biblical principles can be some of the most edifying and helpful kinds of fellowship we can experience.

With Your Partner...
Discuss how, in fellowship gatherings, one can skillfully keep the conversations on good and edifying biblical dialogue, while preventing them from degenerating into gossip, heresy or counterproductive talk.

152

CHAPTER 7

BEING INTENTIONAL ABOUT BIBLICAL FELLOWSHIP

Read **Acts 18:26**. Why is this kind of discussion so important and why was Priscilla and Aquila's home such an appropriate setting for this?

Read **Romans 15:14**. How does this passage motivate you in your own spiritual growth? Why is a growing and vibrant Christian life so important to this kind of "mutual instruction"?

Goals of Our Fellowship

As we share our experiences and ourselves with God's people it is important to keep in mind God's measure of progress and success for our interaction. The Bible is clear about what God wants to see cultivated and developed as a result of our time together.

1. Biblical Love

At the top of God's list is the biblical virtue of Christian love. It should be said of God's people that we truly love each other. It should be a distinguishing feature of our interaction.

> **John 13:34-35**
>
> "A new commandment I give to you, that you love one another: just as I have loved you, you also are to love one another. By this all people will know that you are my disciples, if you have love for one another."

153

PARTNERS:
ONE-ON-ONE DISCIPLESHIP

Deeper Study...
Engage in the classic study of the "four loves" based on the four commonly used ancient Greek words: storge, philia, eros, and agape. Think through the distinctions and the overlapping attributes of each.

Because the word love is so broadly used today, it is important to distinguish Jesus' use of the word "love" in John 13. There are several Greek words translated "love" in the New Testament, but the one used in John 13 (i.e., *agape*) is a word that is usually reserved for the highest form of selfless acts done for the good of the one loved. In other words, this kind of love may not involve happy feelings, emotional promptings, or sentimental attractions. But biblical love always seeks the good of the one loved, no matter what the cost or sacrifice.

List some historical examples from the Bible of true selfless love that were clearly not motivated by a desire to "feel good." Start by reading **Romans 5:6-8**.

Read **Philippians 2:3-8** and **Romans 15:2-3**. How would these directives change the usual way we go about "attending church," having people over to our home, or engaging in conversation over a meal at a restaurant with a fellow Christian?

With Your Partner...
Discuss the subtle ways selfishness and self-interest cloud our interaction with other Christians and discuss how you can develop more "agape" love in the settings in which you fellowship.

Read **Romans 12:16**. How does true Christian love change the "natural" or predictable choices about whom we choose to fellowship with in our church family?

2. Encouragement

A second goal for our fellowship is described by the word "encouragement" and is often coupled with a word translated to "build up" (in some translations, "edification"). Much of what God wants to see happen by our interaction with the family of God is that his children come away encouraged, built up in their faith, and heartened to live for him in this world.

154

CHAPTER 7
BEING INTENTIONAL ABOUT BIBLICAL FELLOWSHIP

Read **1 Thessalonians 5:11 & 14.** Based on your own experience of having received this kind of encouragement from others, what are some of the best settings and strategies used to accomplish this?

With Your Partner...
Think of someone you believe needs encouragement. Consider, for example, the context of verses like 1 Thessalonians 4:18 and come up with an assignment of how to bring some biblical encouragement to this individual.

As **1 Thessalonians 4:18** shows us our "words" are key instruments in bringing encouragement and edification to our brothers and sisters in Christ. Even when we can't be there in person, our words in letters, emails, and other written forms of communication can be powerful avenues that God can use to create a rich atmosphere of true biblical fellowship in our church.

Read **Ephesians 4:29** and write down the name of one Christian you will write to this week for the exclusive purpose of building him or her up with words of encouragement. What subject or topic will you use to convey this encouragement?

3. Equipping

A third goal of our fellowship with other Christians should be that our interaction results in that Christian being more prepared to love and serve God. This is a natural outgrowth of some of what we have discussed already. "Sharing our knowledge of Christ" and "sharing our prayers" are obvious ways we can help prepare people to love Christ more or serve God better. We will spend more time in the next chapter discussing this important calling when we study the ways God has "gifted" us to build up his church. But for now, let us at least be mindful that even our fellowship should result in a healthier and more able team of Christians.

Read **Ephesians 4:11-16.** Note God's desire to see his people prepared to engage in the calling and mission of his church. He uses our interaction with one another to accomplish this. Consider the Sunday sermon. The preacher delivers the sermon, but there are several ways that the interaction of fellow Christians,

155

PARTNERS:

ONE-ON-ONE DISCIPLESHIP

which follows the message, helps to drive the sermon to a place of application and effectiveness in each person's life.

How have you experienced this? How does the "follow up discussion" with other Christians in the lobby of the church, over a meal at a restaurant after church, or at someone's home on a weeknight following the message, help to move the sermon from theory to practice?

With Your Partner...

Discuss the opportunities presented at your church for small group discussions where the application of the pastor's sermon is the goal. If your church doesn't provide this ministry program, discuss how Sunday lunches or Sunday evening gatherings can utilize this avenue of biblical fellowship to equip Christ's church for service.

Perspectives as We Fellowship

With a more biblical view of fellowship we see that real fellowship is more than just hanging out with our favorite friends from church. Real biblical fellowship is selfless and sacrificial. It is also well-pleasing to God. Because it will not come as naturally as socializing with our best friends, it is important that we seek God's enablement by adopting a biblical mindset when we fellowship.

1. Fueled by Christ

With Your Partner...

Discuss the ways in which retreating into ourselves in order to avoid the associated costs of biblical fellowship is actually a rip off, especially in light of Philippians 2:1-2.

Giving, serving, sharing and sacrificing doesn't sound energizing. Actually to most people it sounds draining, tiring and exhausting. But Christ is faithful to empower us as we engage in his agenda. This is precisely how the Apostle Paul appeals to the Philippians when he calls them to engage in biblical fellowship. Read **Philippians 2:1-5**. Itemize the benefits Paul lists in verse 1, which we receive when we focus on the directives of verses 2-5.

Remember that if you wait for feelings to prompt you to biblical fellowship you may never engage in this important Christian responsibility. Read **Isaiah 40:29-31**. If you are feeling a lack of energy, ability or motivation, how does this passage help you look past those feelings?

156

CHAPTER 7
BEING INTENTIONAL ABOUT BIBLICAL FELLOWSHIP

How do the following passages help motivate you to act and let Christ uphold you and sustain you in your efforts?

• 1 Peter 4:11

• Acts 20:35

• Psalm 68:35

2. See Christ as the Recipient

God would have us envision Jesus as the ultimate recipient of our efforts at Christian fellowship. The Book of 1 John repeatedly makes the point that if we acknowledge that God loves us, then our response should be to love God's people. By loving God's people we are in a very real way loving God. He takes the love we show for his people very personally.

Read **Matthew 25:45** and **Matthew 10:42**. How does this perspective change the way you prioritize your love, honor, and service to God's people? How will you keep this in mind the next time you are considering your investment in biblical fellowship?

Seeing Christ as the recipient of our love certainly changes the way we think about the neglect of or potential damage we might cause to God's people. If we are cavalier, careless or inconsiderate when we interact with Christians, we are at risk of offending Christ himself.

157

PARTNERS:
ONE-ON-ONE DISCIPLESHIP

Read **Acts 9:4-5** and **1 Corinthians 8:12** and write your response to these sobering verses. How will keeping these verses in mind add a special care to your words or actions when you gather for a time of fellowship?

3. Follow Christ's Example

A central aspect of Christian living is the emulation of the behavior and priorities of Jesus Christ. So much of what we have studied in this chapter is nothing more than a study of how Christ cared for and loved his people. When we think about living like Christ, we certainly cannot imagine the Christian life without a large priority and obvious focus on selfless and sacrificial interaction with Christ's followers.

Read **Romans 15:2-3**. When you think about how to share your life with other Christians, how can the standard of Christ take a more prominent role in your thinking and what can you do to keep Christ's example in the forefront of your mind?

Deeper Study...
The broadest call to replicate Christ's commitment to fellowship is bound up in the call to "love one another" (John 13:34). Using a concordance, list and comment on all the biblical "one another" directives in the New Testament (e.g., Galatians 6:2; Ephesians 4:32).

---

1 John 4:7-16

Beloved, let us love one another, for love is from God, and whoever loves has been born of God and knows God. Anyone who does not love does not know God, because God is love. In this the love of God was made manifest among us, that God sent his only Son into the world, so that we might live through him. In this is love, not that we have loved God but that he loved us and sent his Son to be the propitiation for our sins. Beloved, if God so loved us, we also ought to love one another. No one has ever seen God; if we love one another, God abides in us and his love is perfected in us. By this we know that we abide in him and he in us, because he has given us of his Spirit. And we have seen and testify that the Father has sent his Son to be the Savior of the world. Whoever confesses that Jesus is the Son of God, God abides in him, and he in God. So we have come to know and to believe the love that God has for us. God is love, and whoever abides in love abides in God, and God abides in him.

CHAPTER 7
BEING INTENTIONAL ABOUT BIBLICAL FELLOWSHIP

A Final Motivation

Usually Christians dive into fellowship early in their Christian life. They get plugged in at every level in the church, they eagerly participate in a number of Christian relationships, and they get involved every time the church doors are opened. In time they discover that this side of heaven Christians are plagued with sin, that problems arise, that feelings get hurt, and that relationships can be difficult. And later, under the guise of "maturity," longtime Christians rationalize their waning involvement in fellowship by saying they "don't need it as much anymore." In reality, this is just an excuse. Our need for fellowship never decreases; according to God it only increases.

Reread the first passage we examined in this study, **Hebrews 10:23-25**, giving special attention to verse 25. Regardless of past hurts or a lack of felt need, you are closer to "the Day" now than when you first repented and put your trust in Christ. Your need for fellowship will only increase as "the Day" draws near. Do not allow the enemy to deceive you, persuading you to move away from investing in the body of Christ. It may not be easy, but it is critically important. You cannot live as Christ intended without an intentional commitment and involvement in biblical fellowship.

With Your Partner...
Reveal your new or renewed goals and commitments. Discuss how you can hold one another accountable to engaging in meaningful Christian fellowship.

What are your new or renewed commitments to biblical fellowship? What do you intend to change in your weekly patterns and priorities as a result of this study?

159

PARTNERS:
ONE-ON-ONE DISCIPLESHIP

Notes

CHAPTER 7
BEING INTENTIONAL ABOUT BIBLICAL FELLOWSHIP

Notes

PARTNERS:
ONE-ON-ONE DISCIPLESHIP

Notes

RESOURCES & FURTHER STUDY

7
Being Intentional About Biblical Fellowship

> Rating Key
> ★ Helpful (four being most)
> ◉ Difficulty (four being hardest)

★★
◉◉ Adams, Jay. *The Biblical View of Self-Esteem, Self-Love and Self-Image.* Harvest House, 1986. (This forthright book biblically dismantles one of our prominent cultural myths, which stands as a common barrier to true Christians fellowship.)

★★
◉◉ Allender, Dan and Tremper Longman. *Bold Love.* Reprint. NavPress, 1993. (As the title implies, this book works to show that biblical love is not a sentimentalized emotion, but is bold, strong and tenacious.)

★★
◉◉ Bellah, Robert. *Habits of the Heart: Individualism & Commitment in American Life.* UC Press, 1996. (Though not a Christian book, this secular sociological study effectively chronicles the shifts in society that Christians must not imitate or accommodate.)

★★★
◉◉◉ Carson, D. A. *Love in Hard Places.* Crossway Books, 2002. (Much like Allender's and Longman's work, Carson skillfully exposes several myths about the world's sappy and erroneous definitions of love.)

★★★
◉◉◉ Edwards, Jonathan. *Charity and Its Fruits.* Banner of Truth, 1969. (This classic work, originally written in the 18th century, demonstrates the supremacy of love [or "charity" as it was called] in the Christian life.)

★★
◉◉ Frazee, Randy. *The Connecting Church.* Zondervan, 2001. (Frazee's book can prove to be helpful in challenging the residual individualism and consumerism often found in modern church life.)

★★
◉◉ Gorman, Julie. *Community That Is Christian.* Victor Books, 1993. (Practical insights can be gleaned from Gorman's book as she helps Christians evaluate the opportunities afforded by small groups.)

★★★
◉◉ Kroll, Woodrow. *Struggling with Selfishness: Choosing to Look Past Yourself.* Back to the Bible, 1996. (This little book provides some help for the chronic temptation to selfishness in our Christian relationships.)

★★★
◉◉◉ Lewis, C. S. *The Four Loves.* Harvest Books, 1971. (This classic work by Lewis systematically explores the four ancient Greek words for "love" – *agape, phileo, storge* and *eros*.)

★★★
◉◉◉ Lloyd-Jones, D. Martyn. *Ephesians 4:1-16. An Exposition on Christian Unity.* Baker Books, 1998. (As the title implies, this book works through these critically important sixteen verses in Ephesians.)

★★★
◉◉ Mahaney, C.J. *Humility: True Greatness.* Multnomah Press, 2005. (This book is a challenging yet devotional look at God's call and our need for humility.)

★★★
◉◉◉ Morris, Leon. *Testaments of Love: A Study of Love in the Bible.* Eerdmans, 1981. (In this book Morris effectively works through the biblical data on both the human and divine aspects of love.)

★★★ Murray, Andrew. *Humility: The Journey Toward Holiness.* Bethany House, 2001. (This classic book,

◉◉◉ originally written in 1895, challenges Christians to see the evils of pride and the indispensible need for humility.)

★★ Putnam, Robert. *Bowling Alone: The Collapse & Revival of American Community.* Touchstone,
◉◉ 2001. (Though not a Christian book, this secular sociological study shows the shifts in society toward individualism that can negatively infect the church.)

★★ Roseveare, Helen. *Living Fellowship: Willing to be the Third Side of a Triangle.* Christian Focus
◉ Publications, 2008. (This book explores the biblical ingredients and implications of Christian fellowship.)

★★ Ryken, Philip Graham, ed. *The Communion of the Saints: Living in Fellowship with the People of*
◉◉ *God.* P & R, 2001. (In this book Ryken calls Christians to reject our tendencies to isolate and purposefully pursue true Christian fellowship as prescribed in the New Testament.)

★★★ Sande, Ken. *The Peacemaker: A Biblical Guide to Resolving Personal Conflicts.* Baker Books,
◉◉ 1997. (This handbook to resolving personal conflict can be a handy resource for working through the issues that often fracture and divide the body of Christ.)

★★★ Schaeffer, Francis. *The Church at the End of the Twentieth Century.* Crossway Books, 1994. (In
◉◉◉ Schaeffer's thoughtful and probing way, he surveys the threats, problems and solutions to keeping our churches faithful to Christ and working together as a body.)

★★ Spicq, Ceslas. Agape *in the New Testament.* Three Volumes. Wipf & Stock, 2006. (This reprint of
◉◉◉ Spicq's extensive examination of love in the New Testament can deepen your understanding of this central Christian virtue.)

★★★ Swindoll, Charles. *Improving Your Serve: The Art of Unselfish Living.* Reprint. Word, 2002. (With
◉ his effective writing style, Swindoll skillfully challenges us to rethink our motives as we connect and serve in the body of Christ.)

★★★ Whitney, Donald. *Spiritual Disciplines Within the Church: Participating Fully in the Body of Christ.*
◉◉ Moody, 1996. (Whitney covers a number of practical and important aspects of being an active and contributing part of one's church.)

Chapter 8

PARTNERS MEETING #8

Getting Actively Involved in Serving Your Church

At Partners Meeting #8...

You and your partner will be discussing what the Bible has to say about the privilege and responsibility of being involved in ministry at your church. You will seek to find clarity concerning the topic of "spiritual gifts", which has unfortunately been unnecessarily complicated in recent church history. You and your partner will spend time evaluating how God has equipped you to be used by him to advance the biblical goals and objectives of your church. This can be a life-changing chapter as you make fresh commitments to be a good steward of the investment God has made in you.

To Prepare for Partners Meeting #8...

- Carefully read chapter 8 and answer the questions.

- Be praying that God would make clear to you the areas of ministry in which God has enabled you to be most effective.

- If any of the "Deeper Study" topics are of interest to you, prepare to discuss them.

- Be able to recite all the books of the Bible in order.

- Memorize 1 Peter 4:10.

> As each has received a gift, use it to serve one another, as good stewards of God's varied grace.
> – 1 Peter 4:10

PARTNERS:
ONE-ON-ONE DISCIPLESHIP

With Your Partner...
Discuss some of the challenges, demands or difficulties associated with serving in your church that have made you reluctant or apprehensive about being significantly involved in ministry.

Most Christians readily see the importance of attending a good church, and many will accept their responsibility to be intentional about biblical fellowship, but far too few truly step up to get involved in serving their church in any significant way. That is unfortunate, not only because it is an act of disobedience, but also because actively serving the church is by far the most rewarding aspect of a Christian's relationship with his or her church. However, it can also be the most challenging aspect, which is why so many choose to stay on the sidelines. But it is important to realize that if any church is to be healthy and effective in doing what God calls churches to be and do, then all the attendees need to move from being passive spectators or even involved participants, to becoming actively serving ministers. That's right "ministers."

Rethinking Who Does What

Many rationalize their lack of involvement in ministry by wrongly assuming that "ministry" is what the pastors were hired for. That may be true, but it is certainly not biblical. Some may think the seminary graduates on the payroll are assigned by God to do all the ministry in the church, but the Bible says something very different. Read **Ephesians 4:11-12**. What is the specific role of the "shepherds and teachers" and what is the stated role of the "saints" (i.e., the Christians) in this text? How should this arrangement change the average person's perspective on church services, Bible studies and Sunday school?

Deeper Study...
Some time was spent in chapter 6 seeking to understand who the "poimen" (shepherds) in the church are intended to be. It is also important to understand the biblical use and definition of the Greek word "hagios" (often translated "saint"). Confusion has been created as this word has often been wrongly limited to an exclusive band of figures from Church history, who were canonized and venerated by the Roman Catholic Church. Do a word study on the word "hagios." Trace the biblical usage and carefully confirm the intended scriptural definition.

Every Christian Needed

The church being referred to as a "body" is a very familiar and frequently used analogy enlisted throughout the New Testament. You may have noticed its reference in the passage you just read (Eph.4:12). Paul extends the application of this analogy at the end of that paragraph in **Ephesians 4:15-16**. Read these verses carefully and notice the two stated criteria for a "body" of Christians that desires to be healthy. The first, in v.15, has to do with "growth" as it relates to the "head" who is identified as Christ. Obviously, for a church to be healthy, its participants must have a vibrant and growing relationship with Jesus Christ. But not so obvious to many is the second criterion described in v.16. Explain this second criterion and its implications for a church that desires to be healthy.

166

CHAPTER 8
GETTING ACTIVELY INVOLVED IN SERVING YOUR CHURCH

What are some of the reasons church attendees give for not "working" to contribute toward the health of their church?

With Your Partner...
Discuss some of the problems that you imagine would result at a church where only a very small percentage of the people were involved in the majority of the ministry work.

If all the teachers, preachers and worship leaders decided to skip church all week, their absence would be painfully apparent. By contrast, most Christians feel insignificant to the overall health of their church. They assume they can be "passive" at their church meetings or, worse yet, skip them altogether and it really doesn't matter. Read **1 Corinthians 12:14-25**. How does this passage and its analogy of the "body" address a Christian's sense of unimportance?

What is the word used in v.22 to describe the seemingly "weak" or unimportant Christians in a church? What are some of the implications of this truth?

This perspective may be empowering for every Christian, but it should never lead to pride. The "necessary" roles we are called to fill in the church must be seen from the perspective of grace. Read **1 Timothy 1:12-14** and jot down, in your own words, the way we should perceive our ministry and service.

With Your Partner...
Talk about how we can live out the balance of understanding our role in ministry as critically important to our church body, yet approaching our ministry tasks with humility and grace.

167

PARTNERS:
ONE-ON-ONE DISCIPLESHIP

Your Ministry Assignment from God

Deeper Study...

Become familiar with some of the varieties of views on how "gifts" and "giftedness" are perceived by Christians today. Articles such as Kenneth Berding's "Confusing Word and Concept in Spiritual Gifts" in The Journal of the Evangelical Theological Society (43 [2000]: 37-51), and books such as Max Turner's "The Holy Spirit and Spiritual Gifts in the New Testament Church and Today" (Hendrickson, 1996) can help expose you to the critical points in the debate.

If you are to fulfill your indispensible, God-given role within your church, it would seem apparent that you need to identify what your specific role is. That simple deduction leads Christians to dive into what has been, in many circles, the confusing and convoluted study of "spiritual gifts." It seems there is no limit to the conflicting variety of theories and concepts, diagnostic tools and assessment questionnaires that claim to provide us with a proper understanding of the "gifts." Many of these books, seminars and assessments get very complicated. But our goal in this section is to see if all of this complexity is warranted by the biblical data. We will then seek to rightly respond to what the Bible says about the "gifts" and our specific ministry assignments.

Some Biblical Observations

It is important that we make a few simple observations about the biblical passages which list and discuss the various ministry assignments within the early church. These observations will help us avoid some of the confusion, which so often surrounds this topic.

1. This Subject is Described with a Variety of Words

This is important to note. Especially because our English words often carry baggage that is not present in the biblical passages. Fill in the following English words from **1 Corinthians 12:4-6**.

> **v.4** Now there are varieties of _____ (*charisma*), but the same Spirit;
>
> **v.5** and there are varieties of _____ (*diakonia*), but the same Lord;
>
> **v.6** and there are varieties of _____ (*energema*), but it is the same God who empowers them all in everyone.

While the word "gifts" is usually employed when we discuss this topic, it is helpful to notice the parallelism that shows us the breadth of what is in view here. In English, the word "gift" or "giftedness" may too narrowly lead us to think only of some "special ability" or "exceptional talent." *Charisma* in the Greek language is not attempting to give us this impression. The word is built on the root word *charis*, which means "grace" and this should put the emphasis on God's undeserved generosity. Yes, God generously grants us the ability and power to serve him, but the word *charisma* ("gift") is not as dominant in these discussions

168

CHAPTER 8
GETTING ACTIVELY INVOLVED IN SERVING YOUR CHURCH

about ministry as some would assume. For instance, in 1 Corinthians 12 it only occurs five times. Even in the opening statement of 12:1, which is usually translated "Now concerning spiritual *gifts*," the word *charisma* is not employed. In this verse "spiritual gifts" translates the word *pneumatikos*, which emphasizes the "Spirit's" work in and through his people.

Notice the second word *diakonia*, which we encountered in 12:5, this is usually translated "ministry" or "service," from which we get the word "deacon." Remember that the *deacons*, when we first read about them in Acts 6, are "ministering" to the church by serving food during the church gatherings. This is hardly something we would deem an "exceptional talent," but it is of course something that is needed during any church programs that involve food. And without *servants* to faithfully and lovingly serve the food, the church will be lacking.

The third word in this parallelism is the word *energema* (12:6) from which we get our English word "energy." It is translated "workings," "operations" or "activities" and carries the idea of something that requires effort or energy. That is one reason *energema* is naturally followed by the rest of verse 6, which clarifies that God does the empowering in all of these *charisma, diakonia* and *energema*. Therefore, God is due all the credit and glory when is comes to each and every ministry.

How do the variety of words used to describe these ministry assignments help to keep you from thinking too narrowly about what "spiritual gifts" are and aren't?

With Your Partner...
Discuss how the word "gift" or "giftedness" can be or has been misleading when thinking about your contribution of service to your church.

The next verse reveals the essence of what is taking place when Christians serve in their church.

---

1 Corinthians 12:7

To each is given the manifestation of the Spirit for the common good.

The Holy Spirit is intent on ministering to the body of Christ—the people of God. He is called the "Helper" in John 14:16, 26; 15:26; and 16:7. The Spirit's help, encouragement and teaching, according to 1 Corinthians 12:7, is accomplished in large part through the Christians who make up the body of

169

PARTNERS:
ONE-ON-ONE DISCIPLESHIP

Christ. The Holy Spirit teaches the church through the teachers he enlists and empowers in the church. The Holy Spirit also encourages the church through the encouragers he prepares and works through within the church. And again, according to 1 Corinthians 12:7 everyone is given a part in this "manifestation of the Spirit." In other words, the Holy Spirit is intent on utilizing *every Christian* to serve God's people. Not "to some," or even "to most," but "to each" is given the manifestation of the Spirit for the common good.

Read **1 Thessalonians 5:19**. How does this verse take on a broader and more sobering application, knowing that the Holy Spirit is intent on manifesting his work for the good of the church through *each and every Christian* who attends your church?

With Your Partner...
Discuss some of the ways you have served in the church for the good of the church. Also candidly discuss those periods you haven't and why you didn't.

2. No Two Lists of Ministries are the Same

As Christians ponder what their ministry assignment from God might be, they naturally look to the list of ministries found in the Scripture. This is good, but it often yields some frustrating results. One reason for the frustration is that there are several ministry lists in the Bible—six to be exact. And no two lists are identical. Most Bible students are quick to say, "I'll consult all of them!" Then they proceed to consolidate them into one master list. But when they do this they often give no thought as to why God would give one list to one church and a different list to another, especially if a consolidated list with all "the gifts" is supposed to be at work in each church.

Do the study for yourself. Let's start with the three lists contained in 1 Corinthians 12. Look up the three passages at the top of each column on the following chart and itemize the ministries or gifts which are listed. For the first passage (12:8-10), list the ministries or gifts in the order they appear. In the next two passages, look for the ministries or gifts which are repeated, and write them in the boxes that correspond to the gift you wrote in the previous column. These will be preceded by an arrow ($\rightarrow$). If the passage does not contain a gift that was listed in one of the previous passages the box will be grayed out. If a box is not grayed out and does not have an arrow ($\rightarrow$), this means the gift listed was not mentioned in the prior passage.

170

	1 Corinthians 12:8-10	1 Corinthians 12:28	1 Corinthians 12:29-30
1			
2			
3			
4		→	→
5		→	→
6		→	→
7			
8		→	→
9			→
10			→
11			→
12			
13			

There are nine ministries or gifts listed in 12:8-10.

How many ministries or gifts are listed in **12:28**? How many are left out and how many are added?

How many ministries or gifts are listed in **12:29-30**? How many are left out and how many are added?

A student of the Bible might be comfortable in saying that there are thirteen ministries or "gifts" listed for the Corinthians in 1 Corinthians 12. One might argue that Paul expected the Christians in the Corinthian church to consolidate these three lists, since they are in such close proximity, and that they should assume that every Christian in the Corinthian church had at least one of these "gifts" as their assigned ministry within their church. But things get a bit more confusing when the other three "gift lists" are considered.

PARTNERS:
ONE-ON-ONE DISCIPLESHIP

Let's build a similar chart for the remaining three gift lists from Romans, Ephesians and 1 Peter. Start by listing the seven stated ministries or gifts in Romans 12:6-8. Then look up the next two passages given at the top of the columns, look for the ministries or gifts that are repeated and put them in the cells that correspond to the previous column. These are preceded by an arrow (→). If there is no correspondence the cell will be grayed out.

	Romans 12:6-8	Ephesians 4:11	1 Peter 4:10-11
1		→	
2			→
3		→	
4			
5			
6			
7			
8			
9			
10			
11			

FYI...

The Greek construction of the sentence in Eph.4:11 suggests that "the shepherds and teachers" is referring to one office or ministry (i.e., men who serve as a "shepherd-teacher" or "pastor-teacher") though the chart allows you to list "teachers" and "shepherds" separately.

Go back over this chart and star any ministries or gifts that *did not* appear in the lists found in the 1 Corinthians 12 chart.

How many unique ministries or gifts are found, if you consider and consolidate all six passages in all four New Testament epistles?

Counting 1 Corinthians 12 as one list, how many ministries or gifts make all four lists in each of the four epistles (i.e., 1 Corinthians, Romans, Ephesians and 1 Peter)? How many and which ones make the list in three out of four of the epistles?

172

CHAPTER 8
GETTING ACTIVELY INVOLVED IN SERVING YOUR CHURCH

That may have seemed tedious, but it was an important exercise to affirm and think through the following observation and its implications: *No two lists are identical!* Each first-century audience received a different (or at least largely varied) list of ministries or gifts. That is not what we would expect if the modern approach of "discover your spiritual gift and put it to work" were God's intention. Most "gift assessment tests" and "ministry placement questionnaires" assume that God has a set "list of gifts" that he revealed in Scripture (and you just itemized), and that from this specific list he chooses one or more gifts to give to you when you become a Christian. He then expects you, or so they tell you, to discover which gift or gifts you have and to put them to work in an appropriately matched ministry.

If this were God's intended approach to getting Christians involved in ministry, we would expect a consistent "gift list" to be given to each church, but that's not what we find. Not only that, the recipients of the other New Testament epistles did not receive any list at all.

With Your Partner...
Discuss any experience you may have had with the various "spiritual gift tests" or "ministry placement questionnaires."

What implications might you draw, if in fact there is no exhaustive and complete list of ministries or gifts that God authoritatively delivered to his people in his word?

3. The More Specific the Audience, the More Detailed the List

Considering the background of each of the New Testament epistles that include a gift list will provide a further clue as to how these lists should be understood.

The letter to the Corinthian Christians has the most detailed and itemized list. First Corinthians is one of the longer New Testament letters and it is actually one of the most specific. A variety of particular concerns are addressed. Many of the chapters contain Paul's detailed answers to a series of questions that the Christians in the church at Corinth had asked. That includes the Apostle Paul's discussion of the variety of ministries or gifts and their exercise within the church, as is evidenced by the phrasing of the beginning of chapter 12 (i.e., "Now concerning," cp. 7:1; 8:1 and 16:1). Of course God planned that this epistle would be included as a part of his God-breathed library, but it is important to note that the context of this discussion on "spiritual gifts" is addressing a specific church, followed by two chapters that speak to a specific set of problems related to those ministries and gifts.

173

PARTNERS:
ONE-ON-ONE DISCIPLESHIP

The letter to the Roman Christians was originally sent to the very large first-century church in Rome, which Paul had yet to visit (Rom.15:20-24). Paul did have a lot of knowledge about this church (cf. Rom.1:11-15; 16:1-16), but a great deal of his instruction throughout the letter is put in more general terms. Both his discussion of the Gospel in the first eight chapters, and his address of practical ministry in chapter 12 are broadly stated.

As most exegetical commentaries or introductions to Ephesians suggest, there are many clues which lead scholars to conclude that the letter to the Ephesians was likely intended to be immediately and broadly circulated. Consider the lack of detail or specific references to the people, problems, or victories in the church at Ephesus, in light of the fact that Paul ministered there for three years (cp. Ac.19 and Eph.1:15; 3:2; 4:21). The information regarding ministry and gifts in Ephesians 4 is very broad and easily applicable to the variety of churches that were likely in view when this letter was penned.

The letter we call 1 Peter was originally addressed to the Christians in the regions of "Pontus, Galatia, Cappadocia, Asia and Bithynia" (1Pt.1:1). This, letter was intended for the broadest original audience of the four epistles that contain any sort of "gift list," and it contains the briefest list of all.

You can see that the more specific the original audience, the more detailed the ministry or gift list. In turn, the broader the original audience, the more general the ministry or gift list. What conclusions might be drawn from this observation?

4. Some Ministries/Gifts Overlap

When we read through the list of ministries or gifts in all four passages it is not hard to see how these must in some way overlap (as illustrated in the following chart). This is difficult to deny when we ponder 1 Peter 4:10-11. Without any preliminary attempts to define the gifts which we find listed in the other passages, "speaking" and "serving" must logically encompass some of the others. Consider that when one "taught" in the church (Eph.4:11) and another "prophesied" in the church (1Cor.12:28), both were obviously "speaking" (1Pt.4:11a) and were to do so as Peter described. When in the church one "led" (Rom.12:8) and another was

174

CHAPTER 8
GETTING ACTIVELY INVOLVED IN SERVING YOUR CHURCH

"healing" people (1Cor.12:9), both were obviously "serving" (1Pt.4:11b) and both were to do it "with the strength that God supplies."

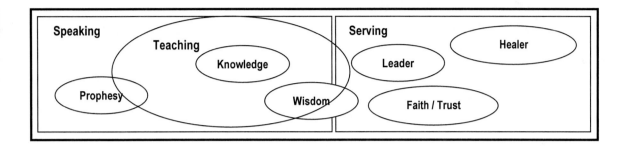

Some Reasonable Conclusions

We have made these four observations about the "gift lists" in the New Testament:

1. This Subject is Described with a Variety of Words

2. No Two Lists of Ministries are the Same

3. The More Specific the Audience, the More Detailed the List

4. Some Ministries or Gifts Overlap

It is not difficult then to draw a few simple conclusions, which may force us to jettison several popular theories and modern ideas about "spiritual gifts" when we discover they are incompatible with our biblical findings.

1. These Lists Must be Examples and Not a Complete List of Spiritual Gifts

With such variation and breadth, the lack of correspondence and the exceedingly simple categorization of Peter, it should be reasonably clear that these lists are not meant to serve as a definitive and exhaustive list of "spiritual gifts." They should not be compiled and presented as though this was God's complete list of ways he empowers people for service in the church. Yet that is exactly what is often taught in churches today. We are led to believe by modern presentations on "spiritual gifts" that we must have one of the eighteen or nineteen gifts listed in these New Testament passages. And as is often the case, if you sing, play an instrument on the worship team, run a soundboard, or excel in working in the nursery, then you have the unsatisfying experience of being forced to validate your ministry by saying you've "got the gift of helps" or "service." However, if these biblical lists are *examples* of ministries in the earliest churches and not a complete list of spiritual gifts, then we shouldn't play word games to try to make all ministries fit into the eighteen or nineteen listed examples.

175

PARTNERS:
ONE-ON-ONE DISCIPLESHIP

What are some of the negative ramifications that might come to God's people and the functioning of Christ's church, when people choose to hold to the view that only the ministries listed in the Bible are valid expressions of the Holy Spirit's work within their church?

With Your Partner...
Discuss your answer to the corresponding question regarding how the church and God's people are negatively affected by insisting that the "valid" ministries or gifts are only those eighteen or nineteen identified in the four New Testament letters.

2. Each Church's Ministry List Will Vary

In 1 Timothy 5, Paul gives directions regarding the care of widows in the church. While there are several instructions about who can and cannot be on the official list, the understanding is that there will be a set of local Christian widows for whom the church must care. Elsewhere, Paul has made clear in his letters that pastors have specific and demanding priorities that would necessitate other Christians (besides the pastors) step up and meet the various needs of the widows. But in the letter to the Ephesians (which is where Timothy pastors), there is no "gift" listed regarding care for widows. Paul lists only four "gifts" in the epistle to the Ephesians, none of which can be reasonably argued to include care for widows. Were the Christians in Ephesus to conclude that the biblically commanded ministry to care for widows would not be met, or at least not be met by a set of gifted Christians within their church? Of course not.

Reread **Ephesians 4:11-12** with the biblically mandated ministry to widows in view. How does Ephesians 4:12 give you confidence that there are several "valid" and "specific" ministries that the Holy Spirit will enable and empower in your church, that are not individually listed in the few New Testament passages that itemize "gifts" or ministries?

Now think through the many ministries at your church that aim at fulfilling their biblical purpose to reach people for Christ, and to edify, equip and care for God's people. Make a list of some of the ministries which are essential for your church to function as the church of Jesus Christ, but are not normally considered part of God's "spiritual gifts" or God empowered ministries. Linger on

176

CHAPTER 8
GETTING ACTIVELY INVOLVED IN SERVING YOUR CHURCH

this question and make your list as specific as you are able, considering the current size and scope of your church's work.

When we consider that some are enabled and gifted by God's Spirit to care for elderly widows and others are enabled and gifted by God's Spirit to care for children, while their parents engage in the focused study of God's word and corporate worship, we start to realize just how "spiritual" these ministries and endowments actually are.

What are some of the dangers in not seeing the working of the soundboard, participation on the prayer team, or working in kids' ministry as divinely enabled and spiritually gifted ministries? How can this expanded and broadened view of "spiritual gifts" improve how Christians in your church do their work?

With Your Partner...
Compare your lists and discuss how a more biblical view of "valid" ministries will change the way Christians approach these ministries and go about fulfilling these roles in your church?

3. Not All Gifts or Ministries on the "Gifts Lists" will Apply to Your Church

It should be obvious that a list of ministries at one church will likely not match the list of ministries at another church. There may be a variety of biblically valid ministries in a large church that would not be present in a small church. Some churches have no "widows" (according to the 1 Timothy 5 definition) and

PARTNERS:
ONE-ON-ONE DISCIPLESHIP

therefore there would be no necessity for a set of Christians who were enabled and empowered by God's Spirit to minister to such a group.

Several of the gifts or ministries listed in the New Testament are broad, and some have been shown to be categories (e.g., 1 Peter 4:10-11's "serving" and "speaking"). And many of the gifts listed in the Bible are present in most, if not all churches today. But there are some ministries or gifts listed in the New Testament that are very unique. A few of the listed gifts and ministries are supernatural—that is, when exercised they suspend or reverse natural law and some gifts or offices are shown in Scripture as exclusive to the first century ministry of Christ. Consider the gift (or office) of "apostle" named in the Ephesians 4 list. Jesus chose and named twelve apostles from among his band of disciples (Lk.6:13-16; Mk.3:13-19; Mt.10:1-4) and endowed them with special power and authority. When Judas defected, the eleven hastily sought to name a replacement, considering requirements regarding personal and physical involvement with Christ (Ac.1:12-14; cf. 1Cor.9:1). In the New Jerusalem, inscribed on the foundations of the city walls, there will be "the twelve names of the twelve apostles of the Lamb" (Rev.21:14). So we know there were only twelve apostles who occupied this unique and special office in the church.

Deeper Study...
Study the word "apostolos" (apostle), its 78 occurrences and its New Testament usage. Note its technical and non-technical use. Make sure you use a resource that reveals how often the non-technical occurrences are translated other than "apostle" into English (i.e., Bible software with original language search capabilities or a Greek-English concordance). Note also how the word "apostolos" is given its technical meaning by Christ. As with the words "kurios" (Lord/lord) and "angelos" (angel/messenger), work to identify the contextual indicators which direct us to understand the difference between the technical and non-technical usage of important words like these.

What does **Ephesians 2:20** tell us about the apostles? Why is that word picture important regarding the uniqueness of this office?

So when New Testament lists refer to apostles, we can know that such a "gift" or ministry is one your church and mine cannot possibly possess in any New Testament sense.

Consider the gift (or office) of "prophet," which is also named in the Ephesians 4 list. In a technical sense, in terms of those who inscribe God's inspired word, we can be assured that this gift was also only given to a limited and finite list of individuals.

178

CHAPTER 8

GETTING ACTIVELY INVOLVED IN SERVING YOUR CHURCH

How do passages like **Ephesians 3:1-5**; **2 Thessalonians 2:15**; **Revelation 22:6, 18-19**; and **Jude 3** suggest that there was a finite number of prophetic figures in the New Testament?

FYI...
It is important to realize that many these days occasionally use the word "prophet" and "prophetic" in a non-technical sense to refer to a Bible teacher with a particular forthright or powerful style. While that is a popular usage in some circles, these kinds of teachers throughout church history are "reiterating" and effectively applying biblical prophecy when they teach, and are not proclaiming new revelatory prophetic truths from God.

Understanding the "foundational" nature of the apostles and prophets (Eph.2:20), helps us to understand the parallel roles of the four "gifts" listed in Ephesians 4:11. The difference between the first and second set has to do with what the apostles and prophets left behind, namely the New Testament Scriptures.

	Ministry Associated with Establishing Churches	Ministry Associated with Sustaining Churches
Without a Written New Testament	**Apostles** (foundational)	**Prophets** (foundational)
With a Written New Testament	**Evangelists** (ongoing)	**Shepherd-Teachers** (ongoing)

Deeper Study...
Substantiate why it is that Timothy is said to be an "evangelist" (2Tim.4:5), citing his specific role in Ephesus as spelled out throughout the books of 1 and 2 Timothy.

Without the objective, propositional words of God inscribed in the New Testament, you can imagine how hard it would have been to evaluate the truthfulness of first century preaching, especially if the preachers' comments about Christ conflicted. Consider how the early church was to distinguish between the newly revealed truths and any spurious claims about the person and work of Christ.

What does **2 Corinthians 12:12** tell us about the apostles?

179

PARTNERS:
ONE-ON-ONE DISCIPLESHIP

What does **Hebrews 2:3-4** say "attested" to the information delivered in the first century regarding Christ? Recall and cite some obvious examples of these from your Bible.

The miraculous ministries or gifts described throughout the New Testament are quite different from many of the claims made today concerning "miracles." One of the reasons biblical miracles were called "signs" was because they clearly and unequivocally pointed to something divine. They weren't vague or ambiguous. If you witnessed a biblical "sign" or "wonder" you knew that you had seen something that was not personal or subjective, but that instead you had witnessed something which was beyond the realm of human ability. The miraculous gifts in the New Testament associated with the apostles and prophets actually reversed or suspended the physical laws of nature—such as the instantaneous healing of the paralytic, Aeneas, by Peter in Acts 9, or the resurrection of Eutychus, by Paul in Acts 20. These kinds of supernatural events confirmed that the message of the apostles and prophets was not their own, but was in fact, God's.

Given below are the five miraculous gifts from the "gift lists" passages, which are observed elsewhere in Scripture to be bona fide "sign gifts" or ministries wherein natural law is suspended or reversed.

Deeper Study...

Consider the modern claims regarding the definition of "tongues" as ecstatic or unintelligible utterances used in prayer. Consider carefully the texts which are quoted to support this view (i.e., 1Cor.13:1, Rom.8:26). Examine the contexts of these passages and compare the "private prayer language view" with the three historical occurrences of the gift of tongues found in Acts (i.e., Ac.2:4-11; 10:45-46; 19:6-7). With that in mind, attempt to carefully walk through 1 Corinthians 14 distinguishing Corinthian abuses and distortions from the apostle's correctives and affirmations.

- **Healing** (1Cor.12:9) – The instantaneous reversal of a sickness, disease or even death.

- **Prophecy** (1Cor.12:10) – The proclamation or writing of new revelation from God's mind.

- **Tongues** (1Cor.12:10) – The ability to fluently speak a language not studied.

- **Interpretation of Tongues** (1Cor.12:10) – The ability to translate a language not studied.

- **Miracles** (1Cor.12:10) – A broad categorization describing undeniable supernatural acts.

It is interesting that all of these miraculous gifts are listed in the earliest of the four New Testament epistles in which our "gift lists" are found – 1 Corinthians (AD 55). Only "prophecy" is found on any of the other "gift lists"

180

CHAPTER 8
GETTING ACTIVELY INVOLVED IN SERVING YOUR CHURCH

(i.e., Romans and Ephesians). This is not to suggest that the miraculous gifts were not practiced outside of Corinth. Of course the book of Acts records only a handful of instances (covering events from the resurrection of Christ up until AD 62). But it does follow that as the apostles died off (or were killed off) and as the New Testament writing continued to move toward its completion, the miraculous gifts were reported less and less.

With Your Partner...
Knowing that modern churches differ regarding their views on the miraculous gifts (see for instance Are Miraculous Gifts for Today? Four Views, *a book edited by Stan Gundry and Wayne Grudem), it is helpful to discuss with your partner your church's position on this issue. Especially as you participate in ministries that call on you to lead and teach others, it is critical to share the view of your pastors and church leaders on this topic, aware that Satan uses disagreements of this sort to disrupt and divide churches (1Cor.1:10).*

If you and your church believe that the five miraculous "gifts" or ministries, which are found among the biblical "gift lists" were only foundational and used for the establishment of the church and the attestation of New Testament revelation, why would it be wrong for others to characterize you as "not believing in spiritual gifts"?

Why would it also be wrong to say that you "put God in a box" or that you "limit God" or that you "don't have faith"?

Does one "limit God" or "not believe in miracles" or "not have faith" because one buys bread at the grocery store, when the Bible says that the Israelites gathered their bread, or manna, off the ground each morning (**Ex.16:14-16**)? Why or why not?

181

PARTNERS:
ONE-ON-ONE DISCIPLESHIP

Questions to Ask

All of what we have covered so far in this chapter is important background to figuring out how you might specifically be involved in ministry at your church. We know the Bible says each of us must be involved. We understand that the New Testament lists are examples and that there are many other important and valid ministries besides those listed in the Bible. We have also considered that not all the gifts, offices or ministries listed in the Bible will be present in the twenty-first century church. Now let us work through four questions that can help us to zero in on what might be the best and most productive area of ministry for us.

1. What Needs Do I See in My Church?

This is an important question that should be pondered without checking the bulletin or consulting your church's website. Begin by reflecting on your knowledge and experiences at your church. What do you perceive that your church is lacking? What do you think your church could do better? In your church's attempts to reach people for Christ, worship God, and equip and build up the people of God, how could these things be done better? How could they be done more efficiently? How could they be done more effectively? Take a few minutes to thoughtfully jot down your initial responses to these questions.

With Your Partner...
Discuss your answers to this important question with your partner. Describe which of these needs you have sought to be the answer to in the past, and which ones you've never attempted to address or solve in any way.

This line of questioning is not meant to foster a hypercritical attitude, but articulating things that irk us in the church often exposes our spiritual inclinations and areas of divine enablement. Gifted preachers, for instance, are bothered by listening to substandard preaching. People who are gifted to shepherd teenagers are usually those who can look at a youth program and quickly identify its weaknesses. Christians who are endowed by God to lead in musical worship are usually those who easily see the flaws in corporate worship. Of course we can all be critical, but the goal here is to identify what we perceive to be the most obvious needs in our church, so that we can seriously consider whether or not God is preparing us to capably meet these needs.

With Your Partner...
Discuss why some of the needs we identify in the church might not be the wisest priority for your church at the moment. Consider how deference to leadership and their proposed sequence and priorities is an important aspect of church life. Discuss why "everyone just doing whatever, whenever" is never a prudent strategy for any organization.

182

CHAPTER 8

GETTING ACTIVELY INVOLVED IN SERVING YOUR CHURCH

2. What Opportunities in My Church Interest Me Most?

This will require a look through a church bulletin, calendar, newsletter or website. Locate as many of these resources from your church as possible and pay close attention to your heart when you read through them. Reflect on all that is going on and ask yourself, "What programs or ministries interest me the most?" Think about which outreaches or missions projects truly stir your heart and get you excited about serving Christ. Decide which activities, events, fellowship groups or service teams really make you think about the possibilities and potential impact they can have for God's glory. Take a few minutes to write down your responses to this question.

With Your Partner...
Dialogue about the things you have written down in response to this probing question. Talk with your partner about how one gets involved or gets started in serving in the areas you have identified.

Paul liked to talk about "open doors" of opportunity. When he saw them he was eager to step up to their challenges. Read **1 Corinthians 16:5-9**. What do you learn from this passage about Paul and the way he assessed ministry needs and how he planned his own life?

3. Would My Help Be Helpful?

An honest appraisal of ourselves and what we would bring to the ministry we want to get involved in, is essential—both before and after we step up to serve.

Before you get plugged into a ministry it is good to have a sense that you can be helpful. There should be some reasonable belief that God has prepared and equipped you to do what you are seeking to accomplish. Read **Romans 12:3-4** and consider the preliminary concerns that Paul has for those considering their individual involvement in the ministry of their church. Why are these instructions so important? What would happen if this step was ignored and each member of the body indiscriminately did whatever he or she wanted to in the church?

183

PARTNERS:
ONE-ON-ONE DISCIPLESHIP

With that said, it is important to remember that everyone who is called to do something important in the church has periods of doubt and will occasionally battle feelings of inadequacy in doing the ministry God wants him or her to be involved in.

---

2 Corinthians 3:4-6a

Such is the confidence that we have through Christ toward God. Not that we are sufficient in ourselves to claim anything as coming from us, but our sufficiency is from God, who has made us competent to be ministers of a new covenant.

Read **Exodus 4:10-12**. What did God say to Moses about his assigned ministry role when he doubted his abilities?

With Your Partner...
Discuss the balance of having adequate confidence in God for the ability to serve in a particular ministry (2Cor.3:4-6a) and the problem of "thinking more highly of yourself than you ought" and not accepting the fact that not everyone can "have the same function" in the church (Rom.12:3-4). How do you keep the proper balance between reasonable self-assessment and trust in God?

Once we get involved in a particular ministry, though it may be difficult to hear, we all need to invite honest and unbiased feedback on how helpful our attempts to help the church have been. This input should come from those who we know are gifted to do the kind of ministry we are attempting to do. We can always find someone who will politely tell us we did "a good job," but we want to seek the objective appraisal of those who are good at what we are seeking to do. If we have the desire to be a part of leading in musical worship, we should certainly seek the evaluation of our efforts by those we know are gifted to lead in musical worship. We don't want to foist our musical efforts on the church if our "help" is actually "not helpful," and others do not recognize our giftedness in that area. The same holds true for teaching a Bible class, working with teenagers, or ministering to widows. Whatever the ministry, we should be sensitive to the fact that just because we want to be helpful, doesn't mean that we will be.

CHAPTER 8
GETTING ACTIVELY INVOLVED IN SERVING YOUR CHURCH

With Your Partner...
Discuss some of the Christians who are capable and obviously gifted at doing what you would want to do in the church. Talk about a way to get some feedback from them about your efforts in that ministry.

Proverbs 15:31-33

The ear that listens to life-giving reproof
    will dwell among the wise.

Whoever ignores instruction despises himself,
    but he who listens to reproof gains intelligence.

The fear of the Lord is instruction in wisdom,
    and humility comes before honor.

While it may be hard to hear that we are not helpful in a particular ministry, we need to wisely embrace the consensus of the body of Christ as we seek to serve God. It is actually a great advantage to have clarity about which ministries God has *not* enabled us to minister in. When we can accept that we are misplaced in what we are attempting to do, we are freed up to move on to find the ministries in which God has equipped us to be effective.

4. What Will I Do This Week?

Now we come to the most important question in this chapter – *What is it that you will do?* Knowing that God has called every Christian to be involved in ministry, we can be sure that if you are a Christian, God has equipped you and is calling you to minister in your church. So what is it that you will do to serve your church and assist in the advancement of its overall ministry?

You may be at a point in your Christian life where you are already involved in a ministry. Be sure to consider and continue to reconsider if you or any of your gifts are misplaced or underutilized. Don't forget that as you grow spiritually and God hones and sharpens your spiritually endowed abilities, your ministry involvement often changes. Every seasoned Christian can attest to the way his or her ministry posts have changed over the years. I myself began serving the church in the most simplistic ways. My first employment at the church was to clean the toilets. I was hired as a janitor and I worked to serve the church to the best of my ability. I later served as a small group leader, a camp counselor, a youth pastor, a college pastor, and am currently serving as a senior preaching pastor. Of course I was not equipped or prepared to preach God's word when I served the church by sweeping the floors and raking the leaves. But through the years I needed to constantly reassess my developing gifts and have others assess my ministry efforts so that I could continue to adjust my ministry post.

185

PARTNERS:
ONE-ON-ONE DISCIPLESHIP

So where will you serve now? And based on how God is developing and equipping you, where do you think you may serve in the years ahead?

With Your Partner...

Discuss your answers to these very important questions. Honestly dialogue about where you now serve, should serve, and where you may serve in the future. Talk to your partner about the church leaders who might help you develop and grow in your area of ministry. Make sure you talk about who you can contact at the church to explore a deeper or more fruitful involvement in the ministry you do or desire to do.

Deeper Study...

Go through each of the non-miraculous gifts listed in 1 Corinthians 12, Romans 12, Ephesians 4 and 1 Peter 4. Look for other passages throughout the New Testament which describe the ways that all Christians are to be involved in some way in each of the listed gifts, even if that is not one's particular area of giftedness or one's specific ministry.

Keep in mind that we all have responsibilities in the Christian life that may not feel like our strengths or particular areas of giftedness. For example, Romans 12:8 states that some are especially enabled to carry out "acts of mercy" that benefit the church. But that does not mean that everyone else in the church doesn't have to "show mercy." The same goes for "giving" or "generosity" (Rom.12:8). While some have an amazing ability to give generously, it does not mean that the other Christians in the congregation are not required to give at all (cf. Gal.6:6). Consider the special ministry of "the evangelists" (Eph.4:11). Because some are gifted as effective and fearless evangelists, doesn't mean that the rest of us don't have to share the message of the gospel (cf. Mt.28:19; 2 Cor.5:11, 18-21).

With Your Partner...

Talk about godly strategies and biblical reasons for not neglecting ministry in the church because we are busy living for Christ in the home or in our workplace. Discuss how you might stay involved in serving the church even during the busiest seasons of your career, education or domestic life.

While our focus in this chapter has been on God's calling to serve in the church and the biblical requirement to minister to those in your church, that emphasis does not overlook the foundational calling for you to see your employment or domestic responsibilities as an arena to serve Christ (Col.3:17-24). Obviously, the average Christian will need to invest a majority of their waking hours in the marketplace earning a living or in the home raising a family. We must see that God's empowerment to serve the church is in addition to, and not in place of, our vocation (i.e., "calling") in the home or in the workplace.

Get Motivated!

When Peter discusses involvement in ministry in 1 Peter 4 his exhortation is surrounded by some incredible truths that should ignite thoughtful Christians to dive in to ambitiously serving the church of Jesus Christ.

CHAPTER 8
GETTING ACTIVELY INVOLVED IN SERVING YOUR CHURCH

> **1 Peter 4:7-11**
>
> **7** The end of all things is at hand; therefore be self-controlled and sober-minded for the sake of your prayers. **8** Above all, keep loving one another earnestly, since love covers a multitude of sins. **9** Show hospitality to one another without grumbling. **10** As each has received a gift, use it to serve one another, as good stewards of God's varied grace: **11** whoever speaks, as one who speaks oracles of God; whoever serves, as one who serves by the strength that God supplies—in order that in everything God may be glorified through Jesus Christ. To him belong glory and dominion forever and ever. Amen.

1. This Could Be Our Last Opportunity!

The first phrase of verse 7 puts the entirety of our lives in perspective. At any moment our opportunities for ministering to the body of Christ could be over. When we remember the profound worth and eternal value of serving God, and we combine that with realizing that Christ could return at any moment, we should be motivated to not wait another day to get involved.

Read **Matthew 24:45-50** and **Matthew 25:1-5**, identify and jot down Christ's opinion of those in these two parables who think "they've got time later" to do what they've been asked to do.

What does it do for you to consider that this year could be your last year, or that this month could be your last month, or that this Sunday could be the last Sunday you have to assemble together with your church here on earth?

2. God has Invested in You for This!

Verse 10 of 1 Peter 4 brings up the importance of seeing our ministry to the people of God as a stewardship. Stewards have been entrusted with something of value by their masters, and their masters expect the stewards to "turn a profit" with that investment. Read the poignant and sobering words found in **Matthew 25:24-26**. How was the servant described in v.26?

PARTNERS:
ONE-ON-ONE DISCIPLESHIP

In light of **Matthew 25:24-26** and **1 Peter 4:10**, how would you respond to the Christian who tells you that while he may have been given some abilities by God to serve the church, he doesn't think his service is of much importance and probably won't be missed?

3. Your Service Brings Glory to God!

One of the most encouraging motivations in 1 Peter 4 is found at the end of verse 11. We are told that when we enthusiastically employ the gifts God has invested in us, we bring glory to God. Whether it is pushing a broom for the good of the church or preaching a sermon to edify other Christians, the Bible tells us that God is honored, pleased and exalted. Nothing is more foundational in the Christian life than "glorifying God through Jesus Christ." And we have that opportunity today, tomorrow and each remaining day God grants us. It may be hard to believe, but even the things that seem mundane, if they are rightly done and done for the right reason, if they are done for the good of Christ's people, then God is exalted and the spotlight is placed on his eternal "glory and dominion."

With Your Partner...
Discuss how you can keep God's glory and honor in view as you serve in your area of ministry. Talk about how this focused perspective on bringing glory to God can affect the way you go about your ministry. What is the difference when you think this way and when you don't?

Read **Ephesians 3:20-21**. Even if you feel your efforts for the good of the church are feeble or small, remember these words. God is able to do something great through you for his "glory in the church" (v.21a). Write out your thoughts and response to the astonishing incentive found in these two verses.

188

CHAPTER 8
GETTING ACTIVELY INVOLVED IN SERVING YOUR CHURCH

Notes

PARTNERS:
ONE-ON-ONE DISCIPLESHIP

Notes

RESOURCES & FURTHER STUDY

8 *Getting Actively Involved in Serving Your Church*

> Rating Key
> ★ Helpful (four being most)
> ☉ Difficulty (four being hardest)

Resources on Ministry, "Spiritual Gifts" & Serving God

★★★
☉☉☉
Berding, Kenneth. *What are the Spiritual Gifts? Rethinking the Conventional View.* Grand Rapids, MI: Kregel, 2006. (Berding critically evaluates the prevailing views on "spiritual gifts" providing some fresh insight. Even if one does not agree with all his findings, this book will effectively and persuasively drive you back to Scripture to rethink several of our commonly held views on this subject.)

★★
☉
Buford, Bob. *Halftime: Changing Your Game Plan from Success to Significance.* Grand Rapids, MI: Zondervan, 1994. (While not theologically deep, Buford will practically help those in the "second half" of life to reevaluate their ministry goals and spiritual purpose.)

★★★
☉☉
Guinness, Os. *The Call: Finding and Fulfilling the Central Purpose of your Life.* Nashville, TN: Thomas Nelson, 1998. (This book is filled with a breadth of insight and a variety of subtopics relating to "vocation" and calling as a Christian. This is not a "how to" book, but rather a guide to ponder the meaning and direction of our Christian lives.)

★★
☉☉
Helm, Paul. *The Callings: The Gospel in the World.* Carlisle, PA: Banner of Truth, 1988. (This brief work attacks the bifurcation of "sacred" and "secular" and helps us redeem our efforts in the home and workplace.)

★★★
☉
Mahaney, C.J. *Humility: True Greatness.* Sisters, OR: Multnomah Books, 2005. (Mahaney thoughtfully explores this important ingredient in life and ministry.)

★★
☉☉
Murray, Andrew. *Humility: The Beauty of Holiness.* Reprint. Grand Rapids, MI: Bethany House, 2001. (This classic devotional helps us to remember the importance of humility in serving God and in all of the Christian life.)

★★★
☉
Sanders, Oswald. *Spiritual Leadership.* Chicago, IL: Moody Press, 1980. (Sanders addresses a wide variety of issues related to our spiritual lives and preparation as we serve in the church.)

★★★
☉☉☉
Schaeffer, Francis. *The Church at the End of the Twentieth Century.* Wheaton, IL: Crossway Publishers, 1980. (Though "the end of the twentieth century" has come and gone, much of the concerns Schaeffer addresses in this book are timeless and worth pondering for the ministry in any age.)

★★★
☉
Swindoll, Charles. *Improving Your Serve: The Art of Unselfish Living.* Nashville, TN: Thomas Nelson, 2002. (This is a helpful, probing discussion about our motives and attitudes, if we are to be Christian "servants" in Christ's church.)

191

★★ Thomas, Robert L. *Understanding Spiritual Gifts: A Verse-by-Verse Study of 1 Corinthians 12-14.* Grand
◉◉ Rapids, MI: Kregel Academic. (As the title suggests, Thomas carefully walks through these three
important chapters that discuss biblical gifts and ministry.)

★★★ Whitney, Donald. *Spiritual Disciplines Within the Church: Participating Fully in the Body of Christ.*
◉ Chicago, IL: Moody Press, 1996. (Whitney covers several topics related to church life. The sections on
the importance of the church as Christ's organization and "serving" are helpful and motivating.)

Resources on the Debate Regarding "Sign Gifts"

★★★ Chantry, Walter. *Signs of the Apostles: Observations on Pentecostalism Old and New.* Carlisle, PA: Banner
◉◉ of Truth, 1973. (Chantry explores the common themes in old and new strains of Pentecostalism, as well as
issues related to prophecy and sign gifts.)

★★★ Gaffin, Richard Jr. *Perspectives on Pentecost: New Testament Teaching on the Gifts of the Holy Spirit,*
◉◉ Phillipsburg. NJ: P & R Publishing, 1979. (In this concise book, Gaffin examines the relevant New
Testament texts on the gift of the Holy Spirit, tongues and prophecy.)

★★★ Geisler, Norman. *Signs and Wonders.* Chicago, IL: Moody Press, 1973. (Geisler works to arrive at a
◉◉ biblical definition of a "miracle" as well as exploring related issues such as providence, prophecy and Scripture.)

★★★ Grudem, Wayne, ed. *Are Miraculous Gifts for Today? Four Views.* Grand Rapids, MI: Zondervan
◉◉◉ Publishers, 1996. (In the "Point / Counterpoint" series, this book offers a critique of the four primary views
regarding the cessation, continuation or partial continuation of the sign gifts.)

★★★ MacArthur, John. *Charismatic Chaos.* Grand Rapids, MI: Zondervan, 1993. (In this book MacArthur
◉◉ critically examines not only the sign gifts, but also the "health and wealth gospel", televangelists, and the claims of
ongoing revelation.)

★★★ Mayhue, Richard. *The Healing Promise: Is It Always God's Will to Heal?* Dublin, Ireland: Mentor
◉◉ Books, 1978. (Mayhue addresses this relevant question regarding God's ability to heal and what the Bible says
about what our prayers and expectations should be when we, or someone we love is sick.)

★★ Napier, John. *Charismatic Challenge: Four Key Questions.* Franklin, TN: Providence House
◉◉ Publishers, 1995. (Napier interacts with issues related to cessationism and views on the continuation of
supernatural manifestations.)

★★★ Smith, Charles. *Tongues in a Biblical Perspective.* Winona Lake, IN: BMH Publishers, 1980. (As the
◉◉ title promises, Smith works to carefully show the biblical data on what tongues are and are not.)

★★★ Unger, Merrill. *The Baptism and the Gifts of the Holy Spirit.* Chicago, IL: Moody Press, 1974. (Unger
◉◉ seeks to eliminate the confusion often associated with modern discussions of "the baptism of the Holy Spirit".)

★★ Warfield, B. B. *Counterfeit Miracles.* Reprint. Carlisle, PA: Banner of Truth, 1972. (In his lectures at
◉◉◉ Columbia Theological Seminary in 1917, this book captures Warfield's early response to the rise of claims regarding
a resurgence of supernatural events in his time.)

PARTNERS MEETING #9

Sharing the Gospel with People Who Need It

At Partners Meeting #9...

You will discuss the joy of sharing the good news of Jesus Christ. This chapter will seek to equip you with a memorable outline of the gospel message that can be effectively and persuasively presented to those in your life who desperately need it! God can really use this meeting to dispel the fears that often surround our high calling as ambassadors of Christ!

To Prepare for Partners Meeting #9...

- Read chapter 9 and answer the questions.

- Bring to your meeting the names of people you know that are not yet Christians.

- Be prepared to "share the gospel" with your partner as though he or she were someone on your list.

- If any of the "Deeper Study" topics are of interest to you, prepare to discuss them.

- Memorize 2 Corinthians 5:20

> Therefore we are ambassadors for Christ, God making his appeal through us. We implore you on behalf of Christ, be reconciled to God.
>
> – 2 Corinthians 5:20

PARTNERS:

ONE-ON-ONE DISCIPLESHIP

One could hardly think of a more important activity for the Christian to get excited about than sharing the saving message of the gospel with people who desperately need to hear it. Sharing with others how to avoid God's wrath and how to become partakers in God's family takes center stage throughout the New Testament. It is God's desire that proclaiming the good news would become a passion for all of us – it is clearly his!

> **2 Peter 3:9**
>
> The Lord is not slow to fulfill his promise, as some count slowness, but is patient toward you, not wishing that any should perish, but that all should reach repentance.

> **1 Timothy 2:3-4**
>
> This is good, and it is pleasing in the sight of God our Savior, who desires all people to be saved and to come to the knowledge of the truth.

Our Fundamental Task on Earth

When we consider the things that the Bible calls us to do as God's children, all of them can be accomplished with much greater effectiveness once this life is over – all but one! Think about it. Our worship will be great. Our relationships will be perfect. Sin will be a distant memory. Sounds terrific! So then why doesn't God just choose to take us all home? Because there is certainly one task that we cannot accomplish once we leave this planet.

Read **Acts 1:6-8** and the context of **2 Peter 3:9** that is printed above. Why does God postpone the coming of his kingdom? What does he expect us to do? Do these verses seem to imply that evangelism is a limited responsibility for just a few Christians?

What are your initial reactions to thinking that God wants you to be his missionary right where you are?

194

CHAPTER 9
SHARING THE GOSPEL WITH PEOPLE WHO NEED IT

Your Sphere of Influence

An important and primary step in sharing the gospel is knowing who the people are that need to hear it. Although we should be ready and willing to share the gospel with anyone and everyone we run into, it is important to understand that God has given us a particular sphere of influence for which we should accept responsibility.

Take a few moments and assess your life relationships. Consider those around you who you suspect have never genuinely repented of their sins and placed their trust in Jesus Christ for salvation. When in doubt, put them on the list!

Your Family

The most obvious area of concern ought to be your immediate and extended family. God has given you a unique area of influence with your family. Though it is often difficult to share the gospel with family members, especially those who are older than you, you shouldn't neglect the opportunity that God has given you by placing them in your family.

Who are the members of your family (immediate and extended) that you suspect need to hear the saving message of Jesus Christ?

With Your Partner...
Discuss those on your lists that you think God is currently preparing to hear the message of the gospel. Compare notes on family members and coworkers who are most receptive to talk about Christ and those who are least receptive.

Your Coworkers or Classmates

Those you rub shoulders with every day ought to be next on your list. There are few people you spend more time with than your coworkers or classmates. It would be a tragedy for someone to work with you for years and never hear about the salvation you have in Jesus Christ.

Who are the people you come into contact with on a regular basis at work or at school that you suspect need to hear the saving message of Jesus Christ?

Your Neighbors

Depending on the dynamics of your neighborhood, these relationships may be few or they could be plenteous. If they are few, out of your love for the lost, you may want to creatively increase your contact with your neighbors.

Who are the people who live nearby that you suspect need to hear the saving message of Jesus Christ?

195

PARTNERS:
ONE-ON-ONE DISCIPLESHIP

Your Acquaintances

Depending on your stage and position in life, there are probably other circles of influence you have which are quite significant. Perhaps you are a part of a club, board, organization, or team that puts you in contact with people that are not a part of God's family. It is even possible that through some church activity you have come in contact with someone who does not genuinely know Christ.

Who are the other acquaintances you have that you suspect need to hear the saving message of the gospel?

The Most Effective Evangelism

You might be tempted to think that the most effective and fruitful evangelism takes place at a big time evangelistic event or in the presence of a gifted public speaker. Though there is no doubt that God has used crusades and articulate preachers to lead many to Christ, the statistics are overwhelmingly stacked on the side of personal, one-on-one conversations between people who already know each other. Survey after survey confirms that the most likely means by which a person makes a decision to follow Christ is through an existing relationship with a follower of Christ.

In other words, don't think that your goal should be to wait for the next evangelistic event to take them to—they are more likely to decide to trust in Christ after talking with you! That may be hard to believe, but it is true! Don't underestimate the power of personal, one-on-one presentations of the saving message of the gospel!

Who were the people who were instrumental in your coming to Christ? How many of these did you know prior to the day you made the decision to repent and put your trust in Christ?

Relying on Prayer

With Your Partner...
Share with your partner any experience you have had in actually helping someone come to the place of repentance?

The thought of being used to lead someone into the family of God is an awesome thought. When it happens, it is an awesome feeling—so awesome, that we must be sure to maintain a biblical perspective about how it all works. Noting the relationship between prayer and evangelism is a good place to start.

196

CHAPTER 9

SHARING THE GOSPEL WITH PEOPLE WHO NEED IT

Read **Matthew 9:35-38** and jot down what Jesus commands his disciples to pray for. How does this metaphor help you understand God's involvement in the most basic ingredients in seeing lost people saved?

Note the context of **1 Timothy 2:4**. What is God asking us to do in verses 1 & 2? How do you think this relates to his desire in verse 4?

Read **Ephesians 6:19-20**. You would think, of all people, Paul would not need to ask for such things. What does this tell you about your need for prayer in this area?

Consider the statements found in **1 Corinthians 3:3-9**. Although these were the big guns of the first century, Paul sets the record straight about God, salvation, and those who deliver the message. What do these verses do to help you understand the role of prayer in evangelism (especially verse 7)?

It is important to remember that evangelism and new life in Christ are all "a God thing." So commit yourself to prayer! Remember that it is God who changes the hearts of men and women. We must pray if we are to see fruit in our evangelism. Below are some suggested items for prayer.

With Your Partner...
Pray through this list of items with your partner.

For you:

1. *Pray that God will keep you willing and available to share the gospel anytime & anyplace.*

2. *Pray that God will give you boldness in sharing the good news.*

3. *Pray that God will give you wisdom as you articulate the message of the gospel.*

4. *Pray that God will always glorify himself when you talk to others about Jesus Christ.*

PARTNERS:
ONE-ON-ONE DISCIPLESHIP

For them:

    1. *Pray that God will even now make them thirsty for the truth of the gospel.*

    2. *Pray that God will minimize distractions and maximize communication when you talk.*

    3. *Pray that God will make them receptive and willing to listen when you speak with them.*

    4. *Pray that God will make them restless until they come to the place of repentance & faith.*

Make a list of any other concerns that you think are important as you contemplate sharing the gospel with others.

William Carper

"The saints who advance on their knees need not retreat."

Knowing the Core Information

Knowing that successful evangelism is "all about God" does not relieve us of our obligation to be obedient to our calling as messengers of the good news.

---

2 Corinthians 5:17-20

Therefore, if anyone is in Christ, he is a new creation. The old has passed away; behold, the new has come. All this is from God, who through Christ reconciled us to himself and gave us the ministry of reconciliation; that is, in Christ God was reconciling the world to himself, not counting their trespasses against them, and entrusting to us the message of reconciliation. Therefore, we are ambassadors for Christ, God making his appeal through us. We implore you on behalf of Christ, be reconciled to God.

If we have been given the "message of reconciliation" we ought to be sure that we know it well. Though the gospel seems to be presented in countless ways, there is really only one gospel message. Some presentations claim to package the gospel but don't deliver. Sometimes the biblical message of salvation can be obscured and even lost completely in a method. Though methods are important

198

CHAPTER 9

SHARING THE GOSPEL WITH PEOPLE WHO NEED IT

and it is good to learn one, we must always remember that the message should stand out clearly! Review the following outline from chapter one.

The Gospel Message

1. The Background
   - *God is our Creator* (Genesis 1:1)
   - *God is Holy* (1 Peter 1:15-16)
   - *God is Just* (2 Thessalonians 1:8-9)
   - *God is Loving* (1 John 4:8)

2. The Bad News
   - *We are Sinful and Separated from God* (Isaiah 59:2)
   - *We Deserve God's Punishment* (Ephesians 2:3)

3. The Good News
   - *Jesus is God* (Philippians 2:6-7)
   - *He Lived and Died as Our Substitute* (2 Corinthians 5:21)
   - *He Conquered Death for Us* (1 Corinthians 15:17-18)

Deeper Study...
Survey the beliefs of the groups that distort or deny some element of the message of the gospel. Choose to survey those groups that individuals on your lists (from pages 195 & 196) are involved in or influenced by.

The message of the gospel can be rightly understood, but understanding the good news is not enough. One must rightly respond to the gospel. Review the required response to the gospel as explained in chapter one.

Two Elements of the Biblical Response to the Gospel

1. REPENTANCE (Acts 20:21)
   - *To repent is to turn from your sin – ending a life lived for yourself and by your standards. (2 Corinthians 5:15)*
   - *To repent is to turn to God – beginning a life of living for God and by his standards. (1 Thessalonians 1:9)*

2. FAITH (Acts 20:21)
   - *To have faith in Christ is to trust in his righteousness and not your own to make you right with God. (Philippians 3:9)*
   - *To have faith in Christ is to trust in his payment for your sins on the cross to make you right with God. (1Cor.15:2-3)*

FYI...
If these summary statements are unclear to you, be sure and review their explanations and biblical support found in chapter one.

The message of the gospel and its necessary response must clearly come through in any proclamation or presentation of the gospel. Make sure you understand and can communicate each part of the above information before you move on to learning a method of presenting it.

199

PARTNERS:
ONE-ON-ONE DISCIPLESHIP

Learning a Method

There are several methods enlisted to present the biblical information listed. You may already know and use one. In the Partners program we ask that you learn the following method, not because it is necessarily the best, but primarily so that you can pass it on to others in this spiritual growth program.

The Umbrella Illustration

The umbrella illustration is designed to communicate the core message of salvation through an analogy that people can easily understand. The umbrella diagram is designed to be simple enough for you to draw yourself when sharing the gospel with others. It can prove to be a helpful visual aid in showing people's need for forgiveness and God's gracious provision through Jesus Christ. Remember that the illustration and diagram are only supplements for a thorough explanation of each element of the gospel message which we will cover on the pages to follow. If you can draw the basic elements below, then you can effectively use the umbrella illustration when sharing the good news!

CHAPTER 9
SHARING THE GOSPEL WITH PEOPLE WHO NEED IT

Talking Through the Umbrella Illustration

Step 1: Draw these first two elements (the cloud with the word "God" in the middle of it and the stick figures) and explain…

"The first verse of the Bible says, 'In the beginning, God created the heavens and the earth.' (*Genesis 1:1*). The Bible teaches that God created everything that is, including you and me. The implications of this truth are huge. If God made us, then he is ultimately in charge! He owns us and we are responsible to him. He retains full rights over us as the Designer and Creator of human life."

[As you discuss the fact that God is our Creator, write the word "Creator" next to the word "God."]

"The Bible tells us that people were created in God's image to enjoy a perfect relationship with him and with each other. God intended and designed the ultimate in quality and quantity of life for the people he had made. Part of this ultimate relationship between God and his people included his desire to have men and women choose to love and serve him for who he is willingly and freely."

When talking about the implications of God being our Creator, you may have a few illustrations of your own. Ownership has a variety of implications that are a key in realizing why the "God issue" must be addressed by everyone!

When talking about God creating people be sure to emphasize the goodness of God! Recall in your own mind the early chapters of Genesis where God gives Adam and Eve every possible advantage – a perfect world, perfect health, perfect relationships, etc. Remember his kindness in desperately wanting them to do right.

FYI…
Throughout this gospel presentation there are questions that may come up that require a thoughtful answer (this is what is meant when the term "apologetics" is used). The first apologetics topic raised is in regards to our origins. See the 'Resources and Further Study' page at the end of chapter 1 for help on the evolution & creation debate.

201

PARTNERS:

ONE-ON-ONE DISCIPLESHIP

Step 2: Write the words "holy" and "sin" in their appropriate places and explain…

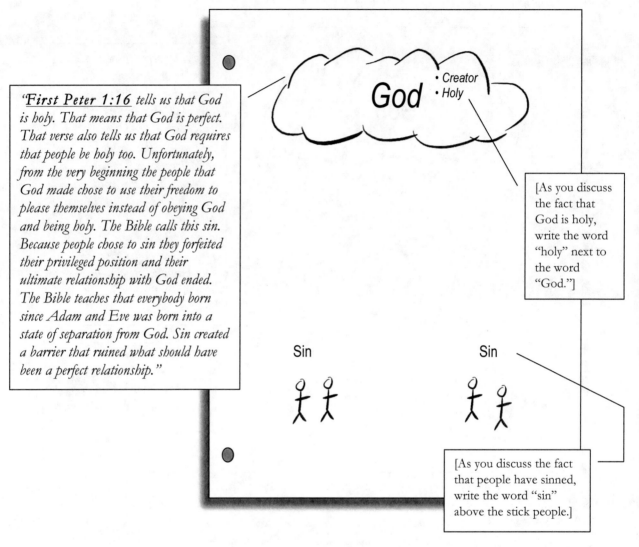

"First Peter 1:16 tells us that God is holy. That means that God is perfect. That verse also tells us that God requires that people be holy too. Unfortunately, from the very beginning the people that God made chose to use their freedom to please themselves instead of obeying God and being holy. The Bible calls this sin. Because people chose to sin they forfeited their privileged position and their ultimate relationship with God ended. The Bible teaches that everybody born since Adam and Eve was born into a state of separation from God. Sin created a barrier that ruined what should have been a perfect relationship."

[As you discuss the fact that God is holy, write the word "holy" next to the word "God."]

[As you discuss the fact that people have sinned, write the word "sin" above the stick people.]

Often it is helpful to actually show the person the verses you are talking about (the verses that are underlined). It is excellent if you commit them to memory! At least know the gist of each verse and where it is found. That way you will not be dependent on this manual or anything else when you use this method of evangelism.

When discussing the problem of sin, a helpful verse listed in the outline of the gospel information is Isaiah 59:2. You might want to utilize the wording of this passage in explaining the separation that sin caused.

It is important to make the distinction between Adam's sinful act that led to separation and our sinful acts that stem from a state of separation. Though our choices confirm Adam's choice, his sin was quite different from ours (see Romans 5:12-19 as well as chapter one of the Partner's manual for more information). This is important, as Romans 5:12-19 says, because Christ's righteousness is imputed to us in the same way as Adam's sin was imputed to us.

CHAPTER 9
SHARING THE GOSPEL WITH PEOPLE WHO NEED IT

Step 3: Write the word "just" in the appropriate place and draw what looks like rain coming from the cloud while continuing your explanation…

This may seem an uncomfortable part of the gospel presentation. Few people like talking about or hearing about "hell" and "God's wrath," but they are essential elements of the gospel. The good news will mean little, if the bad news is not made crystal clear.

Don't be ashamed of sharing the bad news. The pattern of New Testament evangelism that God left for us to study in the book of Acts focuses hard on the sobering reality of what our sins will cost us if we don't "get saved"!

As mentioned in the talk-through, God's kindness prevails for now. His patience and grace prior to his day of judgment should not lull us into believing that God will go easy on sin; it should, as Romans 2:4 says, lead people to repentance (see also 2 Peter 3:9).

PARTNERS:
ONE-ON-ONE DISCIPLESHIP

Step 4: Write the word "loving" in the appropriate place and draw an umbrella labeling it "Jesus" while continuing your explanation…

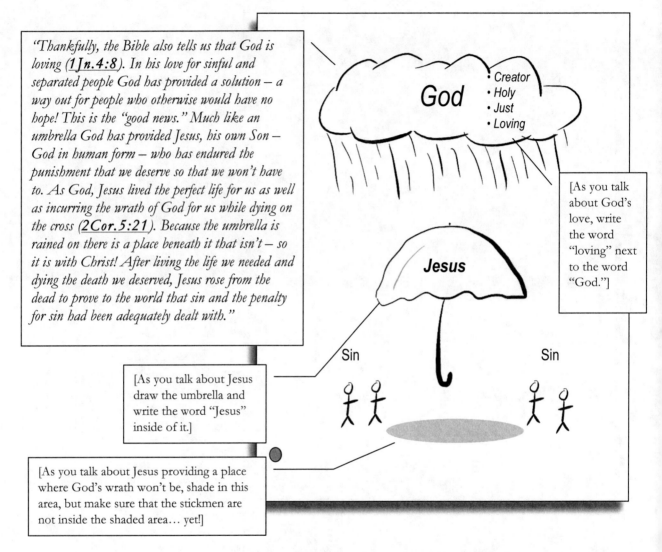

*"Thankfully, the Bible also tells us that God is loving (**1Jn.4:8**). In his love for sinful and separated people God has provided a solution – a way out for people who otherwise would have no hope! This is the "good news." Much like an umbrella God has provided Jesus, his own Son – God in human form – who has endured the punishment that we deserve so that we won't have to. As God, Jesus lived the perfect life for us as well as incurring the wrath of God for us while dying on the cross (**2Cor.5:21**). Because the umbrella is rained on there is a place beneath it that isn't – so it is with Christ! After living the life we needed and dying the death we deserved, Jesus rose from the dead to prove to the world that sin and the penalty for sin had been adequately dealt with."*

[As you talk about God's love, write the word "loving" next to the word "God."]

[As you talk about Jesus draw the umbrella and write the word "Jesus" inside of it.]

[As you talk about Jesus providing a place where God's wrath won't be, shade in this area, but make sure that the stickmen are not inside the shaded area… yet!]

This is the heart of the good news—God's solution! Don't be afraid to spend a good percentage of your time on this step. Make sure you adequately explain: 1) who Jesus is; 2) that Jesus served as our substitute in his life and his death; and 3) that Jesus rose again as a testimony to his completed work on our behalf.

In underscoring God's incredible love it can be helpful (if you have any artistic skill at all) to draw an arm coming out of the cloud holding the umbrella as a shelter from his wrath. Whether you can do this or not, just make sure you give God the credit he deserves for loving sinners enough to provide us with such a costly solution for our sins!

If any of the concepts in this step are unclear to you refer to the longer explanations in chapter one of this manual.

CHAPTER 9
SHARING THE GOSPEL WITH PEOPLE WHO NEED IT

Step 5: Draw an arrow and another stickman that is clearly in the shelter of the umbrella! Write the words "repentance & faith" above the arrow and explain…

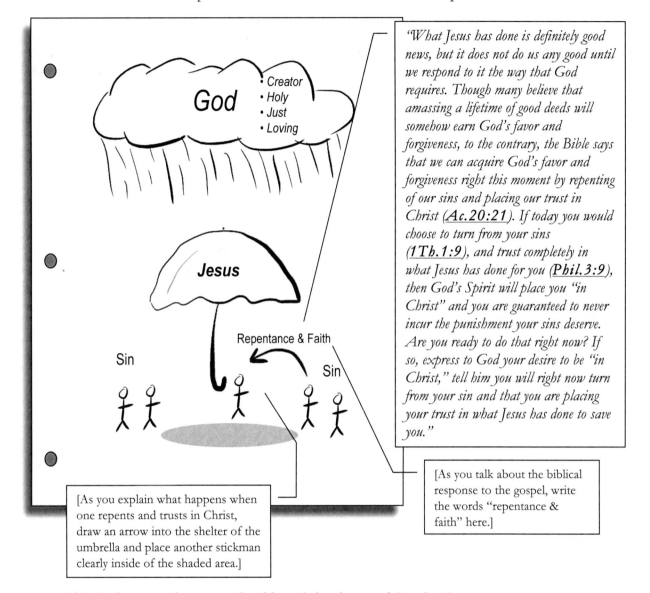

"What Jesus has done is definitely good news, but it does not do us any good until we respond to it the way that God requires. Though many believe that amassing a lifetime of good deeds will somehow earn God's favor and forgiveness, to the contrary, the Bible says that we can acquire God's favor and forgiveness right this moment by repenting of our sins and placing our trust in Christ (Ac.20:21). If today you would choose to turn from your sins (1Th.1:9), and trust completely in what Jesus has done for you (Phil.3:9), then God's Spirit will place you "in Christ" and you are guaranteed to never incur the punishment your sins deserve. Are you ready to do that right now? If so, express to God your desire to be "in Christ," tell him you will right now turn from your sin and that you are placing your trust in what Jesus has done to save you."

[As you explain what happens when one repents and trusts in Christ, draw an arrow into the shelter of the umbrella and place another stickman clearly inside of the shaded area.]

[As you talk about the biblical response to the gospel, write the words "repentance & faith" here.]

This is the step where you should work hard to explain what it means to "repent" and place "faith" in Jesus. Use synonyms like "turning" and "trusting" to get the point across. Be sure and clarify that the "sin" we turn from is our whole life apart from Christ. Drive home the fact that repentance involves a brand new life orientation (see 2 Corinthians 5:15). Be certain that there is a clear understanding that when we trust in Christ to save us, we are called to trust in Christ *alone* (see again Philippians 3:9). As you conclude your explanation of the gospel you should state that genuine repentance and faith will initiate a new relationship with God's Spirit, and this will not leave a person unchanged – and that change will last for the rest of one's life!

Don't end your conversation without clearly asking the person to make the right response! Don't be shy at this point (see 2 Corinthians 5:20)!

PARTNERS:
ONE-ON-ONE DISCIPLESHIP

Adding Your Story

We must always present the gospel objectively. The facts of the gospel are true regardless of what people think about them or what kind of experience people have had with them. That is the nature of absolute truth—it is unaffected by people's subjective experience. But once it is understood that a "testimony" is not the gospel then you are more apt to appropriately use your story to enhance and supplement your presentation of the gospel.

Remember that too much emphasis on your testimony and too little emphasis on the gospel facts can lead to the person you are sharing with saying, *"Well, that's nice for you."* Though sometimes this is a cop-out, often it is the natural response of one who has heard a half-hour of *"It really helped me."*

Think through your testimony and be ready to share it in those situations when you sense that your story can help the person see "how it is done", or relieve suspicions that Christianity is too weird. Write out your testimony below in a way that you might share it after you have carefully explained the gospel facts in the umbrella illustration.

CHAPTER 9
SHARING THE GOSPEL WITH PEOPLE WHO NEED IT

A Few Pointers

Here are a few practical suggestions that may help when sharing the gospel using the umbrella diagram.

- *Don't worry so much about how you will transition into using the umbrella illustration, it doesn't have to be smooth. Something as simple as, "...I am a Christian and I have a simple diagram that helps explain what that means. May I draw it for you?"*

- *Don't worry about drawing the diagram perfectly. It's okay if your drawing is crude — your words are more important than the looks of your paper.*

- *Don't be concerned about finding a perfect piece of paper. This diagram can be effectively shared on a napkin, on the back of a business card, or on the blank space in a newspaper ad.*

- *When you are finished, give the diagram to the person to keep and jot your phone number down on it if they don't already have your number memorized.*

- *Try to prepare the setting for sharing the gospel. Find a conducive environment whenever possible. Sharing this life saving message can be a real spiritual battle. If there is a baby around, he will cry. If there is a dog in the house, it will bark. If there is a flight attendant on the plane, he or she will come calling at just the wrong moment. Some things you can't prepare and control, but those you can, do!*

- *Give the person an opportunity to talk and interact with what you are sharing. Don't be afraid of questions and objections. If you can't answer them, then you have a homework assignment; if they can't be answered, then we all should stop kidding ourselves and bail out.*

- *Don't force or pressure anyone into prolonging the conversation. If they clearly reject the message and want to stop talking, then at least you have done your job in attempting to share this important message. Surely there are others in your sphere of influence that God is preparing and who would be interested in hearing God's message of grace and salvation.*

- *If you happen to be sharing the gospel alongside another Christian (perhaps your Partner) make sure that when one Christian is talking the other Christian is praying. While the conversation is going on ask God to open ears, eyes, and hearts.*

- *If your presentation of the gospel brings up other important issues that lead to lengthy discussions, don't be afraid of this simple presentation lasting over a period of several meetings. Agree on a time to meet again so that you can continue through to the rest of the diagram.*

- *Relax! Try not to be nervous. Though many Christians have given their lives for this message, most of us won't have to. The embarrassment it may cost if someone rejects our message is a small price tag for accurately representing Christ and his gospel in our society.*

What other suggestions might you add to this list?

PARTNERS:
ONE-ON-ONE DISCIPLESHIP

A Final Word on Fear

Sharing the gospel with people who need it can produce in you a wide range of emotions—the most likely being fear. Though fear has thwarted countless evangelistic opportunities, it shouldn't. Make a resolve right now that you will not let fear stop you.

The gospel is God's truth! Remember that one plus God is always the majority! Take courage and note this interesting verse.

> **2 Corinthians 13:8**
>
> For we cannot do anything against the truth, but only for the truth.

Remember that there is only one way to share the truth of the gospel!

> **Ephesians 6:19-20**
>
> [Pray] also for me, that words may be given to me in opening my mouth boldly to proclaim the mystery of the gospel, for which I am an ambassador in chains, that I may declare it boldly, as I ought to speak.

Take your cue from Paul and begin to pray, and ask others to pray for you, that you will boldly and fearlessly proclaim the gospel as it ought to be proclaimed.

Write out a prayer in your own words asking God for courage and committing yourself to the task of courageous evangelism!

With Your Partner...
Make an appointment this week to share the gospel together. Make an appointment with someone on someone's list or with a visitor to your church.

Finally, make it a plan this week, and a lifestyle each week from now on, to share the gospel with someone who needs to hear it. You might want to start with someone on your list from pages 195 and 196. If you are stumped on who to start with, ask your Partner. Often there are people that visit your church that are interested in hearing what Christianity is really all about.

CHAPTER 9
SHARING THE GOSPEL WITH PEOPLE WHO NEED IT

Notes

PARTNERS:
ONE-ON-ONE DISCIPLESHIP

Notes

RESOURCES & FURTHER STUDY

Sharing the Gospel with People Who Need It

> Rating Key
> ★ Helpful (four being most)
> ⊙ Difficulty (four being hardest)

Resources on the Gospel Message

See the Chapter 1 *Resources & Further Study* Page (page 21).

Resources on Sharing the Gospel

★★ ⊙⊙ Aldrich, Joseph C. *Life-Style Evangelism: Learning to Open Your Life to Those Around You.* Portland, OR: Multnomah Press, 1978. (This popular work focuses on how to make the subject of Jesus Christ a more natural and common topic in your conversation with friends and coworkers.)

★★★★ ⊙⊙⊙ Carson, D. A. *The Gagging of God: Christianity Confronts Pluralism.* Grand Rapids, MI: Zondervan Press, 1996. (In this book Carson skillfully analyzes the challenge of presenting the gospel in our postmodern society.)

★★★ ⊙⊙ Coleman, Robert E. *The Master Plan of Evangelism.* Berkshire, UK: Spire Books, 1963. (While not a "how to" evangelism book, Coleman certainly succeeds in motivating us to "fish for men" as he traces the method of Christ.)

★★★ ⊙ Dever, Mark. *The Gospel and Personal Evangelism.* Wheaton, IL: Crossway Books, 2007. (Dever provides an engaging and readable title that discusses the what, why, and how of personal evangelism.)

★★ ⊙ Downs, Tim. *Finding Common Ground: How to Communicate with Those Outside the Christian Community... While We Still Can.* Chicago, IL: Moody Press, 1999. (Starting with the parable of the sower, Downs provides a variety of strategies to build conversational bridges to cast the seed of the gospel.)

★★★ ⊙ Gudernson, Dennis. *Your Child's Profession of Faith.* Amityville, NY: Calvary Press, 1990. (This helpful little book provides parents an appropriate vigilance when comparing the gospel's conviction versus a child's desire to please his or her parents.)

★★ ⊙ Hendricks, Howard G. *Don't Fake It... Say It With Love.* Wheaton, IL: Victor Books, 1981. (This out-of-print book may be worth tracking down because of the engaging way Hendricks motivates and encourages Christians to sincerely and compassionately approach evangelism.)

★★ ⊙ Hybles, Bill and Mark Mittelberg. *Becoming a Contagious Christian.* Grand Rapids, MI: Zondervan Press, 1994. (This popular work may not be theologically deep, but it has provided many with practical ideas and suggestions for strategically turning conversations to Christ.)

★★ ⊙⊙ Jeffery, Peter. *How Shall They Hear? Church-Based Evangelism.* Darlington, UK: Evangelical Press, 1997. (Jeffery sympathizes with the problem we face in sharing the gospel in a modern culture, but seeks to motivate us with the privilege and responsibility which God has given us as his ambassadors.)

★★★ ⊙⊙ Little, Paul E. *How To Give Away Your Faith.* Downers Grove, IL: InterVarsity Press, 1966. (In this classic little book, Little covers a helpful variety of topics related to the task of presenting the gospel.)

211

**** Metzger, Will. *Tell The Truth.* Downers Grove, IL: InterVarsity Press, 1984. (This book not only
◎◎ highlights the "God-centered gospel" versus a "man-centered gospel" as was referenced in chapter one, but Metzger also provides some very practical tips on sharing the biblical gospel in everyday settings.)

*** Peterson, Jim. *Living Proof: Sharing the Gospel Naturally.* Colorado Springs, CO: 1989. (This work
◎ combines two previous books on evangelism by Peterson, addressing a number of topics related to sharing the message of Christ authentically and authoritatively.)

* Posterski, Don. *Why Am I Afraid To Tell You I'm a Christian?* Downers Grove, IL: InterVarsity
◎ Press, 1983. (This simple little book is out of print, but may be worth finding and provides just the encouragement you need if you are dealing with fear when sharing the gospel.)

*** Spurgeon, Charles Haddon. *The Soul Winner: Or How to Lead Sinners to the Savior.* Reprint. New
◎◎ Kensington, PA: Whitaker House, 1995. (In this classic reprint, Spurgeon, in his inimitable way, motivates Christians to urgently present the gospel of Jesus Christ to lost men and women.)

Resources on Apologetics (Defending the Gospel)

*** Craig, William Lane. *Reasonable Faith: Christian Truth & Apologetics (Third Edition).* Wheaton, IL:
◎◎◎ Crossway Books, 2008. (This book provides a well-reasoned and ordered defense of Christianity from a popular and respected apologist of our day.)

*** Geisler, Norman. *Baker Encyclopedia of Christian Apologetics.* Grand Rapids, MI: Baker Books,
◎◎ 1999. (Geisler has assembled an alphabetic reference tool to quickly locate articles on a variety of topics related to defending the faith.)

*** Habermas, Gary and Michael Licona. *The Case for the Resurrection of Jesus.* Grand Rapids, MI:
◎◎ Kregel Books, 2004. (Habermas and Licona skillfully work to reveal the historical veracity of the most validating event in history – the bodily resurrection of Christ.)

** Lewis, Gordon R. *Testing Christianity's Truth Claims.* Chicago, IL: Moody Press, 1976. (Lewis
◎◎ examines philosophical methods and their interface with the truth claims of Christianity.)

*** MacArthur, John. *Nothing But the Truth: Upholding the Gospel in a Doubting Age.* Wheaton, IL:
◎ Crossway Books, 1999. (This is a straightforward and readable book intended to equip Christians to uphold important Christian truths, which are an increasing target of attack in our society.)

** McGrath, Alister. *Intellectuals Don't Need God & Other Modern Myths.* Grand Rapids, MI:
◎◎◎ Zondervan Press, 1993. (As an academic who is comfortable interacting with the intellectual elite of our day, McGrath broadly and creatively reacts to a variety of objections raised by modern intellectuals.)

** Ramm, Bernard. *Protestant Christian Evidences.* Grand Rapids, MI: Eerdmans Press, 1954. (This
◎◎ older work is a forthright and an organized look at the evidence for the Christian faith.)

*** Schaeffer, Francis. *The God Who is There: Speaking Historic Christianity into the 20th Century.* Downers
◎◎◎ Grove, IL: InterVarsity Press, 1968. (If you have never read Schaeffer this is a good place to start as he examines and discusses God, philosophy, art and culture, all with an apologetic bent.)

*** Wilson, Bill, ed. *A Ready Defense: The Best of Josh McDowell.* Nashville, TN: Thomas Nelson, 1993.
◎◎ (This is a useful and accessible reference work which compiles and condenses the popular apologetic writings of Josh McDowell on such topics as archeology, the resurrection of Christ, the cults and world religions.)

Chapter 10

PARTNERS MEETING #10

Living a Holy Life in an Unholy World

At Partners Meeting #10...

You will discuss the problems and the solutions that surround our calling to be godly people in an ungodly world. Use this chapter to set up accountability with your partner that will outlast this program!

To Prepare for Partners Meeting #10...

- Read chapter 10 and answer the questions.

- Think through the temptations you face that are seeking to derail your pursuit of holiness. Be ready to discuss how this chapter applies to those struggles.

- Bring something to the meeting that expresses your love and appreciation for the person you have partnered with throughout this program.

- If any of the "Deeper Study" topics are of interest to you, prepare to discuss them.

- Memorize Titus 2:11-12.

> For the grace of God has appeared, bringing salvation for all people, training us to renounce ungodliness and worldly passions, and to live self-controlled, upright and godly lives in the present age.
>
> – Titus 2:11-12

PARTNERS:

ONE-ON-ONE DISCIPLESHIP

One of the most challenging things about Christianity is the call to live a godly life in the midst of an ungodly world. Although this is not easy, denying sin and vigorously pursuing a holy lifestyle should be a top priority for those who bear the name of Christ.

> **Titus 2:11-12**
>
> For the grace of God has appeared, bringing salvation for all people, training us to renounce ungodliness and worldly passions, and to live self-controlled, upright and godly lives in the present age,

A Critical Reminder

It is important to keep in mind that our pursuit of a holy life is never to be something we do in order to earn or in any way merit the acceptance of God. God tells us that his love and acceptance are granted to us because of what Christ has done on our behalf. Jesus' righteous life and Jesus' substitutionary death on the cross earned our place in his family.

> **Titus 3:5-7**
>
> ...he saved us, not because of works done by us in righteousness, but according to his own mercy, by the washing of regeneration and renewal of the Holy Spirit, whom he poured out on us richly through Jesus Christ our Savior, so that being justified by his grace we might become heirs according to the hope of eternal life.

With Your Partner...

Discuss some of the ways we can subtly fall into the trap of "doing good" in order to win God's love or acceptance.

Your pursuit of a righteous life should always be understood as a response to his grace, never as a means to acquire it.

Describe some of the practical differences between living a righteous life in order to gain God's love versus living a righteous life in response to God's love.

Deeper Study...

Survey the book of Galatians and identify some modern-day religious groups which claim to be evangelical but have crossed the critical line of trying to be "justified" by their works.

214

CHAPTER 10

LIVING A HOLY LIFE IN AN UNHOLY WORLD

Though our good works do not in any way earn our salvation, they are always to be a byproduct of it. When the Bible presents God's grace it is often followed by a clear statement about our calling to vigorously pursue a righteous life. Note this connection in *Titus 2:11-12* and *Ephesians 2:8-10*.

In light of verses like these, how would you respond to someone who would say that righteous living or "good works" are not important in the Christian life?

With Your Partner...
Discuss with your partner some of the negative ramifications of Christians who claim to follow a righteous God but fail to pursue righteousness in their own lives.

Deeper Study...
Study the history of antinomianism in ancient and modern church history.

The Standard

The Bible tells us that God himself is to be our moral standard.

> **1 Peter 1:15-16**
>
> but as he who called you is holy, you also be holy in all your conduct, since it is written, "You shall be holy, for I am holy.

Deeper Study...
Do a word study on the usage of the Greek words hagios *and* teleios *in the New Testament.*

> **Matthew 5:48**
>
> "You therefore must be perfect, as your heavenly Father is perfect."

As we learned in chapter 2, there are certain attributes of God that he does not share with those he creates. His non-shared attributes are true statements about our transcendent God that set him apart from all other creatures. His non-shared attributes obviously cannot become a pattern for human behavior. But the other attributes of God that reflect his moral nature – those that were perfectly demonstrated by the life of Jesus Christ – are to be our template for godly living.

With Your Partner...
Give examples of the "non-shared" attributes of God. See chapter two for help.

Because God is perfect and because he is our Creator, it should be obvious that he is in the position to make the rules regarding how his creatures ought to live. Unfortunately, many people don't think so. Today, it is popular to think that each person can make up his or her own mind as to how they should live. These days "choice" and "alternative" are buzz words that characterize much of the discussion regarding moral issues. These words show that this kind of flawed thinking is pervasive in our modern society.

PARTNERS:
ONE-ON-ONE DISCIPLESHIP

With Your Partner...
Discuss with your partner the problem of "moral relativism." Talk about the logical connection between the abandonment of "moral absolutes" and the cultural acceptance of a variety of moral sins. Dialog about how this one shift from absolutes to relativism has necessarily increased the tolerance of behavior in society that God abhors and will one day judge.

Read *Judges 17:6*. In what way is our culture a reflection of the one described in that passage?

Deeper Study...
Explore some of the resources listed at the end of the chapter regarding pluralism, relativism and post-modernism.

God's Clear Directives

God has not left us guessing as to how his perfect character is to be reflected in our daily behavior. He has given us thousands of clear directives about numerous moral issues he knew we would face in everyday life. We don't have to wonder, for instance, how his attribute of faithfulness is applied to our marriages. He has clearly and concisely instructed us as to what behavior constitutes fidelity in marriage (Exodus 20:14; Matthew 5:28; 1 Thessalonians 4:1-8).

With Your Partner...
Check in with your partner as to your progress and consistency in spending time in the Bible each day. Be accountable as to how well you are doing in practicing the pattern of Bible study you learned in chapter three.

Therefore if we are going to live a holy life that reflects God's character, we must carefully and consistently consult God's word. It is likely that whatever question or temptation we are facing, there is some clear directive that God has already given that will serve to govern our choices.

What were some of the sins that you committed in the early days of your Christian life not knowing that God's word told you to do differently?

Read *James 4:17*. What are some of the clear directives from God's word that you have since discovered and understand, but have had a difficult time obeying?

With Your Partner...
Be brutally honest in sharing this list with your partner. It is the first step in finding the accountability every Christian needs.

216

CHAPTER 10
LIVING A HOLY LIFE IN AN UNHOLY WORLD

Garbage In, Garbage Out

One of the reasons we may find it difficult to obey God's clear directives is because our ears, our eyes and our minds are being bombarded with encouragement to do just the opposite. For instance, the Bible says that we should reflect God's purity by never using words that are vulgar or abrasive (Ephesians 4:29; 5:4) and yet that is much more difficult to do when our ears are constantly fed on profanity and vulgarity.

The Bible admits that removal of *all* unbiblical influences from our lives would require that we be removed from this world (1 Corinthians 5:9-10), which is an option not left to our discretion! But for most Christians, there is a lot of unnecessary garbage willingly invited into their lives. Consider the avenues that so many Christians tolerate that expose them to ideas, images and words that God has expressly forbidden us to participate in.

Deeper Study...
Take a close look at Ephesians 5:1-21 and analyze the way this passage encourages us to reflect God's character instead of the world's. Note how the passage instructs us to interface with our culture (especially vv.11-14).

> **Proverbs 13:20**
>
> Whoever walks with the wise becomes wise, but the companion of fools will suffer harm.

> **1Corinthians 15:33**
>
> Do not be deceived: "Bad company ruins good morals."

With Your Partner...
Discuss with your partner any friendships or associations that you believe may be pulling you away from an obedient walk with Christ.

Many of these unbiblical and unnecessary influences come to us through our choice of friends, the things we read or watch, the places where we spend our time, and the forms of entertainment we choose. Christians must be very selective about what we allow into our lives.

> **Proverbs 4:23**
>
> Keep your heart with all vigilance, for from it flow the springs of life.

What are some of the avenues that bring the wrong thoughts or ideas into your heart and mind? Which of these are unnecessary and could easily be extracted or modified to reduce the unbiblical influences in your life?

With Your Partner...
Discuss how these preventative measures could mistakenly become an end in themselves. In other words, how could these important steps to filter your intake become an unhealthy emphasis and sole focus of your Christian life?

217

PARTNERS:
ONE-ON-ONE DISCIPLESHIP

The "Gray Areas"

There is a lot of talk about "gray areas" in the Christian life. "Gray areas" are popularly defined as those activities that God has supposedly left us without any direction. However, before someone claims to have discovered one of these plentiful "gray zones," he or she must be certain that God's word does not address the issues involved. In other words, one must be sure that an exhaustive study of God's word has been conducted and that there are no explicit directives or implicit principles that can be rightly applied to the activity in question. We might imagine that if we really did such a study, we would find that God has not left us in the dark (or even in the shadows) about too many moral or ethical issues.

What are some of the activities you have heard Christians classify as "gray areas"?

With Your Partner...
Share your list of "gray areas" with your partner. Write down any areas your partner had that you didn't or any new ones you can think of together.

Working to find the righteous path through a "gray area" can prove to be a helpful roadmap which can be applied to just about any moral or ethical dilemma. In addition to the "gray area" activities you listed above, list any moral or ethical crossroads you are facing or may face in the future.

Pick any two issues from the lists above and track your answers to each of the following nine questions. Each of these questions is derived from God's word and can be applied to just about any "gray area" or "moral dilemma" Christians face. Which two will you track?

218

CHAPTER 10
LIVING A HOLY LIFE IN AN UNHOLY WORLD

1. Are there any biblical passages that relate to the issue?

Psalm 119:105

Your word is a lamp to my feet and a light to my path.

It is difficult to overestimate the importance of searching the Bible and not just your memory banks about the Bible to see if there is any explicit or implicit statements that relate to the issue in question. If you are unsure, consult a concordance or topical Bible.

Remember that the passages you are looking for may not directly refer to the issue you are researching, but may prove to be extremely important in deciding whether or not it is appropriate for you as a Christian to participate in the activity. For instance, some may consider abortion a "gray area" because a search of the Bible yields no discovery of the word or a clear reference. Yet a search of "related passages" that deal with the dignity and sanctity of life prior to birth, shed a great deal of light on the abortion issue (e.g., Psalm 139:13-16; Jeremiah 1:5; 20:17, etc.).

Issue #1   Issue #2

FYI...
Check the Resources and Further Study page at the end of this chapter for tools that can help you locate a particular topic or theme in the Bible.

PARTNERS:

ONE-ON-ONE DISCIPLESHIP

2. Can you "glorify" God in it?

> **1 Corinthians 10:31**
>
> So, whether you eat or drink, or whatever you do, do it all to the glory of God.

When considering if an activity is compatible with the Christian life it is important to ask whether or not you can honestly say that you are able to "glorify God" while doing it. Simply put, to glorify God is to *promote him* or to *make him look good*. Don't make the mistake of thinking that you can only promote him or make him look good while doing things like praying, preaching or evangelizing.

First Corinthians 10:31 makes it clear that you should be able to "glorify" God even when you eat. So carefully think through the "gray areas" while asking the question "Will I be putting God in a good light by being involved in this?" Briefly describe how you are able, or not able, to make God look good by your participation or association with the two things you have chosen to take a closer look at.

Issue #1   Issue #2

220

CHAPTER 10
LIVING A HOLY LIFE IN AN UNHOLY WORLD

3. Would Jesus do it?

> **1 John 2:6**
>
> whoever says he abides in him ought to walk in the same way in which he walked.

The Bible has always held Christ up as the standard for Christian living. The diagnostic question "What would Jesus do in this situation?" is not a modern invention. Of course, to know what Jesus would do, you must be a good student of what Jesus actually did. Understanding the patterns and principles of Christ's life are essential for thinking through this question carefully. Remember that this question seeks to explore the values of Christ in a given situation and not the precise actions of Christ.

The Apostle John is not suggesting that Christians replicate the details of Christ's life. The Bible is not asking us to speak to our associates in an ancient language, travel through Galilee, wear sandals, or be crucified on a cross outside of Jerusalem. But the Bible is telling us that the attitudes, values and principles that governed the daily activities of Jesus' life govern ours as well. Considering our questionable issues, we ought to be asking, "Is this something that would fit into the values and priorities of Christ's life?"

Deeper Study...
Explore the idea of "what would Jesus do?" in the classic 1896 book In His Steps *by Charles Sheldon. Consider how Sheldon's theological slant both challenges the modern evangelical and at the same time misses the primary thrust of Jesus' purpose in coming to earth. What can you learn from this book and what errors do you see that should be avoided when answering the question "What would Jesus do?"*

Issue #1   Issue #2

PARTNERS:
ONE-ON-ONE DISCIPLESHIP

4. Would you like to be found doing it when Jesus returns?

1 John 2:28

And now, little children, abide in him, so that when he appears we may have confidence and not shrink from him in shame at his coming.

A continual anticipation of the return of Christ is frequently presented in Scripture as a motivation for doing what is right. Whether it is an urgency in sharing the gospel or the wise evaluation of what is important, thinking about the sudden appearing of Jesus is helpful in almost every aspect of Christian living. Consider the two "gray areas" you have chosen to evaluate and give some thought as to how "confident" and "unashamed" you would be if you were engaged in those activities as Christ breaks through the clouds to gather his people.

Issue #1   Issue #2

CHAPTER 10
LIVING A HOLY LIFE IN AN UNHOLY WORLD

5. How would you feel if your pastor knew you were doing it?

> **Hebrews 4:13**
>
> And no creature is hidden from his sight, but all are naked and exposed to the eyes of him to whom we must give account.

Most Christians attend a church which is led by spiritual leaders they respect. They generally believe that their pastors are godly men who disapprove of compromise. Of course pastors are sinful people too, but sometimes it is helpful to imagine the name and face of a person you regard as godly and consider his or her reaction to your participation in that particular "gray area." If you would feel awkward letting your pastor know what you are doing, then perhaps you should reconsider whether or not God's standards are lower than your pastor's.

Consider the beliefs that exist in the person who would hide his actions from a "godly person" and yet live, as we all do, before a holy God who clearly and plainly sees everything we do.

How does this test affect your view of the two moral dilemmas or questionable activities?

With Your Partner...
Discuss creative ways to "practice the presence of God" in your daily life. How can you always be vigilant concerning the fact that your life is lived out before a God who perceives all we do and think.

Issue #1   Issue #2

PARTNERS:
ONE-ON-ONE DISCIPLESHIP

6. Could you wear a T-shirt that reads "I am a Christian" without being ashamed?

Colossians 1:10

walk in a manner worthy of the Lord, fully pleasing to him, bearing fruit in every good work and increasing in the knowledge of God.

When thinking through the questionable issues of life you must never forget who you represent. Christians bear the name of Christ and should always strive to be good representatives of that name. Your involvements and associations should not make you cower at the thought of being exposed as a Christian. How would wearing a "I am a Christian" T-shirt change your perspective regarding the two issues?

Issue #1   Issue #2

CHAPTER 10
LIVING A HOLY LIFE IN AN UNHOLY WORLD

7. Would your actions confuse a young Christian?

> **Romans 14:13b, 15**
>
> decide never to put a stumbling block or hindrance in the way of a brother... For if your brother is grieved by what you eat, you are no longer walking in love. By what you eat, do not destroy the one for whom Christ died.

The Bible calls us to lovingly consider the impact of our actions on other Christians – especially those who are "weaker" or younger in Christ. The "distress" Paul is talking about in Romans 14 is more than just a violation of someone's personal preferences; rather the concern is that a younger Christian will be emboldened to violate his or her conscience. In other words, the question we should be asking is, "Will my participation in this activity lead a younger Christian to follow, and in so doing, will that Christian later feel guilty for having participated in my questionable activity?" We must give extreme care in living our Christian lives knowing that younger Christians are always watching.

What effect do you think your actions would have on a younger Christian if you were involved in these two issues?

Issue #1   Issue #2

PARTNERS:
ONE-ON-ONE DISCIPLESHIP

8. Would your actions confuse a non-Christian?

> **Titus 2:10b**
>
> ...but showing all good faith, so that in everything they may adorn the doctrine of God our Savior.

With Your Partner...

Identify and discuss with your partner the non-Christians in your daily environment who are observing your moral choices. Discuss the high stakes of living out our Christian lives before a watching world.

It is not just young Christians who will be impacted by your moral choices, non-Christians will be as well. By your behavior the world will either see more of Christ's character or less. The context of Titus 2:10 is encouraging Christians to live exemplary lives before the watching world. The Bible tells you that the Christian's actions will either make his words (i.e., "the teaching about God") more attractive or less. You should be very concerned that you have a godly set of Christian actions to accompany your words about Christ. Consider the two issues in question as to whether or not there would be any hint of contradiction in the minds of the non-Christians who are watching your life.

Issue #1   Issue #2

226

CHAPTER 10
LIVING A HOLY LIFE IN AN UNHOLY WORLD

9. Is there a doubt or conflict within you concerning the matter?

> **Romans 14:23**
>
> But whoever has doubts is condemned if he eats, because the eating is not from faith. For whatever does not proceed from faith is sin.

There is a consistently high regard in the Bible for maintaining a clear conscience. Back in Romans 14, the concern is not only that you not lead someone else to violate their conscience, you yourself must be sure that you never do so either. There should not be any equivocation in your own mind regarding the questionable matter. While a clear conscience by itself does not grant you permission to participate, you should never participate without it. Even if all eight other qualifications have been met, this question reserves the veto power. If any "gray area" impinges on a clear conscience then you must not proceed. To what extent would participation in these two issues leave your conscience clear or stained?

Issue #1   Issue #2

With Your Partner...
Discuss 1 Corinthians 4:4. Explore the reasons why a clear conscience is necessary, but in and of itself does not make our actions or choices right.

Hopefully working through this section of the chapter has helped to clarify what is appropriate and what is inappropriate for the Christian life for the two issues that you examined. Be sure to keep these nine diagnostic questions handy for the next time an issue presents itself as "gray" or questionable. Take the time to subject future ethical dilemmas to these nine questions and see if God doesn't bring clarity and resolve to the difficult issues we inevitably face in the Christian life. Make it your goal to always work to "try to discern what is pleasing to the Lord" (Ephesians 5:10).

PARTNERS:
ONE-ON-ONE DISCIPLESHIP

Your Fight Against Sin

Whether it is an obvious sin or one which has been determined to be sinful by your careful examination, once you know the right thing to do you must purpose to do it whatever the cost (James 4:17). The writer of Hebrews chides the young church for not going to greater lengths in their fight against sin when he writes:

> **Hebrews 12:4**
>
> In your struggle against sin you have not yet resisted to the point of shedding your blood.

This passage is set in the context of recalling Christ's crucifixion who was willing to "endure the cross" to walk in the righteous path that God had set before him (v.2).

Think about your "struggle against sin." How would you describe the effort you are presently expending to live in a manner that pleases God? How does your current "struggle against sin" compare to earlier days in your Christian life?

Of course, victory over sin is ultimately a work of God's empowering Spirit, but as so many passages in the New Testament make clear, *we* are called upon to exert a great deal of *our* energy in the process of relying on him.

Deeper Study...
Examine other passages that reveal both sides (i.e., human and divine) of the Christian's process of sanctification. Note some of the implications of this dual responsibility and the errors and abuses in Christian doctrine when either side is de-emphasized or neglected.

> **Philippians 2:12b-13**
>
> ....work out your own salvation with fear and trembling, for it is God who works in you, both to will and to work for his good pleasure.

In what way have you allowed your determination to wane, or neglected your responsibility to fight sin by overemphasizing the biblical truth that your walk of obedience is "up to the Holy Spirit" to accomplish?

228

CHAPTER 10

LIVING A HOLY LIFE IN AN UNHOLY WORLD

First Corinthians 10:13 is perhaps the single most useful and strengthening verse in the entire Bible when it comes to fighting sin. Notice the great encouragement and perspective that is packed into each phrase of this incredible verse.

> ### 1 Corinthians 10:13
>
> No temptation has overtaken you that is not common to man. God is faithful, and he will not let you be tempted beyond your ability, but with the temptation he will also provide the way of escape, that you may be able to endure it.

Let's examine this verse a phrase at a time, and explore some of the practical implications of each of its four parts.

1. None of Your Temptations are Unique

"No temptation has overtaken you that is not common to man." What a great comfort to know that the temptation to sin that you are facing is nothing new or entirely unique. It is "common" according to the Bible. It is the enemy's strategy to make you think that your situation is unlike any other.

Isolation is one of Satan's great tools in keeping Christians weak and defeated. Isolation starts in our minds when we start believing that no one else can identify with the pressure of our current temptation.

List some of the current temptations you are facing. Be as specific as possible.

With Your Partner...
Share as much of this list with your partner as you can. Discuss the "commonality" of these temptations.

Think about this list in light of other Christians you know. Can you begin to recognize the truth of God's word that even the most secret and unmentionable temptations of your heart are "common" to many other Christians? What does that commonality do to help you gear up to fight it?

229

PARTNERS:

ONE-ON-ONE DISCIPLESHIP

One of the most important implications that grows out of this truth is personal "accountability." Knowing that our sins are not unique can embolden us to share our temptations, as well as the successes and failures we encounter as those temptations come and go.

> **James 5:16**
>
> Therefore, confess your sins to one another and pray for one another, that you may be healed. The prayer of a righteous person has great power as it is working.

God's plan was certainly not for us to isolate ourselves in our fight against sin. His clear instruction is that we help each other and support each other as we progress in our walks with Christ.

Though the benefits are obvious, what is it that concerns you or makes you apprehensive about being regularly accountable with another Christian about your sin and temptations?

With Your Partner...
Make a commitment and share it with your partner regarding personal accountability. Perhaps your partner in this program will be willing to be your accountability partner in the months to come. Much of what you have been doing in this program with your partner (i.e., reciting memorized verses, discussing personal challenges and temptations) has captured the essence of personal accountability. Whoever it is, share your plan to engage in a regular pattern of personal accountability with another Christian.

Many times accountability partners craft a specific list of questions that address the sins that "so easily entangle" (Hebrews 12:1) them. What four or five questions do you think would be helpful if they were asked of you on a weekly basis?

2. God is Perfectly Consistent in Providing You Help

"God is faithful." Thankfully, the God who wants to see us become more like his Son is one who is perfectly consistent. He doesn't change his attitude toward us or his concern that we win in our battle against sin. He is not fickle and never lets us sink into sin without stepping in with the resources promised in the rest of 1 Corinthians 10:13.

230

CHAPTER 10
LIVING A HOLY LIFE IN AN UNHOLY WORLD

What encouragement do you derive from the fact that God is not concerned one day for your sanctification and unconcerned the next? Or furthermore, what strength do you gain from knowing that regardless of what happened yesterday in your fight against sin, today God wants you to win?

This should be a tremendous source of hope for us in the midst of dealing with a tenacious temptation. Again, the enemy, our spiritual "roaring lion" (1 Peter 5:8), likes to capitalize on our hopelessness. He'd love for us to think that if we failed, further sin doesn't really matter. He'd also like us to get our focus on our unfaithfulness instead of God's faithfulness (see 2 Timothy 2:13).

In what way has a lack of hope negatively impacted your fight against sin?

Write out a prayer that reflects your thankfulness for the importance of a God who "is faithful" as you consider your "struggle against sin."

3. Your Temptation is Not Insurmountable

"*He will not let you be tempted beyond your ability,*" Another great truth boldly presented to us in 1 Corinthians 10:13 is that God will not allow any temptation in our lives to be so intense that we *cannot* beat it.

How often are we led to believe the lie that we *cannot* do the right thing because the temptation is so strong that we have no choice but to give in? The Bible is clear that God sovereignly controls the force and power of our temptations and does not ever make obedience impossible.

Describe a situation in which you failed to believe this truth.

With Your Partner...
Be honest in revealing how often you fall in to believing that your temptations are too strong to resist.

231

PARTNERS:
ONE-ON-ONE DISCIPLESHIP

The bottom line is that in the throes of your next battle with temptation, you don't have to sin. As a Christian, you have been given the divine resources to overcome whatever temptation comes your way. You must firmly believe that God has sovereignly limited every temptation that hits your life.

Read *Job 1:12 & 2:6*. Think through the temptations you faced this week. What does it do to your perspective to know that God was intimately involved in setting the limits to what has come your way?

Read *2 Peter 1:3-4*. How does this passage strengthen your resolve and reinforce hope in your battle against sin?

4. God Always Provides a Way Out

"but with the temptation he will also provide the way of escape, that you may be able to endure it." To understand that God providentially oversees the extent of your next temptation is important, but to recognize that with every temptation he has also guaranteed a specific way out is an incredible and indispensable truth. Remembering this one fact can be the difference between finding that righteous option or throwing up your hands in defeat while giving in to sin.

What does this truth reveal about the concern of God regarding your pursuit of a holy life?

Give an example of a temptation, which in retrospect you can now clearly see the "way out" of, but which, in the middle of the temptation, you selfishly chose to ignore.

With Your Partner...
Discuss some strategies that can help you always look for God's way out of sin.

232

CHAPTER 10

LIVING A HOLY LIFE IN AN UNHOLY WORLD

Most of our temptations come with multiple "ways out." There are usually a variety of godly options for us to take when we are being tempted.

List some of the specific righteous options which are available to you while in the middle of the temptations you face. What are some of the paths which God graciously provides for you in the different temptations in your life?

Temptation #1: _____

    Potential Ways Out:

-
-
-
-

Temptation #2: _____

    Potential Ways Out:

-
-
-
-

Temptation #3: _____

    Potential Ways Out:

-
-
-
-

Thankfully, God has not left us without righteous options. Write out a prayer of thanksgiving and commitment that reflects this truth along with your desire to take full advantage of them in your next temptation.

233

PARTNERS:
ONE-ON-ONE DISCIPLESHIP

Regardless of the failures in your life, God wants to see you become more and more holy in this unholy world. His grace and forgiveness are bountiful and he never wants to see you give up on your calling to be a godly person. His desire is to move you forward from this day onward with an increasing passion to reflect the character of Christ.

Three years before his death, Philip Bliss penned these words which reflected his life's desire to be more like Jesus.

More Holiness Give Me **by Philip Bliss (1873)**

More holiness give me, More striving within;
    More patience in suffering, More sorrow for sin;
More faith in my Savior, More sense of His care;
    More joy in His service, More purpose in prayer.

More gratitude give me, More trust in the Lord;
    More pride in His glory, More hope in His Word;
More tears for His sorrows, More pain at His grief;
    More meekness in trial, More praise for relief.

More purity give me, More strength to overcome;
    More freedom from earth's stains, More longings for home;
More fit for the kingdom, More used would I be;
    More blessed and holy, More, Savior like Thee.

What sections of Bliss' poem resonate with you the most at this point in your pursuit of holiness?

CHAPTER 10
LIVING A HOLY LIFE IN AN UNHOLY WORLD

Notes

PARTNERS:
ONE-ON-ONE DISCIPLESHIP

Notes

10 RESOURCES & FURTHER STUDY

Living a Holy Life in an Unholy World

> **Rating Key**
> ★ Helpful (four being most)
> ◉ Difficulty (four being hardest)

Resources on Living a Holy Life

★★★ ◉ Bridges, Jerry. *The Practice Of Godliness.* Colorado Springs: Navpress, 1983. (Bridges addresses a variety of Christian virtues after urging readers to get serious about pursuing a godly life.)

★★★ ◉ Carty, Jay. *Counter Attack: Taking Back Ground Lost to Sin.* Portland: Multnomah Press, 1988. (This is a very easy to read guide to fighting some of the most common temptations Christians face.)

★★★ ◉◉ Needham, David. *Alive for the First Time: A Fresh Look at the New-Birth Miracle.* Portland: Multnomah Press, 1995. (This is a rework of his former book on the same subject entitled, *Birthright.* In this book there are many insights that help Christians think accurately about who they are in their quest to live holy.)

★★ ◉◉ Sproul, R. C. *The Holiness of God.* Wheaton: Tyndale House, 1985. (Sproul lays the groundwork for living holy lives by examining the holy nature of God.)

★★★ ◉◉◉ Venning, Ralph. *The Sinfulness of Sin.* Edinburgh, Scotland: Banner of Truth, 1993. (This Puritan classic is helpful for those who have lost the sense that sin in their lives is worth vigorously fighting.)

★★ ◉◉ White, Jerry. *Honesty, Morality and Conscience.* Colorado Springs, CO: Navpress, 1979. (This book deals with the important topics indicated in the title.)

★★★★ ◉◉ Wiersbe, Warren, ed. *The Best of A. W. Tozer.* Grand Rapids: Baker Books, 1978. (Just about anything written by Tozer provides an enlightening motivation for living a holy life. This work compiles some of his best.)

★★ ◉◉ _____. *The Integrity Crisis.* Nashville: Thomas Nelson, 1988. (Wiersbe tackles the sin problems that too often ensnare Christians as they attempt to follow Christ.)

Resources on Relativism

★★★ ◉◉ Beckwith, Francis and Greg Koukl. *Relativism: Feet Firmly Planted in Mid-Air.* Grand Rapids: Baker Books, 1998. (This is a helpful and very readable overview of the problem of relativistic thinking in modern society.)

★★★ ◉◉◉◉ Carson, D. A. *The Gagging of God: Christianity Confronts Pluralism.* Grand Rapids: Zondervan, 1996. (This extensive work covers a variety of important topics that need to be shored up in modern Christianity to successfully respond to the pluralistic philosophy so prevalent in modern culture and theology.)

237

★★ Erickson, Millard. *Postmodernizing the Faith: Evangelical Responses to the Challenges of Postmodernism.*
◉◉◉ Grand Rapids: Baker Books, 1998. (Erickson takes a theologian's look at the intellectual responses in evangelical camps to the "relativistic" thinking bound up in postmodernism.)

★★ Zacharias, Ravi. *Jesus Among Other Gods: The Absolute Claims of the Christian Message.* Nashville:
◉◉ Word Publishing, 2000. (This is an engaging look at the incompatible relationship between the Christian gospel and popular relativism.)

Resources on Finding a Topic in the Bible

★★★ Douglas, J. D., ed. *The New Bible Dictionary.* Downers Grove: InterVarsity Press. 1996. (This is one
◉◉ of the many available Bible dictionaries that addresses biblical topics, names and themes, not words primarily.)

★★★ Elwell, Walter A. *Topical Analysis of the Bible.* Grand Rapids: Baker Book House. 1995. (This is a
◉ helpful reference work that topically and logically arranges Bible texts of the NIV.)

★★★★ Logos Research Systems Inc. *Logos Library System Software.* 2001. (This is a very powerful, expandable, and
◉◉ extremely helpful Bible study tool. Searches can be done in a variety of ways. Information on Logos software is available at www.logos.com .)

★★★★ Manser, Martin H. *Zondervan Dictionary of Bible Themes: The Accessible and Comprehensive Tool for*
◉ *Topical Studies.* Grand Rapids: Zondervan Publishing House, 1999. (This is an excellent tool for finding topics in the Bible. It is well researched and logically laid out by topic and by passage.)

★★★ Mounce, William D. The Crossway Comprehensive Concordance of the Holy Bible, English
◉ Standard Version. Wheaton, IL: Crossway Books, 2002. (This is a must have unless you are using Bible software.)

★★★ Nave, Orville. Nave's Topical Bible. Chicago: Moody Press, 1986. (This classic reference work
◉ is an important and helpful list of cross-references arranged alphabetically by topic.)

238